Test-Driven Java Development
Second Edition

Invoke TDD principles for end-to-end application development

Alex Garcia
Viktor Farcic

BIRMINGHAM - MUMBAI

Test-Driven Java Development
Second Edition

Copyright © 2018 Packt Publishing

All rights reserved. No part of this book may be reproduced, stored in a retrieval system, or transmitted in any form or by any means, without the prior written permission of the publisher, except in the case of brief quotations embedded in critical articles or reviews.

Every effort has been made in the preparation of this book to ensure the accuracy of the information presented. However, the information contained in this book is sold without warranty, either express or implied. Neither the authors, nor Packt Publishing or its dealers and distributors, will be held liable for any damages caused or alleged to have been caused directly or indirectly by this book.

Packt Publishing has endeavored to provide trademark information about all of the companies and products mentioned in this book by the appropriate use of capitals. However, Packt Publishing cannot guarantee the accuracy of this information.

Commissioning Editor: Richa Tripathi
Acquisition Editor: Chaitanya Nair
Content Development Editor: Priyanka Sawant
Technical Editor: Gaurav Gala
Copy Editor: Safis Editing
Project Coordinator: Vaidehi Sawant
Proofreader: Safis Editing
Indexer: Priyanka Dhadke
Graphics: Jason Monteiro
Production Coordinator: Arvindkumar Gupta

First published: August 2015
Second edition: March 2018

Production reference: 1220318

Published by Packt Publishing Ltd.
Livery Place
35 Livery Street
Birmingham
B3 2PB, UK.

ISBN 978-1-78883-611-1

www.packtpub.com

```
mapt.io
```

Mapt is an online digital library that gives you full access to over 5,000 books and videos, as well as industry leading tools to help you plan your personal development and advance your career. For more information, please visit our website.

Why subscribe?

- Spend less time learning and more time coding with practical eBooks and Videos from over 4,000 industry professionals
- Improve your learning with Skill Plans built especially for you
- Get a free eBook or video every month
- Mapt is fully searchable
- Copy and paste, print, and bookmark content

PacktPub.com

Did you know that Packt offers eBook versions of every book published, with PDF and ePub files available? You can upgrade to the eBook version at `www.PacktPub.com` and as a print book customer, you are entitled to a discount on the eBook copy. Get in touch with us at `service@packtpub.com` for more details.

At `www.PacktPub.com`, you can also read a collection of free technical articles, sign up for a range of free newsletters, and receive exclusive discounts and offers on Packt books and eBooks.

Contributors

About the authors

Alex Garcia is a Software Engineer at Schibsted. He started coding in C++ but later moved to Java. He is also interested in Groovy, Scala, and JavaScript. He is always eager to learn new things and that is why he has also worked as a System Administrator and Full Stack Engineer. He is a big fan of agile practices. He is always interested in learning new languages, paradigms, and frameworks. When the computer is turned off, he likes to walk around sunny Barcelona and play sports.

> *I enjoyed writing this book and I would like to thank those people who made this possible. Thanks to the technical reviewers and staff at Packt Publishing for their valuable contributions. Thanks Viktor for sharing this experience with me. And finally, special thanks to my parents, my brother, and my girlfriend for being there whenever I need them.*

Viktor Farcic is a Senior Consultant at CloudBees, a member of the Docker Captains group, and an author. His big passions are DevOps; microservices; continuous integration, delivery, and deployment; and test-driven development.

He often speaks at community gatherings and conferences. He published *The DevOps Toolkit* series and the *Test-Driven Java Development* book. His random thoughts and tutorials can be found at his blog, Technology Conversations.

> *I would like to thank a lot of people who have supported me during the writing of this book. The people at Everis and Defe (companies I worked with earlier) provided all the support and encouragement I needed. The technical reviewers, Alvaro Garcia, Esko Luontola, Jeff Deskins, and Muhammad Ali, did a great job by constantly challenging my views, my assumptions, and the quality of the code featured throughout the examples. Alvaro provided even more help by writing the Legacy Code chapter. His experience and expertise in the subject were an invaluable help. The Packt Publishing team was very forthcoming, professional, and always available to provide guidance and support. Finally, I'd like to give a special thanks to my daughter, Sara, and wife, Eva. With weekdays at my job and nights and weekends dedicated to this book, they had to endure months without the support and love they deserve. This book is dedicated to my girls.*

About the reviewer

Jeff Deskins has been building web applications in the cloud since 2008 and enjoys using new technologies to do what was previously impossible. He is continuously learning best practices for creating high-performance applications.

Prior to his internet development career, Jeff worked for 13 years as a television news photographer. He continues to provide internet solutions for different television stations.

> *I would like to thank my wife for her support and patience through the many hours of me sitting behind my laptop learning new technologies. Love you the most!*

Packt is searching for authors like you

If you're interested in becoming an author for Packt, please visit `authors.packtpub.com` and apply today. We have worked with thousands of developers and tech professionals, just like you, to help them share their insight with the global tech community. You can make a general application, apply for a specific hot topic that we are recruiting an author for, or submit your own idea.

Table of Contents

Preface	1
Chapter 1: Why Should I Care for Test-Driven Development?	7
Why TDD?	8
Understanding TDD	9
Red-Green-Refactor	9
Speed is the key	11
It's not about testing	12
Testing	12
Black-box testing	12
White-box testing	13
The difference between quality checking and quality assurance	14
Better tests	15
Mocking	15
Executable documentation	16
No debugging	18
Summary	19
Chapter 2: Tools, Frameworks, and Environments	21
Git	22
Virtual machines	22
Vagrant	23
Docker	25
Build tools	26
The integrated development environment	28
The IDEA demo project	29
Unit-testing frameworks	30
JUnit	31
TestNG	33
Hamcrest and AssertJ	35
Hamcrest	36
AssertJ	37

Code coverage tools — 38
JaCoCo — 38
Mocking frameworks — 39
Mockito — 42
EasyMock — 44
Extra power for mocks — 46
User interface testing — 46
Web-testing frameworks — 46
Selenium — 47
Selenide — 48
Behavior-driven development — 50
JBehave — 50
Cucumber — 53
Summary — 55

Chapter 3: Red-Green-Refactor – From Failure Through Success until Perfection — 57
Setting up the environment with Gradle and JUnit — 58
Setting up Gradle/Java project in IntelliJ IDEA — 58
The Red-Green-Refactor process — 61
Writing a test — 62
Running all the tests and confirming that the last one is failing — 62
Writing the implementation code — 62
Running all the tests — 63
Refactoring — 63
Repeating — 63
Tic-Tac-Toe game requirements — 64
Developing Tic-Tac-Toe — 64
Requirement 1 – placing pieces — 65
Test – board boundaries I — 68
Implementation — 69
Test – board boundaries II — 69
Implementation — 70
Test – occupied spot — 70
Implementation — 71
Refactoring — 71
Requirement 2 – adding two-player support — 72

Test – X plays first	73
Implementation	74
Test – O plays right after X	74
Implementation	74
Test – X plays right after O	75
Requirement 3 – adding winning conditions	75
Test – by default there's no winner	76
Implementation	76
Test – winning condition I	76
Implementation	77
Refactoring	77
Test – winning condition II	78
Implementation	79
Test – winning condition III	79
Implementation	80
Test – winning condition IV	80
Implementation	81
Refactoring	81
Requirement 4 – tie conditions	82
Test – handling a tie situation	82
Implementation	83
Refactoring	83

Code coverage — 84
More exercises — 86
Summary — 86

Chapter 4: Unit Testing – Focusing on What You Do and Not on What Has Been Done — 87

Unit testing — 88
- What is unit testing? — 88
- Why unit testing? — 89
- Code refactoring — 89
- Why not use unit tests exclusively? — 89

Unit testing with TDD — 91

TestNG — 92
- The @Test annotation — 92
- The @BeforeSuite, @BeforeTest, @BeforeGroups, @AfterGroups, @AfterTest, and @AfterSuite annotations — 93

The @BeforeClass and @AfterClass annotations	94
The @BeforeMethod and @AfterMethod annotations	94
The @Test(enable = false) annotation argument	94
The @Test(expectedExceptions = SomeClass.class) annotation argument	94
TestNG versus JUnit summary	94
Remote-controlled ship requirements	**95**
Developing the remote-controlled ship	**96**
Project setup	96
Helper classes	98
Requirement – starting point and orientation	99
Specification – keeping position and direction in memory	100
Implementation	101
Refactoring	101
Requirement – forward and backward moves	102
Specification – moving forward	102
Implementation	104
Specification – moving backward	104
Implementation	105
Requirement – rotating the ship	105
Specification – turning left	105
Implementation	106
Specification – turning right	106
Implementation	106
Requirement – commands	106
Specification – single commands	107
Implementation	107
Specification – combined commands	109
Implementation	109
Requirement – representing spheric maps	110
Specification – planet information	111
Implementation	111
Refactoring	112
Specification – dealing with map boundaries	113
Implementation	113
Requirement – detecting obstacles	**114**
Summary	**115**
Chapter 5: Design – If It's Not Testable, It's Not Designed Well	**117**

Why should we care about design? — 118
Design principles — 118
- You Ain't Gonna Need It — 118
- Don't Repeat Yourself — 119
- Keep it simple, stupid — 119
- Occam's razor — 119
- SOLID principles — 120

Connect 4 — 121
Requirements — 121

Test-last implementation of Connect 4 — 122
- Requirement 1 – the game's board — 122
- Requirement 2 – introducing discs — 123
- Requirement 3 – player shifts — 124
- Requirement 4 – the game's output — 125
- Requirement 5 – win conditions (I) — 126
- Requirement 6 – win condition (II) — 127
- Requirement 7 – win condition (III) — 128
- Requirement 8 – win condition (IV) — 129

The TDD or test-first implementation — 130
Hamcrest — 130
- Requirement 1 – the game's board — 131
- Requirement 2 – introducing discs — 132
- Requirement 3 – player shifts — 134
- Requirement 4 – the game's output — 135
- Requirement 5 – win condition (I) — 137
- Requirement 6 – win condition (II) — 137
- Requirement 7 – win condition (III) — 138
- Requirement 8 – win condition (IV) — 139

Final considerations — 140
Summary — 141

Chapter 6: Mocking – Removing External Dependencies — 143
Mocking — 144
Why mocks? — 145
Terminology — 145
Mock objects — 146

Table of Contents

Mockito   147
Tic-Tac-Toe v2 requirements   147
Developing Tic-Tac-Toe v2   148
    Requirement 1 – store moves   149
        Specification – DB name   150
        Implementation   150
        Specification – a name for the Mongo collection   151
        Implementation   151
        Refactoring   151
        Specification – adding items to the Mongo collection   153
        Implementation   155
        Specification – adding operation feedback   157
        Implementation   157
        Refactoring   157
        Specification – error handling   158
        Implementation   159
        Specification – clear state between games   159
        Implementation   160
        Specification – drop operation feedback   160
        Implementation   160
        Specification – error handling   160
        Implementation   161
    Requirement 2 – store every turn   161
        Specification – creating new collection   162
        Implementation   162
        Specification refactoring   163
        Specification – storing current move   163
        Implementation   164
        Specification – error handling   165
        Implementation   166
        Specification – alternate players   166
        Implementation   167
        Exercises   167
Integration tests   168
    Tests separation   168
    The integration test   169
Summary   172

Chapter 7: TDD and Functional Programming – A Perfect Match — 173
Setting up the environment — 174
Optional – dealing with uncertainty — 174
Example of Optional — 175
Functions revisited — 178
Kata – Reverse Polish Notation — 179
Requirements — 179
Requirement – handling invalid input — 180
Requirement – single operations — 181
Requirement – complex operations — 183
Streams — 185
filter — 185
map — 186
flatMap — 186
reduce — 187
Summary — 188

Chapter 8: BDD – Working Together with the Whole Team — 189
Different specifications — 190
Documentation — 191
Documentation for coders — 192
Documentation for non-coders — 193
Behavior-driven development — 193
Narrative — 194
Scenarios — 195
The book store BDD story — 197
JBehave — 201
JBehave runner — 201
Pending steps — 202
Selenium and Selenide — 204
JBehave steps — 205
Final validation — 211
Summary — 213

Chapter 9: Refactoring Legacy Code – Making It Young Again — 215
Legacy code — 216
Legacy code example — 217

Other ways to recognize legacy code	220
A lack of dependency injection	221
The legacy code change algorithm	222
Applying the legacy code change algorithm	222
Identifying change points	222
Finding test points	223
Breaking dependencies	224
Writing tests	226

The kata exercise — 227

- Legacy kata — 227
- Description — 227
- Technical comments — 228
- Adding a new feature — 228
- Black-box or spike testing — 228
- Preliminary investigation — 229
    - How to find candidates for refactoring — 231
    - Introducing the new feature — 232
- Applying the legacy code algorithm — 232
    - Writing end-to-end test cases — 233
    - Automating the test cases — 237
    - Injecting the BookRepository dependency — 239
- Extract and override call — 239
    - Parameterizing a constructor — 241
    - Adding a new feature — 242
- Removing the primitive obsession with status as int — 244

Summary — 248

Chapter 10: Feature Toggles – Deploying Partially Done Features to Production — 249

Continuous integration, delivery, and deployment — 250
Feature Toggles — 252
A Feature Toggle example — 253
- Implementing the Fibonacci service — 257
- Working with the template engine — 260

Summary — 264

Chapter 11: Putting It All Together — 267
TDD in a nutshell — 268

Best practices	269
Naming conventions	270
Processes	272
Development practices	274
Tools	278
Summary	279
Chapter 12: Leverage TDD by Implementing Continuous Delivery	281
Case study – Awesome Gambling Corp	282
Exploring the codebase	282
Release procedure	285
Deployments to production	286
Conclusions	287
Possible improvements	288
Increasing test coverage	288
Implementing continuous integration	289
Towards continuous delivery	289
Jenkins installation	290
Automating builds	293
First execution	296
What is next?	297
This is just the beginning	298
This does not have to be the end	298
Summary	298
Other Books You May Enjoy	299
Index	303

Preface

Test-driven development has been around for a while and many people have still not adopted it. The reason behind this is that TDD is difficult to master. Even though the theory is very easy to grasp, it takes a lot of practice to become really proficient with it. The authors of this book have been practicing TDD for years and will try to pass on their experience to you. They are developers and believe that the best way to learn some coding practice is through code and constant practice. This book follows the same philosophy. We'll explain all the TDD concepts through exercises. This will be a journey through TDD best practices applied to Java development. At the end of it, you will earn a TDD black belt and have one more tool in your software craftsmanship tool belt.

Who this book is for

If you're an experienced Java developer and want to implement more effective methods of programming systems and applications, then this book is for you.

What this book covers

Chapter 1, *Why Should I Care for Test-Driven Development?*, spells out our goal of becoming a Java developer with a TDD black belt. In order to know where we're going, we'll have to discuss and find answers to some questions that will define our voyage.

Chapter 2, *Tools, Frameworks, and Environments*, will compare and set up all the tools, frameworks and environments that will be used throughout this book. Each of them will be accompanied with code that demonstrates their strengths and weaknesses.

Chapter 3, *Red-Green-Refactor – From Failure Through Success until Perfection*, will help us develop a Tic-Tac-Toe game using the red-green-refactor technique, which is the pillar of TDD. We'll write a test and see it fail; we'll write a code that implements that test, run all the tests, and see them succeed; and finally, we'll refactor the code and try to make it better.

Chapter 4, *Unit Testing – Focusing on What You Do and Not on What Has Been Done*, shows that to demonstrate the power of TDD applied to unit testing, we'll need to develop a remote-controlled ship. We'll learn what unit testing really is, how it differs from functional and integration tests, and how it can be combined with test-driven development.

Chapter 5, *Design – If It's Not Testable, It's Not Designed Well*, will help us develop a Connect 4 game without any tests and try to write tests at the end. This will give us insights into the difficulties we are facing when applications are not developed in a way that they can be tested easily.

Chapter 6, *Mocking – Removing External Dependencies*, shows how TDD is about speed. We want to quickly demonstrate some idea/concept. We'll continue developing our Tic-Tac-Toe game by adding MongoDB as our data storage. None of our tests will actually use MongoDB since all communications to it will be mocked.

Chapter 7, *TDD and Functional Programming – A Perfect Match*, dives into the functional programming paradigm and how TDD could be applied when programming in that way. We'll explore parts of the functional API provided by Java since version 8 and create readable and meaningful tests.

Chapter 8, *BDD – Working Together with the Whole Team*, discusses developing a book store application by using the BDD approach. We'll define the acceptance criteria in the BDD format, carry out the implementation of each feature separately, confirm that it is working correctly by running BDD scenarios, and if required, refactor the code to accomplish the desired level of quality.

Chapter 9, *Refactoring Legacy Code – Making It Young Again*, will help us refactor an existing application. The process will start with creation of test coverage for the existing code and from there on, we'll be able to start refactoring until both the tests and the code meet our expectations.

Chapter 10, *Feature Toggles – Deploying Partially Done Features to Production*, will show us how to develop a Fibonacci calculator and use feature toggles to hide functionalities that are not fully finished or that, for business reasons, should not yet be available to our users.

Chapter 11, *Putting It All Together*, will walk you through all the TDD best practices in detail and refresh the knowledge and experience you gained throughout this book.

Chapter 12, *Leverage TDD by Implementing Continuous Delivery*, explains how TDD and continuous delivery form a very powerful combination that leads to better and faster software deliveries. Some of the problems that companies are facing nowadays are illustrated with an example of a fictitious company. At the end, the speed of the development is increased and some of the pain points are mitigated by the implementation of an effective development pipeline based on automated tests and continuous delivery.

To get the most out of this book

The exercises in this book require readers to have a 64-bit computer. Installation instructions for all required software is provided throughout the book.

Download the example code files

You can download the example code files for this book from your account at www.packtpub.com. If you purchased this book elsewhere, you can visit www.packtpub.com/support and register to have the files emailed directly to you.

You can download the code files by following these steps:

1. Log in or register at www.packtpub.com.
2. Select the **SUPPORT** tab.
3. Click on **Code Downloads & Errata**.
4. Enter the name of the book in the **Search** box and follow the onscreen instructions.

Once the file is downloaded, please make sure that you unzip or extract the folder using the latest version of:

- WinRAR/7-Zip for Windows
- Zipeg/iZip/UnRarX for Mac
- 7-Zip/PeaZip for Linux

The code bundle for the book is also hosted on GitHub at https://github.com/PacktPublishing/Test-Driven-Java-Development-Second-Edition. In case there's an update to the code, it will be updated on the existing GitHub repository.

We also have other code bundles from our rich catalog of books and videos available at https://github.com/PacktPublishing/. Check them out!

Download the color images

We also provide a PDF file that has color images of the screenshots/diagrams used in this book. You can download it here: https://www.packtpub.com/sites/default/files/downloads/TestDrivenJavaDevelopmentSecondEdition_ColorImages.pdf.

Conventions used

There are a number of text conventions used throughout this book.

`CodeInText`: Indicates code words in text, database table names, folder names, filenames, file extensions, pathnames, dummy URLs, user input, and Twitter handles. Here is an example: "In this test, we are defining that `RuntimeException` is expected when the `ticTacToe.play(5, 2)` method is invoked."

A block of code is set as follows:

```
public class FooTest {
  @Rule
  public ExpectedException exception = ExpectedException.none();
  @Test
  public void whenDoFooThenThrowRuntimeException() {
    Foo foo = new Foo();
    exception.expect(RuntimeException.class);
    foo.doFoo();
  }
}
```

Any command-line input or output is written as follows:

```
$ gradle test
```

Bold: Indicates a new term, an important word, or words that you see onscreen. For example, words in menus or dialog boxes appear in the text like this. Here is an example: "IntelliJ IDEA provides a very good Gradle tasks model that can be reached by clicking on **View|Tool Windows|Gradle**."

Warnings or important notes appear like this.

Tips and tricks appear like this.

Get in touch

Feedback from our readers is always welcome.

General feedback: Email `feedback@packtpub.com` and mention the book title in the subject of your message. If you have questions about any aspect of this book, please email us at `questions@packtpub.com`.

Errata: Although we have taken every care to ensure the accuracy of our content, mistakes do happen. If you have found a mistake in this book, we would be grateful if you would report this to us. Please visit `www.packtpub.com/submit-errata`, selecting your book, clicking on the Errata Submission Form link, and entering the details.

Piracy: If you come across any illegal copies of our works in any form on the Internet, we would be grateful if you would provide us with the location address or website name. Please contact us at `copyright@packtpub.com` with a link to the material.

If you are interested in becoming an author: If there is a topic that you have expertise in and you are interested in either writing or contributing to a book, please visit `authors.packtpub.com`.

Reviews

Please leave a review. Once you have read and used this book, why not leave a review on the site that you purchased it from? Potential readers can then see and use your unbiased opinion to make purchase decisions, we at Packt can understand what you think about our products, and our authors can see your feedback on their book. Thank you!

For more information about Packt, please visit `packtpub.com`.

1
Why Should I Care for Test-Driven Development?

This book is written by developers for developers. As such, most of the learning will be through code. Each chapter will present one or more **test-driven development** (**TDD**) practices and we'll try to master them by solving **katas**. In karate, a kata is an exercise where you repeat a form many times, making little improvements in each. Following the same philosophy, we'll be making small, but significant improvements from one chapter to the next. You'll learn how to design and code better, reduce **time to market** (**TTM**), produce always up-to-date documentation, obtain high code coverage through quality tests, and write clean code that works.

Every journey has a start and this one is no exception. Our destination is a Java developer with the TDD black belt.

In order to know where we're going, we'll have to discuss, and find answers, to some questions that will define our voyage. What is TDD? Is it a testing technique, or something else? What are the benefits of applying TDD?

The goal of this chapter is to obtain an overview of TDD, to understand what it is, and to grasp the benefits it provides for its practitioners.

The following topics will be covered in this chapter:

- Understanding TDD
- What is TDD?
- Testing

- Mocking
- Executable documentation
- No debugging

Why TDD?

You might be working in an agile or waterfall environment. Maybe you have well-defined procedures that were battle-tested through years of hard work, or maybe you just started your own start-up. No matter what the situation was, you likely faced at least one, if not more, of the following pains, problems, or causes for unsuccessful delivery:

- Part of your team is kept out of the loop during the creation of requirements, specifications, or user stories
- Most, if not all, of your tests are manual, or you don't have tests at all
- Even though you have automated tests, they do not detect real problems
- Automated tests are written and executed when it's too late for them to provide any real value to the project
- There is always something more urgent than dedicating time to testing
- Teams are split between testing, development, and functional analysis departments, and they are often out of sync
- There is an inability to refactor the code because of the fear that something will be broken
- The maintenance cost is too high
- The time to market is too big
- Clients do not feel that what was delivered is what they asked for
- Documentation is never up-to-date
- You're afraid to deploy to production because the result is unknown
- You're often not able to deploy to production because regression tests take too long to run
- The team is spending too much time trying to figure out what some method or a class does

TDD does not magically solve all of these problems. Instead, it puts us on the way towards the solution. There is no silver bullet, but if there is one development practice that can make a difference on so many levels, that practice is TDD.

TDD speeds up the time to market, enables easier refactoring, helps to create better design, and fosters looser coupling.

On top of the direct benefits, TDD is a prerequisite for many other practices (continuous delivery being one of them). Better design, well-written code, faster TTM, up-to-date documentation, and solid test coverage, are some of the results you will accomplish by applying TDD.

It's not an easy thing to master TDD. Even after learning all the theory and going through best practices and anti-patterns, the journey is only just beginning. TDD requires time and a lot of practice. It's a long trip that does not stop with this book. As a matter of fact, it never truly ends. There are always new ways to become more proficient and faster. However, even though the cost is high, the benefits are even higher. People who have spent enough time with TDD claim that there is no other way to develop a software. We are one of them and we're sure that you will be too.

We are strong believers that the best way to learn some coding technique is by coding. You won't be able to finish this book by reading it in a metro on the way to work. It's not a book that one can read in bed. You'll have to get your hands dirty and code.

In this chapter, we'll go through basics; starting from the next, you'll be learning by reading, writing, and running code. We'd like to say that by the time you're finished with this book, you'll be an experienced TDD programmer, but this is not true. By the end of this book, you'll be comfortable with TDD and you'll have a strong base in both theory and practice. The rest is up to you and the experience you'll be building by applying it in your day-to-day job.

Understanding TDD

At this time, you are probably saying to yourself, *OK, I understand that TDD will give me some benefits, but what exactly is TDD?* TDD is a simple procedure of writing tests before the actual implementation. It's an inversion of a traditional approach where testing is performed after the code is written.

Red-Green-Refactor

TDD is a process that relies on the repetition of a very short development cycle. It is based on the test-first concept of **extreme programming** (**XP**) that encourages simple design with a high-level of confidence. The procedure that drives this cycle is called **Red-Green-Refactor**.

The procedure itself is simple and it consists of a few steps that are repeated over and over again:

1. Write a test
2. Run all tests
3. Write the implementation code
4. Run all tests
5. Refactor
6. Run all tests

Since a test is written before the actual implementation, it is supposed to fail. If it doesn't, the test is wrong. It describes something that already exists or it was written incorrectly. Being in the green state while writing tests is a sign of a false positive. Tests like these should be removed or refactored.

While writing tests, we are in the red state. When the implementation of a test is finished, all tests should pass and then we will be in the green state.

If the last test failed, the implementation is wrong and should be corrected. Either the test we just finished is incorrect or the implementation of that test did not meet the specification we had set. If any but the last test failed, we broke something and changes should be reverted.

When this happens, the natural reaction is to spend as much time as needed to fix the code so that all tests are passing. However, this is wrong. If a fix is not done in a matter of minutes, the best thing to do is to revert the changes. After all, everything worked not long ago. An implementation that broke something is obviously wrong, so why not go back to where we started and think again about the correct way to implement the test? That way, we wasted minutes on a wrong implementation instead of wasting much more time to correct something that was not done right in the first place. Existing test coverage (excluding the implementation of the last test) should be sacred. We change the existing code through intentional refactoring, not as a way to fix recently written code.

Do not make the implementation of the last test final, but provide just enough code for this test to pass.

Write the code in any way you want, but do it fast. Once everything is green, we have confidence that there is a safety net in the form of tests. From this moment on, we can proceed to refactor the code. This means that we are making the code better and more optimal without introducing new features. While refactoring is in place, all tests should be passing all the time.

If, while refactoring, one of the tests failed, refactoring broke an existing functionality and, as before, changes should be reverted. Not only that, at this stage we are not changing any features, but we are also not introducing any new tests. All we're doing is making the code better while continuously running all tests to make sure that nothing got broken. At the same time, we're proving code correctness and cutting down on future maintenance costs.

Once refactoring is finished, the process is repeated. It's an endless loop of a very short cycle.

Speed is the key

Imagine a game of ping pong (or table tennis). The game is very fast; sometimes it is hard even to follow the ball when professionals play the game. TDD is very similar. TDD veterans tend not to spend more than a minute on either side of the table (test and implementation). Write a short test and run all tests (ping), write the implementation and run all tests (pong), write another test (ping), write the implementation of that test (pong), refactor and confirm that all tests are passing (score), and then repeat—ping, pong, ping, pong, ping, pong, score, serve again. Do not try to make the perfect code. Instead, try to keep the ball rolling until you think that the time is right to score (refactor).

 Time between switching from tests to implementation (and vice versa) should be measured in minutes (if not seconds).

It's not about testing

T in **TDD** is often misunderstood. TDD is the way we approach the design. It is the way to force us to think about the implementation and what the code needs to do before writing it. It is the way to focus on requirements and the implementation of just one thing at a time—organize your thoughts and better structure the code. This does not mean that tests resulting from TDD are useless—they are far from that. They are very useful and they allow us to develop with great speed without being afraid that something will be broken. This is especially true when refactoring takes place. Being able to reorganize the code while having the confidence that no functionality is broken is a huge boost to its quality.

The main objective of TDD is testable code design with tests as a very useful side product.

Testing

Even though the main objective of TDD is the approach to code design, tests are still a very important aspect of TDD and we should have a clear understanding of two major groups of techniques, as follows:

- Black-box testing
- White-box testing

Black-box testing

Black-box testing (also known as **functional testing**) treats software under test as a black box without knowing its internals. Tests use software interfaces and try to ensure that they work as expected. As long as the functionality of interfaces remains unchanged, tests should pass even if internals are changed. The tester is aware of what the program should do, but does not have the knowledge of how it does it. Black-box testing is the most commonly used type of testing in traditional organizations that have testers as a separate department, especially when they are not proficient in coding and have difficulties understanding it. This technique provides an external perspective on the software under test.

Some of the advantages of black-box testing are as follows:

- It is efficient for large segments of code
- Code access, understanding the code, and ability to code are not required
- It offers separation between users and developers perspectives

Some of the disadvantages of black-box testing are as follows:

- It provides limited coverage, since only a fraction of test scenarios is performed
- It can result in inefficient testing due to tester's lack of knowledge about software internals
- It can lead to blind coverage, since testers have limited knowledge about the application

If tests are driving the development, they are often done in the form of acceptance criteria that is later used as a definition of what should be developed.

Automated black-box testing relies on some form of automation, such as **behavior-driven development (BDD)**.

White-box testing

White-box testing (also known as **clear box testing, glass box testing, transparent box testing,** and **structural testing**) looks inside the software that is being tested and uses that knowledge as part of the testing process. If, for example, an exception should be thrown under certain conditions, a test might want to reproduce those conditions. White-box testing requires internal knowledge of the system and programming skills. It provides an internal perspective on the software under test.

Some of the advantages of white-box testing are as follows:

- It is efficient in finding errors and problems
- Required knowledge of internals of the software under test is beneficial for thorough testing
- It allows finding hidden errors

- It encourages programmer's introspection
- It helps in optimizing the code
- Due to the required internal knowledge of the software, maximum coverage is obtained

Some of the disadvantages of white-box testing are as follows:

- It might not find unimplemented or missing features
- It requires high-level knowledge of internals of the software under test
- It requires code access
- Tests are often tightly coupled to the implementation details of the production code, causing unwanted test failures when the code is refactored

White-box testing is almost always automated and, in most cases, take the form of unit tests.

When white-box testing is done before the implementation, it takes the form of TDD.

The difference between quality checking and quality assurance

The approach to testing can also be distinguished by looking at the objectives they are trying to accomplish. Those objectives are often split between **quality checking** (**QC**) and **quality assurance** (**QA**). While QC is focused on defects identification, QA tries to prevent them. QC is product-oriented and intends to make sure that results are as expected. On the other hand, QA is more focused on processes that assure that quality is built-in. It tries to make sure that correct things are done in the correct way.

While QC had a more important role in the past, with the emergence of TDD, **acceptance test-driven development** (**ATDD**), and later on BDD, focus has been shifting towards QA.

[14]

Better tests

No matter whether one is using black-box, white-box, or both types of testing, the order in which they are written is very important.

Requirements (specifications and user stories) are written before the code that implements them. They come first so they define the code, not the other way around. The same can be said for tests. If they are written after the code is done, in a certain way, that code (and the functionalities it implements) is defining tests. Tests that are defined by an already existing application are biased. They have a tendency to confirm what code does, and not to test whether a client's expectations are met, or that the code is behaving as expected. With manual testing, that is less the case since it is often done by a siloed QC department (even though it's often called QA). They tend to work on test definition in isolation from developers. That in itself leads to bigger problems caused by inevitably poor communication and the **police syndrome**, where testers are not trying to help the team to write applications with quality built in, but to find faults at the end of the process. The sooner we find problems, the cheaper it is to fix them.

Tests written in the TDD fashion (including its flavors such as ATDD and BDD) are an attempt to develop applications with quality built in from the very start. It's an attempt to avoid having problems in the first place.

Mocking

In order for tests to run quickly and provide constant feedback, code needs to be organized in such a way that the methods, functions, and classes can be easily replaced with mocks and stubs. A common word for this type of replacements of the actual code is **test double**. The speed of execution can be severely affected with external dependencies; for example, our code might need to communicate with the database. By mocking external dependencies, we are able to increase that speed drastically. Whole unit test suite execution should be measured in minutes, if not seconds. Designing the code in a way that can be easily mocked and stubbed forces us to structure that code better by applying a separation of concerns.

More important than speed is the benefit of the removal of external factors. Setting up databases, web servers, external APIs, and other dependencies that our code might need, is both time consuming and unreliable. In many cases, those dependencies might not even be available. For example, we might need to create a code that communicates with a database and have someone else create a schema. Without mocks, we would need to wait until that schema is set.

With or without mocks, the code should be written in such a way that we can easily replace one dependency with another.

Executable documentation

Another very useful aspect of TDD (and well-structured tests in general) is documentation. In most cases, it is much easier to find out what the code does by looking at tests than at the implementation itself. What is the purpose of some methods? Look at the tests associated with it. What is the desired functionality of some part of the application UI? Look at the tests associated with it. Documentation written in the form of tests is one of the pillars of TDD and deserves further explanation.

The main problem with (traditional) software documentation is that it is not up-to-date most of the time. As soon as some part of the code changes, the documentation stops reflecting the actual situation. This statement applies to almost any type of documentation, with requirements and test cases being the most affected.

The necessity to document code is often a sign that the code itself is not well-written. Moreover, no matter how hard we try, documentation inevitably gets outdated.

Developers shouldn't rely on system documentation because it is almost never up-to-date. Besides, no documentation can provide as detailed and up-to-date a description of the code as the code itself.

Using code as documentation does not exclude other types of documents. The key is to avoid duplication. If details of the system can be obtained by reading the code, other types of documentation can provide quick guidelines and a high-level overview. Non-code documentation should answer questions such as what the general purpose of the system is and what technologies are used by the system. In many cases, a simple `README` is enough to provide the quick start that developers need. Sections such as project description, environment setup, installation, and build and packaging instructions are very helpful for newcomers. From there on, code is the bible.

Implementation code provides all needed details while test code acts as the description of the intent behind the production code.

Tests are executable documentation with TDD being the most common way to create and maintain it.

Assuming that some form of **continuous integration** (**CI**) is in use, if some part of the test documentation is incorrect, it will fail and be fixed soon afterwards. CI solves the problem of incorrect test documentation, but it does not ensure that all functionality is documented. For this reason (among many others), test documentation should be created in the TDD fashion. If all functionality is defined as tests before the implementation code is written and the execution of all tests is successful, then tests act as a complete and up-to-date information source that can be used by developers.

What should we do with the rest of the team? Testers, customers, managers, and other non-coders might not be able to obtain the necessary information from the production and test code.

As we saw earlier, two of the most common types of testing are black-box and white-box testing. This division is important since it also divides testers into those who do know how to write or at least read code (white-box testing) and those who don't (black-box testing). In some cases, testers can do both types. However, more often than not, they do not know how to code so the documentation that is usable by developers is not usable by them. If documentation needs to be decoupled from the code, unit tests are not a good match. That is one of the reasons why BDD came in to being.

 BDD can provide documentation necessary for non-coders, while still maintaining the advantages of TDD and automation.

Customers need to be able to define new functionality of the system, as well as to be able to get information about all the important aspects of the current system. That documentation should not be too technical (code is not an option), but it still must be always up-to-date. BDD narratives and scenarios are one of the best ways to provide this type of documentation. The ability to act as acceptance criteria (written before the code), be executed frequently (preferably on every commit), and be written in a natural language makes BDD stories not only always up-to-date, but usable by those who do not want to inspect the code.

Documentation is an integral part of the software. As with any other part of the code, it needs to be tested often so that we're sure that it is accurate and up-to-date.

The only cost-effective way to have accurate and up-to-date information is to have executable documentation that can be integrated into your CI system.

TDD as a methodology is a good way to move along in this direction. On a low-level, unit tests are a best fit. On the other hand, BDD provides a good way to work on a functional level while maintaining understanding that is accomplished by using natural language.

No debugging

We (authors of this book) almost never debug applications we're working on!

This statement might sound pompous, but it's true. We almost never debug because there is rarely a reason to debug an application. When tests are written before the code and the code coverage is high, we can have high confidence that the application works as expected. This does not mean that applications written using TDD do not have bugs—they do. All applications do. However, when that happens, it is easy to isolate them by simply looking for the code that is not covered by tests.

Tests themselves might not include some cases. In those situations, the action is to write additional tests.

With high code coverage, finding the cause of some bug is much faster through tests than spending time debugging line by line until the culprit is found.

Summary

In this chapter, you got the general understanding of TDD practice and insights into what TDD is and what it isn't. You learned that it is a way to design code through a short and repeatable cycle called Red-Green-Refactor. Failure is an expected state that should not only be embraced, but enforced throughout the TDD process. This cycle is so short that we move from one phase to another with great speed.

While code design is the main objective, tests created throughout the TDD process are a valuable asset that should be utilized and severely impact our view of traditional testing practices. We went through the most common of those practices, such as white-box and black-box testing, tried to put them into the TDD perspective, and showed benefits that they can bring to each other.

You discovered that mocks are very important tools that are often a must when writing tests. Finally, we discussed how tests can and should be utilized as executable documentation and how TDD can make debugging much less necessary.

Now that we are armed with theoretical knowledge, it is time to set up the development environment and get an overview and comparison of different testing frameworks and tools.

2
Tools, Frameworks, and Environments

"We become what we behold. We shape our tools and then our tools shape us."

– Marshall McLuhan

As every soldier knows his weapons, a programmer must be familiar with the development ecosystem and those tools that make programming much easier. Whether you are already using any of these tools at work or home, it is worth taking a look at many of them and comparing their features, advantages, and disadvantages. Let's get an overview of what we can find nowadays about the following topics and construct a small project to get familiar with some of them.

We won't go into the details of those tools and frameworks, since that will be done later on in the following chapters. The goal is to get you up and running, and provide you with a short overview of what they do and how.

The following topics will be covered in this chapter:

- Git
- Virtual machines
- Build tools
- The integrated development environment
- Unit testing frameworks
- Hamcrest and AssertJ

- Code coverage tools
- Mocking frameworks
- User interface testing
- Behavior-driven development

Git

Git is the most popular revision control system. For that reason, all the code used in this book is stored in Bitbucket (https://bitbucket.org/). If you don't have it already, install Git. Distributions for all the popular operating systems can be found at: http://git-scm.com.

Many graphical interfaces are available for Git; some of them being Tortoise (https://code.google.com/p/tortoisegit), **Source Tree** (https://www.sourcetreeapp.com), and **Tower** (http://www.git-tower.com/).

Virtual machines

Even though they are outside the topic of this book, virtual machines are a powerful tool and a first-class citizen in a good development environment. They provide dynamic and easy-to-use resources in isolated systems so they can be used and dropped at the time we need them. This helps developers to focus on their tasks instead of wasting their time creating or installing required services from scratch. This is the reason why virtual machines have found room in here. We want to take advantage of them to keep you focused on the code.

In order to have the same environment no matter the OS you're using, we'll be creating virtual machines with Vagrant and deploying required applications with Docker. We chose Ubuntu as a base operating system in our examples, just because it is a popular, commonly used Unix-like distribution. Most of these technologies are platform-independent, but occasionally you won't be able to follow the instructions found here because you might be using some other operating system. In that case, your task is to find what the differences are between Ubuntu and your operating system and act accordingly.

Vagrant

Vagrant is the tool we are going to use for creating the development environment stack. It is an easy way to initialize ready-to-go virtual machines with minimum effort using preconfigured boxes. All boxes and configurations are placed in one file, called the `Vagrant` file.

Here is an example of creating a simple Ubuntu box. We made an extra configuration for installing MongoDB using Docker (the usage of Docker will be explained shortly). We assume that you have VirtualBox (https://www.virtualbox.org) and Vagrant (https://www.vagrantup.com) installed on your computer and that you have internet access.

In this particular case, we are creating an instance of Ubuntu 64-bits using the Ubuntu box (`ubuntu/trusty64`) and specifying that the VM should have 1 GB of RAM:

```
config.vm.box = "ubuntu/trusty64"
config.vm.provider "virtualbox" do |vb|
vb.memory = "1024"
end
```

Further on, we're exposing MongoDB's default port in the Vagrant machine and running it using Docker:

```
config.vm.network "forwarded_port", guest: 27017, host: 27017
config.vm.provision "docker" do |d|
  d.run "mongoDB", image: "mongo:2", args: "-p 27017:27017"
end
```

Finally, in order to speed up the Vagrant setup, we're caching some resources. You should install the plugin called `cachier`. For further information, visit: https://github.com/fgrehm/vagrant-cachier.

```
if Vagrant.has_plugin?("vagrant-cachier")
  config.cache.scope = :box
end
```

Now it's time to see it working. It usually takes a few minutes to run it for the first time because the base box and all the dependencies need to be downloaded and installed:

```
$> vagrant plugin install vagrant-cachier
$> git clone
https://bitbucket.org/vfarcic/tdd-java-ch02-example-vagrant.git
$> cd tdd-java-ch02-example-vagrant
$> vagrant up
```

When this command is run, you should see the following output:

```
vfarcic@viktor:~/IdeaProjects/tdd-java-ch02-example-vagrant$ vagrant up
Bringing machine 'default' up with 'virtualbox' provider...
==> default: Importing base box 'ubuntu/trusty64'...
==> default: Matching MAC address for NAT networking...
==> default: Checking if box 'ubuntu/trusty64' is up to date...
==> default: Setting the name of the VM: tdd-java-ch02-example-vagrant_default_1435347519969_47040
==> default: Clearing any previously set forwarded ports...
==> default: Clearing any previously set network interfaces...
==> default: Preparing network interfaces based on configuration...
    default: Adapter 1: nat
==> default: Forwarding ports...
    default: 27017 => 27017 (adapter 1)
    default: 22 => 2222 (adapter 1)
==> default: Running 'pre-boot' VM customizations...
==> default: Booting VM...
==> default: Waiting for machine to boot. This may take a few minutes...
    default: SSH address: 127.0.0.1:2222
    default: SSH username: vagrant
    default: SSH auth method: private key
    default: Warning: Connection timeout. Retrying...
    default:
    default: Vagrant insecure key detected. Vagrant will automatically replace
    default: this with a newly generated keypair for better security.
    default:
    default: Inserting generated public key within guest...
    default: Removing insecure key from the guest if its present...
    default: Key inserted! Disconnecting and reconnecting using new SSH key...
==> default: Machine booted and ready!
==> default: Checking for guest additions in VM...
==> default: Mounting shared folders...
    default: /vagrant => /home/vfarcic/IdeaProjects/tdd-java-ch02-example-vagrant
    default: /tmp/vagrant-cache => /home/vfarcic/.vagrant.d/cache/ubuntu/trusty64
==> default: Configuring cache buckets...
==> default: Running provisioner: docker...
    default: Installing Docker (latest) onto machine...
    default: Configuring Docker to autostart containers...
==> default: Starting Docker containers...
==> default: -- Container: mongoDB
==> default: Configuring cache buckets...
vfarcic@viktor:~/IdeaProjects/tdd-java-ch02-example-vagrant$
```

Be patient until the execution is finished. Once done, you'll have a new virtual machine with Ubuntu, Docker, and one MongoDB instance up and running. The best part is that all this was accomplished with a single command.

To see the status of the currently running VM, we can use the `status` argument:

```
$> vagrant status
Current machine states:
default                    running (virtualbox)
```

The virtual machine can be accessed either through `ssh` or by using Vagrant commands, as in the following example:

```
$> vagrant ssh
Welcome to Ubuntu 14.04.2 LTS (GNU/Linux 3.13.0-46-generic x86_64)
 * Documentation:   https://help.ubuntu.com/
 System information disabled due to load higher than 1.0
 Get cloud support with Ubuntu Advantage Cloud Guest:
   http://www.ubuntu.com/business/services/cloud
 0 packages can be updated.
 0 updates are security updates.
vagrant@vagrant-ubuntu-trusty-64:~$
```

Finally, to stop the virtual machine, exit from it and run the `vagrant halt` command:

```
$> exit
$> vagrant halt
  ==> default: Attempting graceful shutdown of VM...
$>
```

> For the list of Vagrant boxes or further details about configuring Vagrant, visit: https://www.vagrantup.com.

Docker

Once the environment is set, it is time to install the services and the software that we need. This can be done using Docker, a simple and portable way to ship and run many applications and services in isolated containers. We will use it to install the required databases, web servers, and all the other applications required throughout this book, in a virtual machine created using Vagrant. In fact, the Vagrant VM that was previously created already has an example of getting an instance of MongoDB up and running using Docker.

Let's bring up the VM again (we stopped it previously with the `vagrant halt` command) and also MongoDB:

```
$> vagrant up
$> vagrant ssh
vagrant@vagrant-ubuntu-trusty-64:~$ docker start mongoDB
mongoDB
vagrant@vagrant-ubuntu-trusty-64:~$ docker ps
CONTAINER ID        IMAGE               COMMAND                  CREATED
360f5340d5fc        mongo:2             "/entrypoint.sh mong..." 4 minutes ago
STATUS              PORTS                      NAMES
Up 4 minutes        0.0.0.0:27017->27017/tcp   mongoDB
vagrant@vagrant-ubuntu-trusty-64:~$ exit
```

With `docker start`, we started the container; with `docker ps`, we listed all the running processes.

By using this kind of procedure, we are able to reproduce a full-stack environment in the blink of an eye. You may be wondering if this is as awesome as it sounds. The answer is yes, it is. Vagrant and Docker allow developers to focus on what they are supposed to do and forget about complex installations and tricky configurations. Furthermore, we made an extra effort to provide you with all the necessary steps and resources to reproduce and test all the code examples and demonstrations in this book.

Build tools

With time, code tends to grow both in complexity and size. This occurs in the software industry by its nature. All products evolve constantly and new requirements are made and implemented across a product's life. Build tools offer a way to make managing the project life cycle as straightforward as possible, by following a few code conventions, such as the organization of your code, in a specific way, and by the usage of naming a convention for your classes or a determined project structure formed by different folders and files.

Some of you might be familiar with Maven or Ant. They are a great couple of Swiss army knives for handling projects, but we are here to learn so we decided to use Gradle. Some of the advantages of Gradle are its reduced boilerplate code, resulting in a much shorter file and a more readable configuration file. Among others, Google uses it as its build tool. It is supported by IntelliJ IDEA and is quite easy to learn and work with. Most of the functionalities and tasks are obtained by adding plugins.

Mastering Gradle is not the goal of this book. So, if you want to learn more about this awesome tool, take a tour through its website (http://gradle.org/) and read about the plugins you can use and the options you can customize. For a comparison of different Java build tools, visit: https://technologyconversations.com/2014/06/18/build-tools/. Before proceeding forward, make sure that Gradle is installed on your system.

Let's analyze the relevant parts of a `build.gradle` file. It holds project information in a concise way, using Groovy as the descriptor language. This is our project's build file, autogenerated with IntelliJ:

```
apply plugin: 'java'
sourceCompatibility = 1.7
version = '1.0'
```

A Java plugin is applied since it is a Java project. It brings common Java tasks, such as build, package, test, and so on. The source compatibility is set to JDK 7. The compiler will complain if we try to use the Java syntax that is not supported by this version:

```
repositories {
    mavenCentral()
}
```

Maven Central (http://search.maven.org/) holds all our project dependencies. This section tells Gradle where to pull them from. The Maven Central repository is enough for this project, but you can add your custom repositories, if any. Nexus and Ivy are also supported:

```
dependencies {
    testCompile group: 'junit', name: 'junit', version: '4.12'
}
```

Last, but not least, this is how project dependencies are declared. IntelliJ decided to use JUnit as the testing framework.

Gradle tasks are easy to run. For example, to run tests from the command prompt, we can simply execute the following:

gradle test

This can be accomplished from IDEA by running the `test` task from the Gradle Tool Window that can be accessed from **View** | **Tool Windows** | **Gradle**.

The tests result is stored in the HTML files that are located in the `build/reports/tests` directory.

The following is the test report generated by running `gradle test` against the sample code:

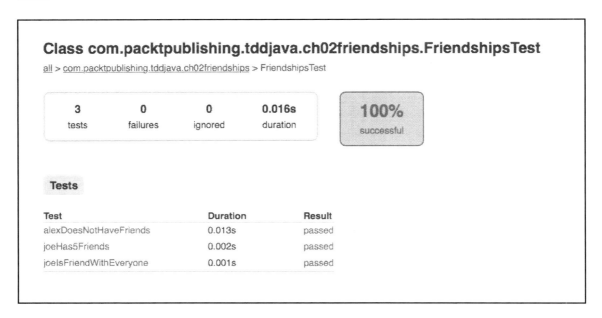

The integrated development environment

As many tools and technologies will be covered, we recommend using IntelliJ IDEA as the tool for code development. The main reason is that this **integrated development environment** (IDE) works without any tedious configuration. The Community Edition (IntelliJ IDEA CE) comes with a bunch of built-in features and plugins that make coding easy and efficient. It automatically recommends plugins that can be installed depending on the file extension. As IntelliJ IDEA is the choice we made for this book, you will find references and steps referring to its actions or menus. Readers should find a proper way to emulate those steps if they are using other IDEs. Refer to: `https://www.jetbrains.com/idea/` for instructions on how to download and install IntelliJ IDEA.

The IDEA demo project

Let's create the base layout of the demo project. This project will be used throughout this chapter to illustrate all the topics that are covered. Java will be the programming language and Gradle (http://gradle.org/) will be used to run different sets of tasks, such as building, testing, and so on.

Let us import into IDEA the repository that contains examples from this chapter:

1. Open IntelliJ IDEA, select **Check out from Version Control**, and click on **Git**.
2. Type https://bitbucket.org/vfarcic/tdd-java-ch02-example-junit.git in the Git repository URL and click on **Clone. Confirm** for the rest of the IDEA questions until a new project is created with code cloned from the Git repository.

The imported project should look similar to the following image:

Now that we have got the project set up, it's time to take a look at unit-testing frameworks.

Unit-testing frameworks

In this section, two of the most used Java frameworks for unit testing are shown and briefly commented on. We will focus on their syntax and main features by comparing a test class written using both JUnit and TestNG. Although there are slight differences, both frameworks offer the most commonly used functionalities, and the main difference is how tests are executed and organized.

Let's start with a question. What is a test? How can we define it?

A **test** is a repeatable process or method that verifies the correct behavior of a tested target in a determined situation with a determined input expecting a predefined output or interactions.

In the programming approach, there are several types of tests depending on their scope—functional tests, acceptance tests, and unit tests. Further on, we will explore each of those types of tests in more detail.

Unit testing is about testing small pieces of code. Let's see how to test a single Java class. The class is quite simple, but enough for our interest:

```java
public class Friendships {
  private final Map<String, List<String>> friendships =
    new HashMap<>();

  public void makeFriends(String person1, String person2) {
    addFriend(person1, person2);
    addFriend(person2, person1);
  }

  public List<String> getFriendsList(String person) {
    if (!friendships.containsKey(person)) {
      return Collections.emptyList();
    }
    return friendships.get(person)
  }

  public boolean areFriends(String person1, String person2) {
    return friendships.containsKey(person1) &&
        friendships.get(person1).contains(person2);
  }

  private void addFriend(String person, String friend) {
    if (!friendships.containsKey(person)) {
```

```
      friendships.put(person, new ArrayList<String>());
    }
    List<String> friends = friendships.get(person);
    if (!friends.contains(friend)) {
      friends.add(friend);
    }
  }
}
```

JUnit

JUnit (http://junit.org/) is a simple and easy-to-learn framework for writing and running tests. Each test is mapped as a method, and each method should represent a specific known scenario in which a part of our code will be executed. The code verification is made by comparing the expected output or behavior with the actual output.

The following is the test class written with JUnit. There are some scenarios missing, but for now we are interested in showing what tests look like. We will focus on better ways to test our code and on best practices later in this book.

Test classes usually consist of three stages: set up, test, and tear down. Let's start with methods that set up data needed for tests. A setup can be performed on a class or method level:

```
Friendships friendships;

@BeforeClass
public static void beforeClass() {
  // This method will be executed once on initialization time
}

@Before
public void before() {
  friendships = new Friendships();
  friendships.makeFriends("Joe",",," "Audrey");
  friendships.makeFriends("Joe", "Peter");
  friendships.makeFriends("Joe", "Michael");
  friendships.makeFriends("Joe", "Britney");
  friendships.makeFriends("Joe", "Paul");
}
```

The `@BeforeClass` annotation specifies a method that will be run once before any of the test methods in the class. It is a useful way to do some general set up that will be used by most (if not all) tests.

The `@Before` annotation specifies a method that will be run before each test method. We can use it to set up test data without worrying that the tests that are run afterwards will change the state of that data. In the preceding example, we're instantiating the `Friendships` class and adding five sample entries to the `Friendships` list. No matter what changes will be performed by each individual test, this data will be recreated over and over until all the tests are performed.

Common examples of usage of those two annotations are the setting up of database data, the creation of files needed for tests, and so on. Later on, we'll see how external dependencies can and should be avoided using mocks. Nevertheless, functional or integration tests might still need those dependencies and the `@Before` and `@BeforeClass` annotations are a good way to set them up.

Once the data is set up, we can proceed with the actual tests:

```java
@Test
public void alexDoesNotHaveFriends() {
  Assert.assertTrue("Alex does not have friends",
      friendships.getFriendsList("Alex").isEmpty());
}

@Test
public void joeHas5Friends() {
  Assert.assertEquals("Joe has 5 friends", 5,
      friendships.getFriendsList("Joe").size());
}

@Test
public void joeIsFriendWithEveryone() {
  List<String> friendsOfJoe =
    Arrays.asList("Audrey", "Peter", "Michael", "Britney", "Paul");
  Assert.assertTrue(friendships.getFriendsList("Joe")
    .containsAll(friendsOfJoe));
}
```

In this example, we are using a few of the many different types of asserts. We're confirming that `Alex` does not have any friends, while `Joe` is a very popular guy with five friends (`Audrey`, `Peter`, `Michael`, `Britney`, and `Paul`).

Finally, once the tests are finished, we might need to perform some cleanup:

```java
@AfterClass
public static void afterClass() {
  // This method will be executed once when all test are executed
}
```

```
@After
public void after() {
  // This method will be executed once after each test execution
}
```

In our example, in the `Friendships` class, we have no need to clean up anything. If there were such a need, those two annotations would provide that feature. They work in a similar fashion to the `@Before` and `@BeforeClass` annotations. `@AfterClass` is run once all tests are finished. The `@After` annotation is executed after each test. This runs each test method as a separate class instance. As long as we are avoiding global variables and external resources, such as databases and APIs, each test is isolated from the others. Whatever was done in one, does not affect the rest.

The complete source code can be found in the `FriendshipsTest` class at https://bitbucket.org/vfarcic/tdd-java-ch02-example-junit.

TestNG

In TestNG (http://testng.org/doc/index.html), tests are organized in classes, just as in the case of JUnit.

The following Gradle configuration (`build.gradle`) is required in order to run TestNG tests:

```
dependencies {
    testCompile group: 'org.testng', name: 'testng', version: '6.8.21'
}

test.useTestNG() {
// Optionally you can filter which tests are executed using
//    exclude/include filters
// excludeGroups 'complex'
}
```

Unlike JUnit, TestNG requires additional Gradle configuration that tells it to use TestNG to run tests.

Tools, Frameworks, and Environments

The following test class is written with TestNG and is a reflection of what we did earlier with JUnit. Repeated imports and other boring parts are omitted with the intention of focusing on the relevant parts:

```
@BeforeClass
public static void beforeClass() {
  // This method will be executed once on initialization time
}

@BeforeMethod
public void before() {
  friendships = new Friendships();
  friendships.makeFriends("Joe", "Audrey");
  friendships.makeFriends("Joe", "Peter");
  friendships.makeFriends("Joe", "Michael");
  friendships.makeFriends("Joe", "Britney");
  friendships.makeFriends("Joe", "Paul");
}
```

You probably already noticed the similarities between JUnit and TestNG. Both are using annotations to specify what the purposes of certain methods are. Besides different names (`@Beforeclass` versus `@BeforeMethod`), there is no difference between the two. However, unlike Junit, TestNG reuses the same test class instance for all test methods. This means that the test methods are not isolated by default, so more care is needed in the `before` and `after` methods.

Asserts are very similar as well:

```
public void alexDoesNotHaveFriends() {
  Assert.assertTrue(friendships.getFriendsList("Alex").isEmpty(),
      "Alex does not have friends");
}

public void joeHas5Friends() {
  Assert.assertEquals(friendships.getFriendsList("Joe").size(),
      5, "Joe has 5 friends");
}

public void joeIsFriendWithEveryone() {
  List<String> friendsOfJoe =
    Arrays.asList("Audrey", "Peter", "Michael", "Britney", "Paul");
  Assert.assertTrue(friendships.getFriendsList("Joe")
      .containsAll(friendsOfJoe));
}
```

The only notable difference when compared with JUnit is the order of the `assert` variables. While the JUnit assert's order of arguments is **optional message**, **expected values**, and **actual values**, TestNG's order is an actual value, expected value, and optional message. Besides the difference in the order of arguments we're passing to the `assert` methods, there are almost no differences between JUnit and TestNG.

You might have noticed that `@Test` is missing. TestNG allows us to set it on the class level and thus convert all public methods into tests.

The `@After` annotations are also very similar. The only notable difference is the TestNG `@AfterMethod` annotation that acts in the same way as the JUnit `@After` annotation.

As you can see, the syntax is pretty similar. Tests are organized in to classes and test verifications are made using assertions. That is not to say that there are no more important differences between those two frameworks; we'll see some of them throughout this book. I invite you to explore JUnit (http://junit.org/) and TestNG (http://testng.org/) by yourself.

The complete source code with the preceding examples can be found at https://bitbucket.org/vfarcic/tdd-java-ch02-example-testng.

The assertions we have written until now have used only the testing frameworks. However, there are some test utilities that can help us make them nicer and more readable.

Hamcrest and AssertJ

In the previous section, we gave an overview of what a unit test is and how it can be written using two of the most commonly used Java frameworks. Since tests are an important part of our projects, why not improve the way we write them? Some cool projects emerged, aiming to empower the semantics of tests by changing the way that assertions are made. As a result, tests are more concise and easier to understand.

Hamcrest

Hamcrest adds a lot of methods called **matchers**. Each matcher is designed to perform a comparison operation. It is extensible enough to support custom matchers created by yourself. Furthermore, JUnit supports Hamcrest natively since its core is included in the JUnit distribution. You can start using Hamcrest effortlessly. However, we want to use the full-featured project so we will add a test dependency to Gradle's file:

```
testCompile 'org.hamcrest:hamcrest-all:1.3'
```

Let us compare one assert from JUnit with the equivalent one from Hamcrest:

- The JUnit `assert`:

    ```
    List<String> friendsOfJoe =
      Arrays.asList("Audrey", "Peter", "Michael", "Britney", "Paul");
    Assert.assertTrue( friendships.getFriendsList("Joe")
       .containsAll(friendsOfJoe));
    ```

- The Hamcrest `assert`:

    ```
    assertThat(
      friendships.getFriendsList("Joe"),
      containsInAnyOrder("Audrey", "Peter", "Michael", "Britney",
    "Paul")
    );
    ```

As you can see, Hamcrest is a bit more expressive. It has a much bigger range of asserts that allows us to avoid some boilerplate code and, at the same time, makes code easier to read and is more expressive.

Here's another example:

- JUnit `assert`:

    ```
    Assert.assertEquals(5, friendships.getFriendsList("Joe").size());
    ```

- Hamcrest `assert`:

    ```
    assertThat(friendships.getFriendsList("Joe"), hasSize(5));
    ```

You'll notice two differences. The first is that, unlike JUnit, Hamcrest works almost always with direct objects. While in the case of JUnit, we needed to get the integer size and compare it with the expected number (5); Hamcrest has a bigger range of asserts so we can simply use one of them (hasSize) together with the actual object (List). Another difference is that Hamcrest has the inverse order with the actual value being the first argument (like TestNG).

Those two examples are not enough to show the full potential offered by Hamcrest. Later on in this book, there will be more examples and explanations of Hamcrest. Visit http://hamcrest.org/ and explore its syntax.

The complete source code can be found in the FriendshipsHamcrestTest class in the https://bitbucket.org/vfarcic/tdd-java-ch02-example-junit repositories.

AssertJ

AssertJ works in a similar way to Hamcrest. A major difference is that AssertJ assertions can be concatenated.

To work with AssertJ, the dependency must be added to Gradle's dependencies:

```
testCompile 'org.assertj:assertj-core:2.0.0'
```

Let's compare JUnit asserts with AssertJ:

```
Assert.assertEquals(5, friendships.getFriendsList("Joe").size());
List<String> friendsOfJoe =
   Arrays.asList("Audrey", "Peter", "Michael", "Britney", "Paul");
Assert.assertTrue(  friendships.getFriendsList("Joe")
   .containsAll (friendsOfJoe)
);
```

The same two asserts can be concatenated to a single one in AssertJ:

```
assertThat(friendships.getFriendsList("Joe"))
  .hasSize(5)
  .containsOnly("Audrey", "Peter", "Michael", "Britney", "Paul");
```

This was a nice improvement. There was no need to have two separate asserts, nor was there a need to create a new list with expected values. Moreover, AssertJ is more readable and easier to understand.

Tools, Frameworks, and Environments

The complete source code can be found in the `FriendshipsAssertJTest` class at https://bitbucket.org/vfarcic/tdd-java-ch02-example-junit.

Now that we have the tests up and running, we might want to see what the code coverage is that is generated by our tests.

Code coverage tools

The fact that we wrote tests does not mean that they are good, nor that they cover enough code. As soon as we start writing and running tests, the natural reaction is to start asking questions that were not available before. What parts of our code are properly tested? What are the cases that our tests did not take into account? Are we testing enough? These and other similar questions can be answered with code coverage tools. They can be used to identify the blocks or lines of code that were not covered by our tests; they can also calculate the percentage of code covered and provide other interesting metrics.

They are powerful tools used to obtain metrics and show relations between tests and implementation code. However, as with any other tool, their purpose needs to be clear. They do not provide information about quality, but only about which parts of our code have been tested.

> Code coverage shows whether the code lines are reached during test execution, but it is not a guarantee of good testing practices because test quality is not included in these metrics.

Let's take a look at one of the most popular tools used to calculate code coverage.

JaCoCo

Java Code Coverage (JaCoCo) is a well-known tool for measuring test coverage.
To use it in our project, we need to add a few lines to our Gradle configuration file, that is, `build.gradle`:

1. Add the Gradle `plugin` for JaCoCo:

    ```
    apply plugin: 'jacoco'
    ```

2. To see the JaCoCo results, run the following from your command prompt:

```
gradle test jacocoTestReport
```

3. The same Gradle tasks can be run from the **Gradle Tasks IDEA Tool Window**.
4. The end result is stored in the `build/reports/jacoco/test/html` directory. It's an HTML file that can be opened in any browser:

Friendships

Element	Missed Instructions	Cov.	Missed Branches	Cov.	Missed	Cxty	Missed	Lines	Missed	Methods
areFriends(String, String)		0%		0%	3	3	1	1	1	1
addFriend(String, String)		100%		75%	1	3	0	4	0	1
getFriendsList(String)		100%		100%	0	2	0	2	0	1
makeFriends(String, String)		100%		n/a	0	1	0	3	0	1
Friendships()		100%		n/a	0	1	0	2	0	1
Total	17 of 75	77%	5 of 10	50%	4	10	1	12	1	5

Further chapters of this book will explore code coverage in more detail. Until then, go to http://www.eclemma.org/jacoco/ for more information.

Mocking frameworks

Our project looks cool, but it's too simple and it is far from being a real project. It still doesn't use external resources. A database is required by Java projects so we'll try to introduce it, as well.

What is the common way to test code that uses external resources or third-party libraries? Mocks are the answer. A mock object, or simply a mock, is a simulated object that can be used to replace real ones. They are very useful when objects that depend on external resources are deprived of them.

In fact, you don't need a database at all while you are developing the application. Instead, you can use mocks to speed up development and testing and use a real database connection only at runtime. Instead of spending time setting up a database and preparing test data, we can focus on writing classes and think about them later on during integration time.

Tools, Frameworks, and Environments

For demonstration purposes, we'll introduce two new classes: the `Person` class and the `FriendCollection` class that are designed to represent persons and database object mapping. Persistence will be done with MongoDB (https://www.mongodb.org/).

Our sample will have two classes. `Person` will represent database object data; `FriendCollection` will be our data access layer. The code is, hopefully, self-explanatory.

Let's create and use the `Person` class:

```
public class Person {
  @Id
  private String name;

  private List<String> friends;

  public Person() { }

  public Person(String name) {
    this.name = name;
    friends = new ArrayList<>();
  }

  public List<String> getFriends() {
    return friends;
  }

  public void addFriend(String friend) {
    if (!friends.contains(friend)) friends.add(friend);
  }
}
```

Let's create and use the `FriendsCollection` class:

```
public class FriendsCollection {
  private MongoCollection friends;

  public FriendsCollection() {
    try {
      DB db = new MongoClient().getDB("friendships");
      friends = new Jongo(db).getCollection("friends");
    } catch (UnknownHostException e) {
      throw new RuntimeException(e.getMessage());
    }
  }

  public Person findByName(String name) {
    return friends.findOne("{_id: #}", name).as(Person.class);
```

```
        }

        public void save(Person p) {
          friends.save(p);
        }
}
```

In addition, some new dependencies have been introduced so the Gradle dependencies block needs to be modified, as well. The first one is the MongoDB driver, which is required to connect to the database. The second is Jongo, a small project that makes accessing Mongo collections pretty straightforward.

The Gradle dependencies for `mongodb` and `jongo` are as follows:

```
dependencies {
    compile 'org.mongodb:mongo-java-driver:2.13.2'
    compile 'org.jongo:jongo:1.1'
}
```

We are using a database so the `Friendships` class should also be modified. We should change a map to `FriendsCollection` and modify the rest of the code to use it. The end result is the following:

```
public class FriendshipsMongo {
  private FriendsCollection friends;

  public FriendshipsMongo() {
    friends = new FriendsCollection();
  }

  public List<String> getFriendsList(String person) {
    Person p = friends.findByName(person);
    if (p == null) return Collections.emptyList();
    return p.getFriends();
  }

  public void makeFriends(String person1, String person2) {
    addFriend(person1, person2);
    addFriend(person2, person1);
  }

  public boolean areFriends(String person1, String person2) {
    Person p = friends.findByName(person1);
    return p != null && p.getFriends().contains(person2);
  }

  private void addFriend(String person, String friend) {
```

Tools, Frameworks, and Environments

```
            Person p = friends.findByName(person);
            if (p == null) p = new Person(person);
            p.addFriend(friend);
            friends.save(p);
        }
    }
```

The complete source code can be found in the `FriendsCollection` and `FriendshipsMongo` classes in the `https://bitbucket.org/vfarcic/tdd-java-ch02-example-junit` repository.

Now that we have our `Friendships` class working with MongoDB, let's take a look at one possible way to test it by using mocks.

Mockito

Mockito is a Java framework that allows easy creation of the test double.

The Gradle dependency is the following:

```
dependencies {
  testCompile group: 'org.mockito', name: 'mockito-all', version: '1.+'
}
```

Mockito runs through the JUnit runner. It creates all the required mocks for us and injects them into the class with tests. There are two basic approaches; instantiating mocks by ourselves and injecting them as class dependencies via a class constructor or using a set of annotations. In the next example, we are going to see how it is done using annotations.

In order for a class to use Mockito annotations, it needs to be run with `MockitoJUnitRunner`. Using the runner simplifies the process because you just simply add annotations to objects to be created:

```
@RunWith(MockitoJUnitRunner.class)
public class FriendshipsTest {
...
}
```

In your test class, the tested class should be annotated with `@InjectMocks`. This tells Mockito which class to inject mocks into:

```
@InjectMocks
FriendshipsMongo friendships;
```

From then on, we can specify which specific methods or objects inside the class, in this case `FriendshipsMongo`, will be substituted with mocks:

```
@Mock
FriendsCollection friends;
```

In this example, `FriendsCollection` inside the `FriendshipsMongo` class will be mocked.

Now, we can specify what should be returned when `friends` is invoked:

```
Person joe = new Person("Joe");
doReturn(joe).when(friends).findByName("Joe");
assertThat(friends.findByName("Joe")).isEqualTo(joe);
```

In this example, we're telling Mockito to return the `joe` object whenever `friends.findByName("Joe")` is invoked. Later on, we're verifying with `assertThat` that this assumption is correct.

Let's try to do the same test as we did previously in the class that was without MongoDB:

```
@Test
public void joeHas5Friends() {
  List<String> expected =
    Arrays.asList("Audrey", "Peter", "Michael", "Britney", "Paul");
  Person joe = spy(new Person("Joe"));

  doReturn(joe).when(friends).findByName("Joe");
  doReturn(expected).when(joe).getFriends();

  assertThat(friendships.getFriendsList("Joe"))
    .hasSize(5)
    .containsOnly("Audrey", "Peter", "Michael", "Britney", "Paul");
}
```

A lot of things happened in this small test. First, we're specifying that `joe` is a spy. In Mockito, spies are real objects that use real methods unless specified otherwise. Then, we're telling Mockito to return `joe` when the `friends` method calls `getFriends`. This combination allows us to return the `expected` list when the `getFriends` method is invoked. Finally, we're asserting that the `getFriendsList` returns the expected list of names.

The complete source code can be found in the `FriendshipsMongoAssertJTest` class in the https://bitbucket.org/vfarcic/tdd-java-ch02-example-junit repository.

We'll use Mockito later on; throughout this book, you'll get your chance to become more familiar with it and with mocking in general. More information about Mockito can be found at http://mockito.org/.

EasyMock

EasyMock is an alternative mocking framework. It is very similar to Mockito. However, the main difference is that EasyMock does not create `spy` objects but mocks. Other differences are syntactical.

Let's see an example of EasyMock. We'll use the same set of test cases as those that were used for the Mockito examples:

```
@RunWith(EasyMockRunner.class)
public class FriendshipsTest {
  @TestSubject
  FriendshipsMongo friendships = new FriendshipsMongo();
  @Mock(type = MockType.NICE)
  FriendsCollection friends;
}
```

Essentially, the runner does the same as the Mockito runner:

```
@TestSubject
FriendshipsMongo friendships = new FriendshipsMongo();

@Mock(type = MockType.NICE)
FriendsCollection friends;
```

The `@TestSubject` annotation is similar to Mockito's `@InjectMocks`, while the `@Mock` annotation denotes an object to be mocked in a similar fashion to Mockito's `@Mock`. Furthermore, the type `NICE` tells the mock to return empty.

Let's compare one of the asserts we did with Mockito:

```
@Test
public void mockingWorksAsExpected() {
  Person joe = new Person("Joe");
  expect(friends.findByName("Joe")).andReturn(joe);
  replay(friends);
  assertThat(friends.findByName("Joe")).isEqualTo(joe);
}
```

Besides small differences in syntax, the only disadvantage of EasyMock is that the additional instruction `replay` was needed. It tells the framework that the previously specified expectation should be applied. The rest is almost the same. We're specifying that `friends.findByName` should return the `joe` object, applying that expectation and, finally, asserting whether the actual result is as expected.

In the EasyMock version, the second test method that we used with Mockito is the following:

```
@Test
public void joeHas5Friends() {
  List<String> expected =
  Arrays.asList("Audrey", "Peter", "Michael", "Britney", "Paul");
  Person joe = createMock(Person.class);

  expect(friends.findByName("Joe")).andReturn(joe);
  expect(joe.getFriends()).andReturn(expected);
  replay(friends);
  replay(joe);

  assertThat(friendships.getFriendsList("Joe"))
    .hasSize(5)
    .containsOnly("Audrey", "Peter", "Michael", "Britney", "Paul");
}
```

Again, there are almost no differences when compared to Mockito, except that EasyMock does not have spies. Depending on the context, that might be an important difference.

Even though both frameworks are similar, there are small details that make us choose Mockito as a framework, which will be used throughout this book.

Visit http://easymock.org/ for more information about this asserts library.

The complete source code can be found in the `FriendshipsMongoEasyMockTest` class in the https://bitbucket.org/vfarcic/tdd-java-ch02-example-junit repository.

Extra power for mocks

Both projects introduced earlier do not cover all types of methods or fields. Depending on the applied modifiers, such as static or final, a class, method, or field, can be out of range for Mockito or EasyMock. In such cases, we can use PowerMock to extend the mocking framework. This way, we can mock objects that can only be mocked in a tricky manner. However, one should be cautious with PowerMock since the necessity to use many of the features it provides is usually a sign of poor design. If you're working on a legacy code, PowerMock might be a good choice. Otherwise, try to design your code in such a way that PowerMock is not needed. We'll show you how to do that later on.

For more information, visit `https://code.google.com/p/powermock/`.

User interface testing

Even though unit testing can and should cover the major part of the application, there is still a need to work on functional and acceptance tests. Unlike unit tests, they provide higher-level verifications, and are usually performed at entry points, and rely heavily on user interfaces. At the end, we are creating applications that are, in most cases, used by humans, so being confident of our application's behavior is very important. This comfort status can be achieved by testing what the application is expected to do, from the point of view of real users.

Here, we'll try to provide an overview of functional and acceptance testing through a user interface. We'll use the web as an example, even though there are many other types of user interfaces, such as desktop applications, smartphone interfaces, and so on.

Web-testing frameworks

The application classes and data sources have been tested throughout this chapter, but there is still something missing; the most common user entry point—the web. Most enterprise applications such as intranets or corporate sites are accessed using a browser. For this reason, testing the web provides significant value, helping us to make sure that it is doing what it is expected to do.

Furthermore, companies are investing a lot of time performing long and heavy manual tests every time the application changes. This is a big waste of time since a lot of those tests can be automated and executed without supervision, using tools such as Selenium or Selenide.

Selenium

Selenium is a great tool for web testing. It uses a browser to run verifications and it can handle all the popular browsers, such as Firefox, Safari, and Chrome. It also supports headless browsers to test web pages with much greater speed and less resources consumption.

There is a `SeleniumIDE` plugin that can be used to create tests by recording actions performed by the user. Currently, it is only supported by Firefox. Sadly, even though tests generated this way provide very fast results, they tend to be very brittle and cause problems in the long run, especially when some part of a page changes. For this reason, we'll stick with the code written without the help from that plugin.

The simplest way to execute Selenium is to run it through `JUnitRunner`. All Selenium tests start by initializing `WebDriver`, the class used for communication with browsers:

1. Let's start by adding the Gradle dependency:

    ```
    dependencies {
      testCompile 'org.seleniumhq.selenium:selenium-java:2.45.0'
    }
    ```

2. As an example, we'll create a test that searches Wikipedia. We'll use a Firefox driver as our browser of choice:

    ```
    WebDriver driver = new FirefoxDriver();
    ```

`WebDriver` is an interface that can be instantiated with one of the many drivers provided by Selenium:

1. To open a URL, the instruction would be the following:

    ```
    driver.get("http://en.wikipedia.org/wiki/Main_Page");
    ```

2. Once the page is opened, we can search for an input element by its name and then type some text:

    ```
    WebElement query = driver.findElement(By.name("search"));
    query.sendKeys("Test-driven development");
    ```

3. Once we type our search query, we should find and click the **Go** button:

    ```
    WebElement goButton = driver.findElement(By.name("go"));
    goButton.click();
    ```

Tools, Frameworks, and Environments

4. Once we reach our destination, it is time to validate that, in this case, the page title is correct:

   ```
   assertThat(driver.getTitle(),
       startsWith("Test-driven development"));
   ```

5. Finally, the `driver` should be closed once we're finished using it:

   ```
   driver.quit();
   ```

That's it. We have a small but valuable test that verifies a single use case. While there is much more to be said about Selenium, hopefully, this has provided you with enough information to realize the potential behind it.

> Visit http://www.seleniumhq.org/ for further information and more complex uses of `WebDriver`.

The complete source code can be found in the `SeleniumTest` class in the https://bitbucket.org/vfarcic/tdd-java-ch02-example-web repository.

While Selenium is the most commonly used framework to work with browsers, it is still very low-level and requires a lot of tweaking. Selenide was born out of the idea that Selenium would be much more useful if there was a higher-level library that could implement some of the common patterns and solve often-repeated needs.

Selenide

What we have seen about Selenium is very cool. It brings the opportunity to probe that our application is doing things well, but sometimes it is a bit tricky to configure and use. Selenide is a project based on Selenium that offers a good syntax for writing tests and makes them more readable. It hides the usage of `WebDriver` and configurations from you, while still maintaining a high-level of customization:

1. Like all the other libraries we have used until now, the first step is to add the Gradle dependency:

   ```
   dependencies {
       testCompile 'com.codeborne:selenide:2.17'
   }
   ```

2. Let's see how we can write the previous Selenium test using Selenide instead. The syntax might be familiar to for those who know JQuery (https://jquery.com/):

```java
public class SelenideTest {
  @Test
  public void wikipediaSearchFeature() throws
      InterruptedException {
    // Opening Wikipedia page
    open("http://en.wikipedia.org/wiki/Main_Page");

    // Searching TDD
    $(By.name("search")).setValue("Test-driven development");

    // Clicking search button
    $(By.name("go")).click();

    // Checks
    assertThat(title(),
      startsWith("Test-driven development"));
  }
}
```

This was a more expressive way to write a test. On top of a more fluent syntax, there are some things that happen behind this code and would require additional lines of Selenium. For example, a click action will wait until an element in question is available, and will fail only if the predefined period of time has expired. Selenium, on the other hand, would fail immediately. In today's world, with many elements being loaded dynamically through JavaScript, we cannot expect everything to appear at once. Hence, this Selenide feature proves to be useful and saves us from using repetitive boilerplate code. There are many other benefits Selenide brings to the table. Due to the benefits that Selenide provides when compared with Selenium, it will be our framework of choice throughout this book. Furthermore, there is a whole chapter dedicated to web testing using this framework. Visit http://selenide.org/ for more information on ways to use web drivers in your tests.

No matter whether tests were written with one framework or another, the effect is the same. When tests are run, a Firefox browser window will emerge and execute all steps defined in the test sequentially. Unless a headless browser was chosen as your driver of choice, you will be able to see what is going on throughout the test. If something goes wrong, a failure trace is available. On top of that, we can take browser screenshots at any point. For example, it is a common practice to record the situation at the time of a failure.

The complete source code can be found in the `SelenideTest` class in the https://bitbucket.org/vfarcic/tdd-java-ch02-example-web repository.

Armed with a basic knowledge of web-testing frameworks, it is time to take a short look at BDD.

Behavior-driven development

Behavior-driven development (BDD) is an agile process designed to keep the focus on stakeholder value throughout the whole project. The premise of BDD is that the requirement has to be written in a way that everyone, be it the business representative, analyst, developer, tester, manager, and so on, understands it. The key is to have a unique set of artifacts that are understood and used by everyone—a collection of user stories. Stories are written by the whole team and used as both requirements and executable test cases. It is a way to perform TDD with a clarity that cannot be accomplished with unit testing. It is a way to describe and test functionality in (almost) natural language and make it runnable and repeatable.

A story is composed of scenarios. Each scenario represents a concise behavioral use case and is written in natural language using steps. Steps are a sequence of the preconditions, events, and outcomes of a scenario. Each step must start with the words `Given`, `When`, or `Then`. `Given` is for preconditions, `When` is for actions, and `Then` is for performing validations.

This was only a brief introduction. There is a whole chapter, *Chapter 8, BDD – Working Together with the Whole Team*, dedicated to this topic. Now it is time to introduce JBehave and Cucumber as two of the many available frameworks for writing and executing stories.

JBehave

JBehave is a Java BDD framework used for writing acceptance tests that are able to be executed and automated. The steps used in stories are bound to Java code through several annotations provided by the framework:

1. First of all, add JBehave to Gradle dependencies:

    ```
    dependencies {
        testCompile 'org.jbehave:jbehave-core:3.9.5'
    }
    ```

2. Let's go through a few example steps:

   ```
   @Given("I go to Wikipedia homepage")
   public void goToWikiPage() {
     open("http://en.wikipedia.org/wiki/Main_Page");
   }
   ```

3. This is the `Given` type of step. It represents a precondition that needs to be fulfilled for some actions to be performed successfully. In this particular case, it will open a Wikipedia page. Now that we have our precondition specified, it is time to define some actions:

   ```
   @When("I enter the value $value on a field named $fieldName")
   public void enterValueOnFieldByName(String value, String fieldName)
   {
     $(By.name(fieldName)).setValue(value);
   }
   @When("I click the button $buttonName")
   public void clickButonByName(String buttonName) {
     $(By.name(buttonName)).click();
   }
   ```

4. As you can see, actions are defined with the `When` annotation. In our case, we can use those steps to set some value to a field or click on a specific button. Once actions are performed, we can deal with validations. Note that steps can be more flexible by introducing parameters:

   ```
   @Then("the page title contains $title")
   public void pageTitleIs(String title) {
     assertThat(title(), containsString(title));
   }
   ```

Validations are declared using the `Then` annotation. In this example, we are validating the page title as expected.

These steps can be found in the `WebSteps` class in the https://bitbucket.org/vfarcic/tdd-java-ch02-example-web **repository**.

Once we have defined our steps, it is time to use them. The following story combines those steps in order to validate a desired behavior:

   ```
   Scenario: TDD search on wikipedia
   ```

It starts with naming the scenario. The name should be as concise as possible, but enough to identify the user case unequivocally; it is for informative purposes only:

```
Given I go to Wikipedia homepage
When I enter the value Test-driven development on a field named search
When I click the button go
Then the page title contains Test-driven development
```

As you can see, we are using the same steps text that we defined earlier. The code related to those steps will be executed in a sequential order. If any of them are halted, the execution is halted and the scenario itself is considered failed.

Even though we defined our steps ahead of stories, it can be done the other way around with a story being defined first and the steps following. In that case, the status of a scenario would be pending, meaning that the required steps are missing.

This story can be found in the `wikipediaSearch.story` file in the https://bitbucket.org/vfarcic/tdd-java-ch02-example-web repository.

To run this story, execute the following:

```
$> gradle testJBehave
```

While the story is running, we can see that actions are taking place in the browser. Once it is finished, a report with the results of an execution is generated. It can be found in `build/reports/jbehave`:

> bdd/jbehave/stories/wikipediaSearch.story
>
> ### Scenario: Wikipedia search
>
> Given I go to Wikipedia homepage
> When I enter the value Test-driven development on a field named search
> When I click the button go
> Then the page title contains Test-driven development

JBehave story execution report

For brevity, we excluded the `build.gradle` code to run JBehave stories. The completed source code can be found in the https://bitbucket.org/vfarcic/tdd-java-ch02-example-web repository.

For further information on JBehave and its benefits, visit `http://jbehave.org/`.

Cucumber

Cucumber was originally a Ruby BDD framework. These days it supports several languages including Java. It provides functionality that is very similar to JBehave.

Let's see the same examples written in Cucumber.

The same as any other dependency we have used until now, Cucumber needs to be added to `build.gradle` before we can start using it:

```
dependencies {
    testCompile 'info.cukes:cucumber-java:1.2.2'
    testCompile 'info.cukes:cucumber-junit:1.2.2'
}
```

We will create the same steps as we did with JBehave, using the Cucumber way:

```
@Given("^I go to Wikipedia homepage$")
public void goToWikiPage() {
  open("http://en.wikipedia.org/wiki/Main_Page");
}

@When("^I enter the value (.*) on a field named (.*)$")
public void enterValueOnFieldByName(String value,
    String fieldName) {
  $(By.name(fieldName)).setValue(value);
}

@When("^I click the button (.*)$")
public void clickButonByName(String buttonName) {
  $(By.name(buttonName)).click();
}

@Then("^the page title contains (.*)$")
public void pageTitleIs(String title) {
  assertThat(title(), containsString(title));
}
```

Tools, Frameworks, and Environments

The only noticeable difference between these two frameworks is the way Cucumber defines steps text. It uses regular expressions to match variables types, unlike JBehave which deduces them from a method signature.

The steps code can be found in the `WebSteps` class in the https://bitbucket.org/vfarcic/tdd-java-ch02-example-web repository:

Let's see how the story looks when written using the Cucumber syntax:

```
Feature: Wikipedia Search

  Scenario: TDD search on wikipedia
    Given I go to Wikipedia homepage
    When I enter the value Test-driven development on a field named search
    When I click the button go
    Then the page title contains Test-driven development
```

Note that there are almost no differences. This story can be found in the `wikipediaSearch.feature` file in the https://bitbucket.org/vfarcic/tdd-java-ch02-example-web repository.

As you might have guessed, to run a Cucumber story, all you need to do is run the following Gradle task:

```
$> gradle testCucumber
```

The result reports are located in the `build/reports/cucumber-report` directory. This is the report for the preceding story:

▼ **Feature**: Wikipedia Search
   ▼ **Scenario**: TDD search on wikipedia
      Given I go to Wikipedia homepage
      When I enter the value Test-driven development on a field named search
      When I click the button go
      Then the page title contains Test-driven development

Cucumber story execution report

Chapter 2

The full code example can be found in the `https://bitbucket.org/vfarcic/tdd-java-ch02-example-web` repository.

> For a list of languages supported by Cucumber or for any other details, visit `https://cukes.info/`.

Since both JBehave and Cucumber offer a similar set of features, we decided to use JBehave throughout the rest of this book. There is a whole chapter dedicated to BDD and JBehave.

Summary

In this chapter, we took a break from TDD and introduced many tools and frameworks that will be used for code demonstrations in the rest of the chapters. We set up everything from version control, virtual machines, building tools, and IDEs, until we reached frameworks that are commonly used as today's testing tools.

We are big proponents of the open source movement. Following this spirit, we made a special effort to select free tools and frameworks in every category.

Now that we have set up all the tools that we will need, in the next chapter, we will go deeper into TDD, starting with the Red-Green-Refactor procedure-TDD's cornerstone.

3
Red-Green-Refactor – From Failure Through Success until Perfection

"Knowing is not enough; we must apply. Willing is not enough; we must do."

– Bruce Lee

The **Red-Green-Refactor** technique is the basis of **test-driven development (TDD)**. It is a game of ping pong in which we are switching between tests and implementation code at great speed. We'll fail, then we'll succeed, and, finally, we'll improve.

We'll develop a Tic-Tac-Toe game by going through each requirement one at a time. We'll write a test and see if it fails. Then, we'll write code that implements that test, run all the tests, and see them succeed. Finally, we'll refactor the code and try to make it better. This process will be repeated many times until all the requirements are successfully implemented.

We'll start by setting up the environment with Gradle and JUnit. Then, we'll go a bit deeper into the Red-Green-Refactor process. Once we're ready with the setup and theory, we'll go through the high-level requirements of the application.

With everything set, we'll dive right into the code—one requirement at a time. Once everything is done, we'll take a look at the code coverage and decide whether it is acceptable or whether more tests need to be added.

The following topics will be covered in this chapter:

- Setting up the environment with Gradle and JUnit
- The Red-Green-Refactor process
- Tic-Tac-Toe's requirements
- Developing Tic-Tac-Toe
- Code coverage
- More exercises

Setting up the environment with Gradle and JUnit

You are probably familiar with the setup of Java projects. However, you might not have worked with IntelliJ IDEA before or you might have used Maven instead of Gradle. In order to make sure that you can follow the exercise, we'll quickly go through the setup.

Setting up Gradle/Java project in IntelliJ IDEA

The main purpose of this book is to teach TDD, so we will not go into detail about Gradle and IntelliJ IDEA. Both are used as an example. All exercises in this book can be done with different choices for IDE and build tools. You can, for example, use Maven and Eclipse instead. For most, it might be easier to follow the same guidelines as those presented throughout the book, but the choice is yours.

The following steps will create a new Gradle project in IntelliJ IDEA:

1. Open **IntelliJ IDEA**. Click on **Create New Project** and select **Gradle** from the left-hand side menu. Then, click on **Next**.
2. If you are using IDEA 14 and higher, you will be asked for an **Artifact ID**. Type `tdd-java-ch03-tic-tac-toe` and click on **Next** twice. Type `tdd-java-ch03-tic-tac-toe` as the project name. Then, click on the **Finish** button:

Chapter 3

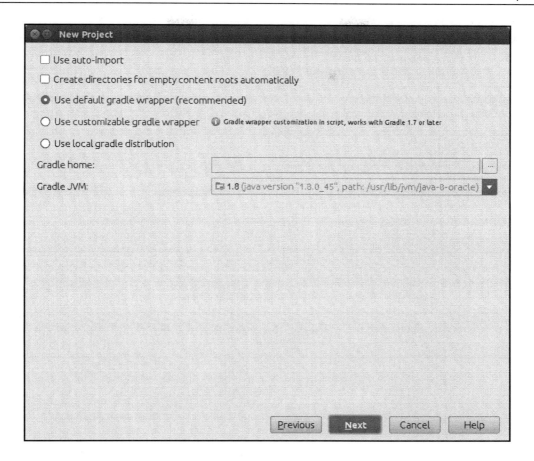

In the **New Project** dialog, we can observe that IDEA has already created the build.gradle file. Open it and you'll see that it already contains the JUnit dependency. Since this is our framework of choice in this chapter, there is no additional configuration that we should do. By default, build.gradle is set to use Java 1.5 as a source compatibility setting. You can change it to any version you prefer. The examples in this chapter will not use any of the Java features that came after Version 5, but that doesn't mean that you cannot solve the exercise using, for example, JDK 8.

Our build.gradle file should look like the following:

```
apply plugin: 'java'

version = '1.0'

repositories {
  mavenCentral()
```

Red-Green-Refactor – From Failure Through Success until Perfection

```
}

dependencies {
  testCompile group: 'junit', name: 'junit', version: '4.11'
}
```

Now, all that's left to do is to create packages that we'll use for tests and the implementation. From the **Project** dialog, right-click to bring up the **Context** menu and select **New** | **Directory**. Type `src/test/java/com/packtpublishing/tddjava/ch03tictactoe` and click on the **OK** button to create the tests package. Repeat the same steps with the `src/main/java/com/packtpublishing/tddjava/ch03tictactoe` directory to create the implementation package.

Finally, we need to the make test and implementation classes. Create the `TicTacToeSpec` class inside the `com.packtpublishing.tddjava.ch03tictactoe` package in the `src/test/java` directory. This class will contain all our tests. Repeat the same for the `TicTacToe` class in the `src/main/java` directory.

Your **Project** structure should be similar to the one presented in the following screenshot:

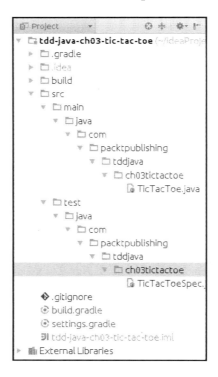

The source code can be found in the `00-setup` branch of the `tdd-java-ch03-tic-tac-toe` Git repository at https://bitbucket.org/vfarcic/tdd-java-ch03-tic-tac-toe/branch/00-setup.

> Always separate tests from the implementation code.
>
> The benefits are as follows: this avoids accidentally packaging tests together with production binaries; many build tools expect tests to be in a certain source directory.
>
> A common practice is to have at least two source directories. The implementation code should be located in `src/main/java` and the test code in `src/test/java`. In bigger projects, the number of source directories can increase, but the separation between implementation and tests should remain.
>
> Build tools such as Maven and Gradle expect source directories, separation, as well as naming conventions.

That's it. We're set to start working on our Tic-Tac-Toe application using JUnit as the testing framework of choice and Gradle for compilation, dependencies, testing, and other tasks. In Chapter 1, *Why Should I Care for Test-Driven Development?*, you first encountered the Red-Green-Refactor procedure. Since it is the cornerstone of TDD and is the main objective of the exercise in this chapter, it might be a good idea to go into a bit more detail before we start the development.

The Red-Green-Refactor process

The Red-Green-Refactor process is the most important part of TDD. It is the main pillar, without which no other aspect of TDD will work.

The name comes from the states our code is in within the cycle. When in the red state, code does not work; when in the green state, everything is working as expected, but not necessarily in the best possible way. Refactor is the phase when we know that features are well covered with tests and thus gives us the confidence to change it and make it better.

Writing a test

Every new feature starts with a test. The main objective of this test is to focus on requirements and code design before writing the code. A test is a form of an executable documentation and can be used later on to get an understanding of what the code does or what are the intentions behind it.

At this point, we are in the red state since the execution of tests fails. There is a discrepancy between what tests expect from the code and what the implementation code actually does. To be more specific, there is no code that fulfills the expectation of the last test; we haven't written it yet. It is possible that at this stage all the tests are actually passing, but that's the sign of a problem.

Running all the tests and confirming that the last one is failing

Confirming that the last test is failing, confirms that the test would not, mistakenly, pass without the introduction of a new code. If the test is passing, then the feature already exists or the test is producing a false positive. If that's the case and the test actually always passes independently of the implementation, it is, in itself, worthless and should be removed.

A test must not only fail, but must fail for the expected reason. In this phase, we are still in the red stage. Tests were run and the last one failed.

Writing the implementation code

The purpose of this phase is to write code that will make the last test pass. Do not try to make it perfect, nor try to spend too much time with it. If it's not well-written or is not optimum, that is still okay. It'll become better later on. What we're really trying to do is to create a safety net in the form of tests that are confirmed to pass. Do not try to introduce any functionality that was not described in the last test. To do that, we are required to go back to the first step and start with a new test. However, we should not write new tests until all the existing ones are passing.

In this phase, we are still in the red stage. While the code that was written would probably pass all the tests, that assumption is not yet confirmed.

Running all the tests

It is very important that all the tests are run and not only the last test that was written. The code that we just wrote might have made the last test pass while breaking something else. Running all the tests confirms not only that the implementation of the last test is correct, but also that it did not break the integrity of the application as a whole. This slow execution of the whole test suite is a sign of poorly written tests or having too much coupling in the code. Coupling prevents the easy isolation of external dependencies, thus increasing the time required for the execution of tests.

In this phase, we are in the green state. All the tests are passing and the application behaves as we expect it to behave.

Refactoring

While all the previous steps are mandatory, this one is optional. Even though refactoring is rarely done at the end of each cycle, sooner or later it will be desired, if not mandatory. Not every implementation of a test requires refactoring. There is no rule that tells you when to refactor and when not to. The best time is as soon as one gets a feeling that the code can be rewritten in a better or more optimum way.

What constitutes a candidate for refactoring? This is a hard question to answer since it can have many answers—it's hard to understand code, the illogical location of a piece of code, duplication, names that do not clearly state a purpose, long methods, classes that do too many things, and so on. The list can go on and on. No matter what the reasons are, the most important rule is that refactoring cannot change any existing functionality.

Repeating

Once all the steps (with refactor being optional) are finished, we repeat them. At first glance, the whole process might seem too long or too complicated, but it is not. Experienced TDD practitioners write one to ten lines of code before switching to the next step. The whole cycle should last anything between a couple of seconds and no more than a few minutes. If it takes more than that, the scope of a test is too big and should be split into smaller chunks. Be fast, fail fast, correct, and repeat.

With this knowledge in mind, let us go through the requirements of the application we're about to develop using the Red-Green-Refactor process.

Tic-Tac-Toe game requirements

Tic-Tac-Toe is most often played by young children. The rules of the game are fairly simple.

Tic-Tac-Toe is a paper-and-pencil game for two players, X and O, who take turns marking the spaces in a 3×3 grid. The player who succeeds in placing three respective marks in a horizontal, vertical, or diagonal row, wins the game.

For more information about the game, please visit Wikipedia (http://en.wikipedia.org/wiki/Tic-tac-toe).

More detailed requirements will be presented later on.

The exercise consists of the creation of a single test that corresponds to one of the requirements. The test is followed by the code that fulfills the expectations of that test. Finally, if needed, the code is refactored. The same procedure should be repeated with more tests related to the same requirement. Once we're satisfied with tests and the implementation of that requirement, we'll move to the next one until they're all done.

In real-world situations, you wouldn't get such detailed requirements, but dive right into tests that would act as both requirements and validation. However, until you get comfortable with TDD, we'll have to define requirements separately from tests.

Even though all the tests and the implementation are provided, try to read only one requirement at a time and write tests and implementation code yourself. Once done, compare your solution with the one from this book and move to the next requirement. There is no one and only one solution; yours might be better than the ones presented here.

Developing Tic-Tac-Toe

Are you ready to code? Let's start with the first requirement.

Requirement 1 – placing pieces

We should start by defining the boundaries and what constitutes an invalid placement of a piece.

 A piece can be placed on any empty space of a 3x3 board.

We can split this requirement into three tests:

- When a piece is placed anywhere outside the *x*-axis, then RuntimeException is thrown
- When a piece is placed anywhere outside the *y*-axis, then RuntimeException is thrown
- When a piece is placed on an occupied space, then RuntimeException is thrown

As you can see, the tests related to this first requirement are all about validations of the input argument. There is nothing in the requirements that says what should be done with those pieces.

Before we proceed with the first test, a brief explanation of how to test exceptions with JUnit is in order.

Starting from Release 4.7, JUnit introduced a feature called Rule. It can be used to do many different things (more information can be found at https://github.com/junit-team/junit/wiki/Rules), but in our case we're interested in the ExpectedException rule:

```
public class FooTest {
  @Rule
  public ExpectedException exception = ExpectedException.none();
  @Test
  public void whenDoFooThenThrowRuntimeException() {
    Foo foo = new Foo();
    exception.expect(RuntimeException.class);
    foo.doFoo();
  }
}
```

In this example, we defined that the `ExpectedException` is a rule. Later on, in the `doFooThrowsRuntimeException` test, we're specifying that we are expecting the `RuntimeException` to be thrown after the `Foo` class is instantiated. If it is thrown before, the test will fail. If the exception is thrown after, the test is successful.

`@Before` can be used to annotate a method that should be run before each test. It is a very useful feature with which we can, for example, instantiate a class used in tests or perform some other types of actions that should be run before each test:

```
private Foo foo;

@Before
public final void before() {
  foo = new Foo();
}
```

In this example, the `Foo` class will be instantiated before each test. This way, we can avoid having repetitive code that would instantiate `Foo` inside each test method.

Each test should be annotated with `@Test`. This tells `JunitRunner` which methods constitute tests. Each of them will be run in a random order so make sure that each test is self-sufficient and does not depend on the state that might be created by other tests:

```
@Test
public void whenSomethingThenResultIsSomethingElse() {
  // This is a test method
}
```

With this knowledge, you should be able to write your first test and follow it with the implementation. Once done, compare it with the solution provided.

Use descriptive names for test methods.

One of the benefits is that it helps to understand the objective of tests.

Using method names that describe tests is beneficial when trying to figure out why some tests failed or when the coverage should be increased with more tests. It should be clear what conditions are set before the test, what actions are performed, and what the expected outcome is.

There are many different ways to name test methods. My preferred method is to name them using the given/when/then syntax used in BDD scenarios. `Given` describes (pre)conditions, `When` describes actions, and `Then` describes the expected outcome. If a test does not have preconditions (usually set using the `@Before` and `@BeforeClass` annotations), `Given` can be skipped.

Do not rely only on comments to provide information about test objectives. Comments do not appear when tests are executed from your favorite IDE, nor do they appear in reports generated by the CI or build tools.

Besides writing tests, you'll need to run them as well. Since we are using Gradle, they can be run from the command prompt:

```
$ gradle test
```

IntelliJ IDEA provides a very good Gradle tasks model that can be reached by clicking on **View** | **Tool Windows** | **Gradle**. It lists all the tasks that can be run with Gradle (`test` being one of them).

The choice is yours—you can run tests in any way you see fit, as long as you run all of them.

Test – board boundaries I

We should start by checking whether a piece is placed within the boundaries of the 3x3 board:

```
package com.packtpublishing.tddjava.ch03tictactoe;

import org.junit.Before;
import org.junit.Rule;
import org.junit.Test;
import org.junit.rules.ExpectedException;

public class TicTacToeSpec {
  @Rule
  public ExpectedException exception = ExpectedException.none();
  private TicTacToe ticTacToe;

  @Before
  public final void before() {
    ticTacToe = new TicTacToe();
  }
  @Test
  public void whenXOutsideBoardThenRuntimeException() {
    exception.expect(RuntimeException.class);
    ticTacToe.play(5, 2);
  }
}
```

When a piece is placed anywhere outside the *x*-axis, then `RuntimeException` is thrown.

In this test, we are defining that `RuntimeException` is expected when the `ticTacToe.play(5, 2)` method is invoked. It's a very short and easy test, and making it pass should be easy as well. All we have to do is create the `play` method and make sure that it throws `RuntimeException` when the x argument is smaller than 1 or bigger than 3 (the board is 3x3). You should run this test three times. The first time, it should fail because the `play` method doesn't exist. Once it is added, it should fail because `RuntimeException` is not thrown. The third time, it should be successful because the code that corresponds with this test is fully implemented.

Implementation

Now that we have a clear definition of when an exception should be thrown, the implementation should be straightforward:

```
package com.packtpublishing.tddjava.ch03tictactoe;

public class TicTacToe {
  public void play(int x, int y) {
    if (x < 1 || x > 3) {
      throw new RuntimeException("X is outside board");
    }
  }
}
```

As you can see, this code does not contain anything else, but the bare minimum required for the test to pass.

> Some TDD practitioners tend to take minimum as a literal meaning. They would have the `play` method with only the `throw new RuntimeException();` line. I tend to translate minimum to as little as possible within reason.

We're not adding numbers, nor are we returning anything. It's all about making small changes very fast. (Remember the game of ping pong?) For now, we're doing red-green steps. There's not much we can do to improve this code so we're skipping the refactoring.

Let's move on to the next test.

Test – board boundaries II

This test is almost the same as the previous one. This time we should validate the *y*-axis:

```
@Test
public void whenYOutsideBoardThenRuntimeException() {
  exception.expect(RuntimeException.class);
  ticTacToe.play(2, 5);
}
```

> When a piece is placed anywhere outside the *y*-axis, then `RuntimeException` is thrown.

Implementation

The implementation of this specification is almost the same as the previous one. All we have to do is throw an exception if y does not fall within the defined range:

```
public void play(int x, int y) {
  if (x < 1 || x > 3) {
    throw new RuntimeException("X is outside board");
  } else if (y < 1 || y > 3) {
    throw new RuntimeException("Y is outside board");
  }
}
```

In order for the last test to pass, we had to add the else clause that checks whether Y is inside the board.

Let's do the last test for this requirement.

Test – occupied spot

Now that we know that pieces are placed within the board's boundaries, we should make sure that they can be placed only on unoccupied spaces:

```
@Test
public void whenOccupiedThenRuntimeException() {
  ticTacToe.play(2, 1);
  exception.expect(RuntimeException.class);
  ticTacToe.play(2, 1);
}
```

When a piece is placed on an occupied space, then RuntimeException is thrown.

That's it; this was our last test. Once the implementation is finished, we can consider the first requirement as done.

Implementation

To implement the last test, we should store the location of the placed pieces in an array. Every time a new piece is placed, we should verify that the place is not occupied, or else throw an exception:

```
private Character[][] board = {
  {'\0', '\0', '\0'},
  {'\0', '\0', '\0'},
  {'\0', '\0', '\0'}
};

public void play(int x, int y) {
  if (x < 1 || x > 3) {
    throw new RuntimeException("X is outside board");
  } else if (y < 1 || y > 3) {
    throw new RuntimeException("Y is outside board");
  }
  if (board[x - 1][y - 1] != '\0') {
    throw new RuntimeException("Box is occupied");
  } else {
    board[x - 1][y - 1] = 'X';
  }
}
```

We're checking whether a place that was played is occupied and, if it is not, we're changing the array entry value from empty (\0) to occupied (X). Keep in mind that we're still not storing who played (X or O).

Refactoring

While the code that we have done so far fulfills the requirements set by the tests, it looks a bit confusing. If someone read it, it would not be clear as to what the play method does. We should refactor it by moving the code into separate methods. The refactored code will look like the following:

```
public void play(int x, int y) {
  checkAxis(x);
  checkAxis(y);
  setBox(x, y);
}

private void checkAxis(int axis) {
  if (axis < 1 || axis > 3) {
    throw new RuntimeException("X is outside board");
```

```
      }
    }
    private void setBox(int x, int y) {
      if (board[x - 1][y - 1] != '\0') {
        throw new RuntimeException("Box is occupied");
      } else {
        board[x - 1][y - 1] = 'X';
      }
    }
```

With this refactoring, we did not change the functionality of the play method. It behaves exactly the same as it behaved before, but the new code is a bit more readable. Since we had tests that covered all the existing functionality, there was no fear that we might do something wrong. As long as all tests are passing all the time and refactoring did not introduce any new behavior, it is safe to make changes to the code.

The source code can be found in the 01-exceptions branch of the tdd-java-ch03-tic-tac-toe Git repository at https://bitbucket.org/vfarcic/tdd-java-ch03-tic-tac-toe/branch/01-exceptions.

Requirement 2 – adding two-player support

Now it's time to work on the specification of which player is about to play his turn.

There should be a way to find out which player should play next.

We can split this requirement into three tests:

- The first turn should be played by player X
- If the last turn was played by X, then the next turn should be played by O
- If the last turn was played by O, then the next turn should be played by X

Until this moment, we haven't used any of the JUnit's asserts. To use them, we need to import the static methods from the org.junit.Assert class:

```
import static org.junit.Assert.*;
```

Chapter 3

In their essence, methods inside the `Assert` class are very simple. Most of them start with `assert`. For example, `assertEquals` compares two objects—`assertNotEquals` verifies that two objects are not the same and `assertArrayEquals` verifies that two arrays are the same. Each of those asserts has many overloaded variations so that almost any type of Java object can be used.

In our case, we'll need to compare two characters. The first is the one we're expecting and the second one is the actual character retrieved from the `nextPlayer` method.

Now it's time to write those tests and the implementation.

Write the test before writing the implementation code.

The benefits of doing this are as follows—it ensures that testable code is written and ensures that every line of code gets tests written for it.

By writing or modifying the test first, the developer is focused on requirements before starting to work on a code. This is the main difference when compared to writing tests after the implementation is done. An additional benefit is that with tests first, we are avoiding the danger that the tests work as quality checking instead of quality assurance.

Test – X plays first

Player X has the first turn:

```
@Test
public void givenFirstTurnWhenNextPlayerThenX() {
  assertEquals('X', ticTacToe.nextPlayer());
}
```

The first turn should be played by Player X.

This test should be self-explanatory. We are expecting the `nextPlayer` method to return X. If you try to run this, you'll see that the code does not even compile. That's because the `nextPlayer` method does not even exist. Our job is to write the `nextPlayer` method and make sure that it returns the correct value.

Implementation

There's no real need to check whether it really is the player's first turn or not. As it stands, this test can be fulfilled by always returning X. Later tests will force us to refine this code:

```
public char nextPlayer() {
  return 'X';
}
```

Test – O plays right after X

Now, we should make sure that players are changing. After X is finished, it should be O's turn, then again X, and so on:

```
@Test
public void givenLastTurnWasXWhenNextPlayerThenO() {
  ticTacToe.play(1, 1);
  assertEquals('O', ticTacToe.nextPlayer());
}
```

If the last turn was played by X, then the next turn should be played by O.

Implementation

In order to track who should play next, we need to store who played last:

```
private char lastPlayer = '\0';

public void play(int x, int y) {
  checkAxis(x);
  checkAxis(y);
  setBox(x, y);
  lastPlayer = nextPlayer();
}

public char nextPlayer() {
  if (lastPlayer == 'X') {
    return 'O';
  }
  return 'X';
}
```

You are probably starting to get the hang of it. Tests are small and easy to write. With enough experience, it should take a minute, if not seconds, to write a test and as much time or less to write the implementation.

Test – X plays right after O

Finally, we can check whether X's turn comes after O played.

If the last turn was played by O, then the next turn should be played by X.

There's nothing to do to fulfill this test and, therefore, the test is useless and should be discarded. If you write this test, you'll discover that it is a false positive. It would pass without changing the implementation; try it out. Write this test and if it is successful without writing any implementation code, discard it.

The source code can be found in the `02-next-player` branch of the `tdd-java-ch03-tic-tac-toe` Git repository at `https://bitbucket.org/vfarcic/tdd-java-ch03-tic-tac-toe/branch/02-next-player`.

Requirement 3 – adding winning conditions

It's time to work on winning according to the rules of the game. This is the part where, when compared with the previous code, work becomes a bit more tedious. We should check all the possible winning combinations and, if one of them is fulfilled, declare a winner.

A player wins by being the first to connect a line of friendly pieces from one side or corner of the board to the other.

To check whether a line of friendly pieces is connected, we should verify horizontal, vertical, and diagonal lines.

Test – by default there's no winner

Let's start by defining the default response of the `play` method:

```
@Test
public void whenPlayThenNoWinner() {
  String actual = ticTacToe.play(1,1);
  assertEquals("No winner", actual);
}
```

 If no winning condition is fulfilled, then there is no winner.

Implementation

The default return values are always easiest to implement and this one is no exception:

```
public String play(int x, int y) {
  checkAxis(x);
  checkAxis(y);
  setBox(x, y);
  lastPlayer = nextPlayer();
  return "No winner";
}
```

Test – winning condition I

Now that we have declared what the default response is (`No winner`), it's time to start working on different winning conditions:

```
@Test
public void whenPlayAndWholeHorizontalLineThenWinner() {
  ticTacToe.play(1, 1); // X
  ticTacToe.play(1, 2); // O
  ticTacToe.play(2, 1); // X
  ticTacToe.play(2, 2); // O
  String actual = ticTacToe.play(3, 1); // X
  assertEquals("X is the winner", actual);
}
```

Chapter 3

 The player wins when the whole horizontal line is occupied by his pieces.

Implementation

To fulfill this test, we need to check whether any horizontal line is filled by the same mark as the current player. Until this moment, we didn't care what was put on the board array. Now, we need to introduce not only which board boxes are empty, but also which player played them:

```
public String play(int x, int y) {
  checkAxis(x);
  checkAxis(y);
  lastPlayer = nextPlayer();
  setBox(x, y, lastPlayer);
  for (int index = 0; index < 3; index++) {
    if (board[0][index] == lastPlayer
        && board[1][index] == lastPlayer
        && board[2][index] == lastPlayer) {
      return lastPlayer + " is the winner";
    }
  }
  return "No winner";
}
private void setBox(int x, int y, char lastPlayer) {
  if (board[x - 1][y - 1] != '\0') {
    throw new RuntimeException("Box is occupied");
  } else {
    board[x - 1][y - 1] = lastPlayer;
  }
}
```

Refactoring

The preceding code satisfies the tests, but is not necessarily the final version. It served its purpose of getting code coverage as quickly as possible. Now, since we have tests that guarantee the integrity of the expected behavior, we can refactor the code:

```
private static final int SIZE = 3;

public String play(int x, int y) {
  checkAxis(x);
```

[77]

```
      checkAxis(y);
      lastPlayer = nextPlayer();
      setBox(x, y, lastPlayer);
      if (isWin()) {
        return lastPlayer + " is the winner";
      }
      return "No winner";
    }

    private boolean isWin() {
      for (int i = 0; i < SIZE; i++) {
        if (board[0][i] + board[1][i] + board[2][i] == (lastPlayer * SIZE)) {
          return true;
        }
      }
      return false;
    }
```

This refactored solution looks better. The `play` method keeps being short and easy to understand. Winning logic is moved to a separate method. Not only have we kept the `play` method's purpose clear, but this separation also allows us to grow the winning condition's code in separation from the rest.

Test – winning condition II

We should also check whether there is a win by filling the vertical line:

```
@Test
public void whenPlayAndWholeVerticalLineThenWinner() {
  ticTacToe.play(2, 1); // X
  ticTacToe.play(1, 1); // O
  ticTacToe.play(3, 1); // X
  ticTacToe.play(1, 2); // O
  ticTacToe.play(2, 2); // X
  String actual = ticTacToe.play(1, 3); // O
  assertEquals("O is the winner", actual);
}
```

The player wins when the whole vertical line is occupied by his pieces.

Implementation

This implementation should be similar to the previous one. We already have horizontal verification and now we need to do the same vertically:

```
private boolean isWin() {
   int playerTotal = lastPlayer * 3;
   for (int i = 0; i < SIZE; i++) {
      if (board[0][i] + board[1][i] + board[2][i] == playerTotal) {
         return true;
      } else if (board[i][0] + board[i][1] + board[i][2] ==
playerTotal) {
         return true;
      }
   }
   return false;
}
```

Test – winning condition III

Now that horizontal and vertical lines are covered, we should move our attention to diagonal combinations:

```
@Test
public void whenPlayAndTopBottomDiagonalLineThenWinner() {
   ticTacToe.play(1, 1); // X
   ticTacToe.play(1, 2); // O
   ticTacToe.play(2, 2); // X
   ticTacToe.play(1, 3); // O
   String actual = ticTacToe.play(3, 3); // X
   assertEquals("X is the winner", actual);
}
```

The player wins when the whole diagonal line from the top-left to bottom-right is occupied by his pieces.

Implementation

Since there is only one line that can constitute with the requirement, we can check it directly without any loops:

```
private boolean isWin() {
   int playerTotal = lastPlayer * 3;
   for (int i = 0; i < SIZE; i++) {
     if (board[0][i] + board[1][i] + board[2][i] == playerTotal) {
       return true;
     } else if (board[i][0] + board[i][1] + board[i][2] ==
playerTotal) {
       return true;
     }
   }
   if (board[0][0] + board[1][1] + board[2][2] == playerTotal) {
     return true;
   }
   return false;
}
```

Test – winning condition IV

Finally, there is the last possible winning condition to tackle:

```
@Test
public void whenPlayAndBottomTopDiagonalLineThenWinner() {
   ticTacToe.play(1, 3); // X
   ticTacToe.play(1, 1); // O
   ticTacToe.play(2, 2); // X
   ticTacToe.play(1, 2); // O
   String actual = ticTacToe.play(3, 1); // X
   assertEquals("X is the winner", actual);
}
```

The player wins when the whole diagonal line from the bottom-left to top-right is occupied by his pieces.

Implementation

The implementation of this test should be almost the same as the previous one:

```
private boolean isWin() {
  int playerTotal = lastPlayer * 3;
  for (int i = 0; i < SIZE; i++) {
    if (board[0][i] + board[1][i] + board[2][i] == playerTotal) {
      return true;
    } else if (board[i][0] + board[i][1] + board[i][2] ==
playerTotal) {
      return true;
    }
  }
  if (board[0][0] + board[1][1] + board[2][2] == playerTotal) {
    return true;
  } else if (board[0][2] + board[1][1] + board[2][0] ==
playerTotal) {
    return true;
  }
  return false;
}
```

Refactoring

The way we're handling possible diagonal wins, the calculation doesn't look right. Maybe the reutilization of the existing loop would make more sense:

```
private boolean isWin() {
  int playerTotal = lastPlayer * 3;
  char diagonal1 = '\0';
  char diagonal2 = '\0';
  for (int i = 0; i < SIZE; i++) {
    diagonal1 += board[i][i];
    diagonal2 += board[i][SIZE - i - 1];
    if (board[0][i] + board[1][i] + board[2][i]) == playerTotal) {
      return true;
    } else if (board[i][0] + board[i][1] + board[i][2] ==
playerTotal) {
      return true;
    }
  }
  if (diagonal1 == playerTotal || diagonal2 == playerTotal) {
    return true;
  }
  return false;
```

}
```

The source code can be found in the `03-wins` branch of the `tdd-java-ch03-tic-tac-toe` Git repository at https://bitbucket.org/vfarcic/tdd-java-ch03-tic-tac-toe/branch/03-wins.

Now, let's go through the last requirement.

## Requirement 4 – tie conditions

The only thing missing is how to tackle the draw result.

The result is a draw when all the boxes are filled.

### Test – handling a tie situation

We can test the draw result by filling all the board's boxes:

```
@Test
public void whenAllBoxesAreFilledThenDraw() {
  ticTacToe.play(1, 1);
  ticTacToe.play(1, 2);
  ticTacToe.play(1, 3);
  ticTacToe.play(2, 1);
  ticTacToe.play(2, 3);
  ticTacToe.play(2, 2);
  ticTacToe.play(3, 1);
  ticTacToe.play(3, 3);
  String actual = ticTacToe.play(3, 2);
  assertEquals("The result is draw", actual);
}
```
```

Implementation

Checking whether it's a draw is fairly straightforward. All we have to do is check whether all the board's boxes are filled. We can do that by iterating through the board array:

```java
public String play(int x, int y) {
  checkAxis(x);
  checkAxis(y);
  lastPlayer = nextPlayer();
  setBox(x, y, lastPlayer);
  if (isWin()) {
    return lastPlayer + " is the winner";
  } else if (isDraw()) {
    return "The result is draw";
  } else {
    return "No winner";
  }
}

private boolean isDraw() {
  for (int x = 0; x < SIZE; x++) {
    for (int y = 0; y < SIZE; y++) {
      if (board[x][y] == '\0') {
        return false;
      }
    }
  }
  return true;
}
```

Refactoring

Even though the `isWin` method is not the scope of the last test, it can still be refactored even more. For once, we don't need to check all the combinations, but only those related to the position of the last piece played. The final version could look like the following:

```java
private boolean isWin(int x, int y) {
  int playerTotal = lastPlayer * 3;
  char horizontal, vertical, diagonal1, diagonal2;
  horizontal = vertical = diagonal1 = diagonal2 = '\0';
  for (int i = 0; i < SIZE; i++) {
    horizontal += board[i][y - 1];
    vertical += board[x - 1][i];
    diagonal1 += board[i][i];
    diagonal2 += board[i][SIZE - i - 1];
  }
```

```
       if (horizontal == playerTotal
           || vertical == playerTotal
           || diagonal1 == playerTotal
           || diagonal2 == playerTotal) {
         return true;
       }
       return false;
   }
```

Refactoring can be done on any part of the code at any time, as long as all the tests are successful. While it's often easiest and fastest to refactor the code that was just written, going back to something that was written the other day, previous month, or even years ago, is more than welcome. The best time to refactor something is when someone sees an opportunity to make it better. It doesn't matter who wrote it or when; making the code better is always a good thing to do.

The source code can be found in the 04-draw branch of the tdd-java-ch03-tic-tac-toe Git repository at https://bitbucket.org/vfarcic/tdd-java-ch03-tic-tac-toe/branch/04-draw.

Code coverage

We did not use code coverage tools throughout this exercise. The reason is that we wanted you to be focused on the Red-Green-Refactor model. You wrote a test, saw it fail, wrote the implementation code, saw that all the tests were executed successfully, refactored the code whenever you saw an opportunity to make it better, and then you repeated the process. Did our tests cover all cases? That's something that code coverage tools such as JaCoCo can answer. Should you use those tools? Probably, only in the beginning. Let me clarify that. When you are starting with TDD, you will probably miss some tests or implement more than what the tests defined. In those cases, using code coverage is a good way to learn from your own mistakes. Later on, the more experienced you become with TDD, the less of a need you'll have for such tools. You'll write tests and just enough of the code to make them pass. Your coverage will be high with or without tools such as JaCoCo. There will be a small amount of code not covered by tests because you'll make a conscious decision about what is not worth testing.

Tools such as JaCoCo were designed mostly as a way to verify that the tests written after the implementation code are providing enough coverage. With TDD, we are taking a different approach with the inverted order (tests before the implementation).

Still, we suggest you use JaCoCo as a learning tool and decide for yourself whether to use it in the future.

To enable JaCoCo within Gradle, add the following to `build.gradle`:

```
apply plugin: 'jacoco'
```

From now on, Gradle will collect JaCoCo metrics every time we run tests. Those metrics can be transformed into a nice report using the `jacocoTestReport` Gradle target. Let's run our tests again and see what the code coverage is:

```
$ gradle clean test jacocoTestReport
```

The end result is the report located in the `build/reports/jacoco/test/html` directory. Results will vary depending on the solution you made for this exercise. My results say that there is a 100% of instructions coverage and 96% of branches coverage; 4% is missing because there was no test case where the player played on a box 0 or negative. The implementation of that case is there, but there is no specific test that covers it. Overall, this is a pretty good coverage:

tdd-java-ch03-tic-tac-toe > com.packtpublishing.tddjava.ch03tictactoe > TicTacToe

TicTacToe

Element	Missed Instructions	Cov.	Missed Branches	Cov.	Missed	Cxty	Missed	Lines	Missed	Methods
isWin(int, int)		100%		100%	0	6	0	10	0	1
TicTacToe()		100%		n/a	0	1	0	3	0	1
play(int, int)		100%		100%	0	3	0	9	0	1
setBox(int, int, char)		100%		100%	0	2	0	4	0	1
isDraw()		100%		100%	0	4	0	5	0	1
checkAxis(int)		100%		75%	1	3	0	3	0	1
nextPlayer()		100%		100%	0	2	0	3	0	1
Total	0 of 272	100%	1 of 28	96%	1	21	0	37	0	7

JaCoCo will be added in the source code. This is found in the `05-jacoco` branch of the `tdd-java-ch03-tic-tac-toe` Git repository at `https://bitbucket.org/vfarcic/tdd-java-ch03-tic-tac-toe/branch/05-jacoco`.

More exercises

We just developed one (most commonly used) variation of the Tic-Tac-Toe game. As an additional exercise, pick one or more variations from Wikipedia (`http://en.wikipedia.org/wiki/Tic-tac-toe`) and implement it using the Red-Green-Refactor procedure. When finished, implement a kind of AI that would play O's turns. Since Tic-Tac-Toe usually leads to a draw, AI can be considered finished when it successfully reaches a draw for any combination of X's moves.

While working on those exercises, remember to be fast and play ping pong. Also, most of all, remember to use the Red-Green-Refactor procedure.

Summary

We managed to finish our Tic-Tac-Toe game using the Red-Green-Refactor process. The examples themselves were simple and you probably didn't have a problem following them.

The objective of this chapter was not to dive into something complicated (that comes later), but to get into the habit of using the short and repetitive cycle called Red-Green-Refactor.

We learned that the easiest way to develop something is by splitting it into very small chunks. The design was emerging from tests instead of using a big upfront approach. No line of the implementation code was written without writing a test first and seeing it fail. By confirming that the last test fails, we are confirming that it is valid (it's easy to make a mistake and write a test that is always successful) and the feature we are about to implement does not exist. After the test failed, we wrote the implementation of that test. While writing the implementation, we tried to make it a minimal one with the objective being to make the test pass, not to make the solution final. We repeated this process until we felt that there was a need to refactor the code. Refactoring did not introduce any new functionality (we did not change what the application does), but made the code more optimal and easier to read and maintain.

In the next chapter, we'll elaborate in more detail about what constitutes a unit within the context of TDD and how to approach the creation of tests based on those units.

4
Unit Testing – Focusing on What You Do and Not on What Has Been Done

"To create something exceptional, your mindset must be relentlessly focused on the smallest detail."

– *Giorgio Armani*

As promised, each chapter will explore a different Java testing framework and this one is no exception. We'll use TestNG to build our specifications.

In the previous `Chapter 3`, *Red-Green-Refactor – From Failure Through Success until Perfection*, we practiced the Red-Green-Refactor procedure. We used unit tests without going deeper into how unit testing works in the context of TDD. We'll build on the knowledge from the last chapter and go into more detail by trying to explain what unit tests really are and how they fit into the TDD approach to building software.

The goal of this chapter is to learn how to focus on the unit we're currently working on and how to ignore or isolate those that were done before.

Once we're comfortable with TestNG and unit testing, we'll dive right into the requirements of our next application and start coding.

The following topics will be covered in this chapter:

- Unit testing
- Unit testing with TDD
- TestNG
- Remote-controlled ship requirements
- Developing the remote-controlled ship

Unit testing

Frequent manual testing is too impractical for any but the smallest systems. The only way around this is the use of automated tests. They are the only effective method to reduce the time and cost of building, deploying, and maintaining applications. In order to effectively manage applications, it is of the utmost importance that both the implementation and test codes are as simple as possible. Simplicity is one of the core **extreme programming** (**XP**) values (http://www.extremeprogramming.org/rules/simple.html) and the key to TDD and programming in general. It is most often accomplished through division into small units. In Java, units are methods. Being the smallest, the feedback loop they provide is the fastest so we spend most of our time thinking and working on them. As a counterpart to implementation methods, unit tests should constitute by far the biggest percentage of all tests.

What is unit testing?

Unit testing is a practice that forces us to test small, individual, and isolated units of code. They are usually methods, even though in some cases classes or even whole applications can be considered to be units, as well. In order to write unit tests, code under tests needs to be isolated from the rest of the application. Preferably, that isolation is already ingrained in the code or it can be accomplished with the use of **mocks** (more on mocks will be covered in Chapter 6, *Mocking – Removing External Dependencies*). If unit tests of a particular method cross the boundaries of that unit, then they become integration tests. As such, it becomes less clear what is under the tests. In case of a failure, the scope of a problem suddenly increases and finding the cause becomes more tedious.

Why unit testing?

A common question, especially within organizations that rely heavily on manual testing, is *Why should we use unit instead of functional and integration testing?* This question in itself is flawed. Unit testing does not replace other types of testing. Instead, unit testing reduces the scope of other types of tests. By its nature, unit testing is easier and faster to write than any other type of tests, thus reducing the cost and **time to market** (**TTM**). Due to the reduced time to write and run them, they tend to detect problems much sooner. The faster we detect problems, the cheaper it is to fix them. A bug that was detected minutes after it was created is much easier to fix than if that same bug was found days, weeks, or even months after it was made.

Code refactoring

Code refactoring is the process of changing the structure of an existing code without changing its external behavior. The purpose of refactoring is to improve an existing code. This improvement can be made for many different reasons. We might want to make the code more readable, less complex, easier to maintain, cheaper to extend, and so on. No matter what the reason for refactoring is, the ultimate goal is always to make it better in one way or another. The effect of this goal is a reduction in technical debt; a reduction in pending work that needs to be done due to suboptimal design, architecture, or coding.

Typically, we approach refactoring by applying a set of small changes without modifying intended behavior. Reducing the scope of refactoring changes allows us continuously to confirm that those changes did not break any existing functionality. The only way to effectively obtain this confirmation is through the use of automated tests.

One of the great benefits of unit tests is that they are the best refactoring enablers. Refactoring is too risky when there are no automated tests to confirm that the application still behaves as expected. While any type of test can be used to provide the code coverage required for refactoring, in most cases only unit tests can provide the required level of details.

Why not use unit tests exclusively?

At this moment, you might be wondering whether unit testing could provide a solution for all your testing needs. Unfortunately, that is not the case. While unit tests usually cover the biggest percentage of your testing needs, functional and integration tests should be an integral part of your testing toolbox.

We'll cover other types of tests in more detail in later chapters. For now, a few important distinctions between them are as follows:

- Unit tests try to verify small units of functionality. In the Java world, those units are methods. All external dependencies, such as invocations of other classes and methods or database calls, should be done in memory with the use of mocks, stubs, spies, fakes, and dummies. Gerard Meszaros coined a more general term, **test doubles**, that envelops all those (http://en.wikipedia.org/wiki/Test_double). Unit tests are simple, easy to write, and fast to run. They are usually the biggest percentage of a testing suite.
- **Functional** and **acceptance** tests have a job to verify that the application we're building works as expected, as a whole. While those two differ in their purpose, both share a similar goal. Unlike unit tests that are verifying the internal quality of the code, functional and acceptance tests are trying to ensure that the system is working correctly from the customer's or user's point of view. Those tests are usually smaller in number when compared with unit tests due to the cost and effort needed to both write and run them.
- **Integration** tests intend to verify that separate units, modules, applications, or even whole systems are properly integrated with each other. You might have a frontend application that uses backend APIs that, in turn, communicate with a database. The job of integration tests would be to verify that all three of those separate components of the system are indeed integrated and can communicate with each other. Since we already know that all the units are working and all functional and acceptance tests are passed, integration tests are usually the smallest of all three as their job is only to confirm that all the pieces are working well together:

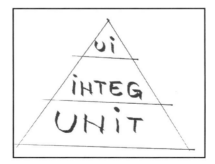

The testing pyramid states that you should have many more unit tests than higher-level tests (UI tests, integration tests, and so on). Why is that? Unit tests are much cheaper to write, faster to run, and, at the same time, provide much bigger coverage. Take, for example, registration functionality. We should test what happens when a username is empty, when a password is empty, when a username or password is not in the correct format, when the user already exists, and so on. Only for this single functionality there can be tens, if not hundreds of tests. Writing and running all those tests from the UI can be very expensive (time-consuming to write and slow to run). On the other hand, unit testing a method that does this validation is easy, fast to write, and fast to run. If all those cases are covered with unit tests, we could be satisfied with a single integration test that checks whether our UI is calling the correct method on the backend. If it is, details are irrelevant from an integration point of view since we know that all cases are already covered on the unit level.

Unit testing with TDD

What is the difference in the way we write unit tests in the context of TDD? The major differentiator is in *when*. While traditionally unit tests are written after the implementation code is done, in TDD we write tests before—the order of things is inverted. Without TDD, the purpose of unit tests is to validate an existing code. TDD teaches us that unit tests should drive our development and design. They should define the behavior of the smallest possible unit. They are micro-requirements pending development. A test tells you what to do next and when you're done doing it. Depending on the type of tests (unit, functional, integration, and so on), the scope of what should be done next differs. In the case of TDD with unit tests, this scope is the smallest possible, meaning a method or, more often, a part of it. Moreover, with TDD driven by unit tests, we are forced to comply to some design principles, such as **keep it simple, stupid** (**KISS**). By writing simple tests with a very small scope, the implementation of those tests tends to be simple as well. By forcing tests not to use external dependencies, we are forcing the implementation code to have a separation of concerns that is well-designed. There are many other examples of how TDD helps us to write better code. Those same benefits cannot be accomplished with unit testing alone. Without TDD, unit tests are forced to work with an existing code and have no influence on the design.

To summarize, the main goal of unit testing without TDD is the validation of the existing code. Unit testing written in advance using the TDD procedure has the main objective specification and design, with validation being a side product. This side product is often of a higher quality than when tests are written after the implementation.

TDD forces us to think through our requirements and design, write clean code that works, create executable requirements, and refactor safely and often. On top of all that, we end up with high test code coverage that is used to regression-test all our code whenever some change is introduced. Unit testing without TDD gives us only tests and, often, with doubtful quality.

TestNG

JUnit and TestNG are two major Java testing frameworks. You already wrote tests with JUnit in the previous chapter, `Chapter 3`, *Red-Green-Refactor – From Failure Through Success until Perfection*, and, hopefully, got a good understanding of how it works. How about TestNG? It was born out of a desire to make JUnit better. Indeed, it contains some functionalities that JUnit doesn't have.

The following subsections summarize some of the differences between the two of them. We'll try not only to provide an explanation of the differences, but also their evaluation in the context of unit testing with TDD.

The @Test annotation

Both JUnit and TestNG use the `@Test` annotation to specify which method is considered to be a test. Unlike JUnit, which requires every method to be annotated with `@Test`, TestNG allows us to use this annotation on a class level, as well. When used in this way, all public methods are considered tests unless specified otherwise:

```
@Test
public class DirectionSpec {
  public void whenGetFromShortNameNThenReturnDirectionN() {
    Direction direction = Direction.getFromShortName('N');
    assertEquals(direction, Direction.NORTH);
  }

  public void whenGetFromShortNameWThenReturnDirectionW() {
    Direction direction = Direction.getFromShortName('W');
    assertEquals(direction, Direction.WEST);
  }
}
```

In this example, we put the `@Test` annotation above the `DirectionSpec` class. As a result, both the `whenGetFromShortNameNThenReturnDirectionN` and `whenGetFromShortNameWThenReturnDirectionW` methods are considered tests. If that code was written using JUnit, both the methods would need to have the `@Test` annotation.

The @BeforeSuite, @BeforeTest, @BeforeGroups, @AfterGroups, @AfterTest, and @AfterSuite annotations

Those six annotations do not have their equivalents in JUnit. TestNG can group tests into suites, using XML configuration. Methods annotated with `@BeforeSuite` and `@AfterSuite` are run before and after all the tests in the specified suite have run. Similarly, the `@BeforeTest` and `@AfterTest` annotated methods are run before any test method belonging to the test classes has run. Finally, TestNG tests can be organized into groups. The `@BeforeGroups` and `@AfterGroups` annotations allow us to run methods before the first test and after the last test, in specified groups, are run.

While those annotations can be very useful when tests are written after the implementation code, they do not provide much usage in the context of TDD. Unlike traditional testing, which is often planned and written as a separate project, TDD teaches us to write one test at a time and keep everything simple. Most importantly, unit tests are supposed to run quickly so there is no need to group them into suites or groups. When tests are fast, running anything less than everything is a waste. If, for example, all tests are run in less than 15 seconds, there is no need to run only a part of them. On the other hand, when tests are slow, it is often a sign that external dependencies are not isolated. No matter what the reason is behind slow tests, the solution is not to run only a part of them, but to fix the problem.

Moreover, functional and integration tests do tend to be slower and require us to have some kind of separation. However, it is better to separate them in, for example, `build.gradle` so that each type of test is run as a separate task.

The @BeforeClass and @AfterClass annotations

These annotations have the same function in both JUnit and TestNG. Annotated methods will be run before the first test and after the last test, in a current class. The only difference is that TestNG does not require those methods to be static. The reason behind this can be found in the different approaches those two frameworks take when running test methods. JUnit isolates each test into its own instance of the test class, forcing us to have those methods defined as static and, therefore, reusable across all test runs. TestNG, on the other hand, executes all test methods in the context of a single test class instance, eliminating the need for those methods to be static.

The @BeforeMethod and @AfterMethod annotations

The `@Before` and `@After` annotations are equivalent to JUnit. Annotated methods are run before and after each test method.

The @Test(enable = false) annotation argument

Both JUnit and TestNG can disable tests. While JUnit uses a separate `@Ignore` annotation, TestNG uses the `@Test` annotation Boolean argument, `enable`. Functionally, both work in the same way and the difference is only in the way we write them.

The @Test(expectedExceptions = SomeClass.class) annotation argument

This is the case where JUnit has the advantage. While both provide the same way to specify the expected exception (in the case of JUnit, the argument is called simply `expected`), JUnit introduces rules that are a more elegant way to test exceptions (we already worked with them in `Chapter 2`, *Tools, Frameworks, and Environment*).

TestNG versus JUnit summary

There are many other differences between those two frameworks. For brevity, we do not cover all of them in this book. Consult their documentation for further information.

Chapter 4

More information about JUnit and TestNG can be found at http://junit.org/ and http://testng.org/.

TestNG provides more features and is more advanced than JUnit. We'll work with TestNG throughout this chapter, and you'll get to know it better. One thing that you'll notice is that we won't use any of those advanced features. The reason is that, with TDD, we rarely need them when working with unit tests. Functional and integration tests are of a different kind and would serve as a better demonstration of TestNG's superiority. However, there are tools that are more suited for those types of tests, as you'll see in the following chapters.

Which one should you use? I'll leave that choice up to you. By the time you finish this chapter, you'll have hands-on knowledge of both JUnit and TestNG.

Remote-controlled ship requirements

We'll work on a variation of a well-known kata called **Mars Rover**, originally published in *Dallas Hack Club* (http://dallashackclub.com/rover).

Imagine that a naval ship is placed somewhere on Earth's seas. Since this is the 21st century, we can control that ship remotely.

Our job will be to create a program that can move the ship around the seas.

Since this is a TDD book and the subject of this chapter is unit tests, we'll develop an application using a TDD approach with the focus on unit tests. In the previous chapter, *Chapter 3, Red-Green-Refactor – From Failure Through Success until Perfection*, you learned the theory and had practical experience with the Red-Green-Refactor procedure. We'll build on top of that and try to learn how to employ unit testing effectively. Specifically, we'll try to concentrate on a unit we're developing and learn how to isolate and ignore dependencies that a unit might use. Not only that, but we'll try to concentrate on one requirement at a time. For this reason, you were presented only with high-level requirements; we should be able to move the remote-controlled ship, located somewhere on the planet, around.

Unit Testing – Focusing on What You Do and Not on What Has Been Done

To make things easier, all the supporting classes have been already made and tested. This will allow us to concentrate on the main task at hand and, at the same time, keep this exercise concise.

Developing the remote-controlled ship

Let's start by importing the existing Git repository.

Project setup

Let's start setting up the project:

1. Open IntelliJ IDEA. If an existing project is already opened, select **File** | **Close Project**.
2. You will be presented with a screen similar to the following:

Chapter 4

3. To import the project from the Git repository, click on **Check out from Version Control** and select **Git**. Type `https://bitbucket.org/vfarcic/tdd-java-ch04-ship.git` in to the **Git Repository URL** field and click on **Clone**:

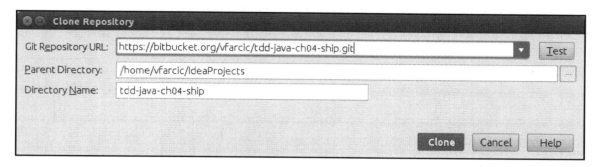

4. Answer **Yes** when asked whether you would like to open the project. Next you will be presented with the **Import Project from Gradle** dialog. Click on **OK**:

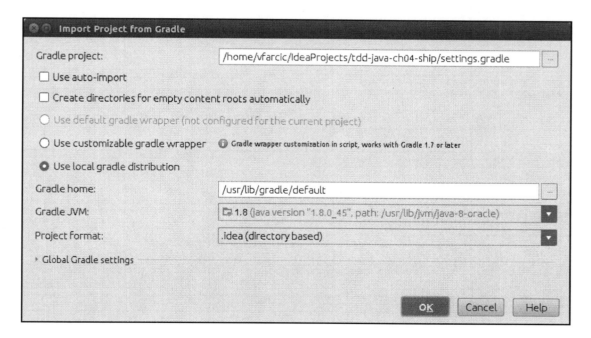

5. IDEA will need to spend some time downloading the dependencies specified in the `build.gradle` file. Once that is done, you'll see that some classes and corresponding tests are already created:

Helper classes

Imagine that a colleague of yours started working on this project. He's a good programmer and a TDD practitioner, and you trust his abilities to have good test code coverage. In other words, you can rely on his work. However, that colleague did not finish the application before he left for his vacations and it's up to you to continue where he stopped. He created all the helper classes: `Direction`, `Location`, `Planet`, and `Point`. You'll notice that the corresponding test classes are there as well. They have the same name as the class they're testing with the `Spec` suffix (that is, `DirectionSpec`). The reason for using this suffix is to make clear that tests are not only intended to validate the code, but also to serve as an executable specification.

Chapter 4

On top of the helper classes, you'll find the Ship (implementation) and ShipSpec (specifications/tests) classes. We'll spend most of our time in those two classes. We'll write tests in ShipSpec and then we'll write the implementation code in the Ship class (just as we did before).

Since we already learned that tests are not only used as a way to validate the code, but also as executable documentation, from this moment on, we'll use the phrase specification or spec instead of test.

Every time we finish writing a specification or the code that implements it, we'll run `gradle test` either from the command prompt or by using the Gradle projects IDEA Tool Window:

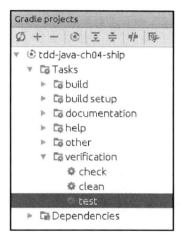

With the project set up, we're ready to dive into the first requirement.

Requirement – starting point and orientation

We need to know what the current location of the ship is in order to be able to move it. Moreover, we should also know which direction it is facing: north, south, east, or west. Therefore, the first requirement is the following:

 You are given the initial starting point (x, y) of a ship and the direction (N, S, E, or W) it is facing.

Before we start working on this requirement, let's go through the helper classes that can be used. The `Point` class holds the x and y coordinates. It has the following constructor:

```
public Point(int x, int y) {
  this.x = x;
  this.y = y;
}
```

Similarly, we have the `Direction` enum class with the following values:

```
public enum Direction {
  NORTH(0, 'N'),
  EAST(1, 'E'),
  SOUTH(2, 'S'),
  WEST(3, 'W'),
  NONE(4, 'X');
}
```

Finally, there is the `Location` class that requires both of those classes to be passed as constructor arguments:

```
public Location(Point point, Direction direction) {
  this.point = point;
  this.direction = direction;
}
```

Knowing this, it should be fairly easy to write a test for this first requirement. We should work in the same way as we did in the previous chapter, Chapter 3, *Red-Green-Refactor – From Failure Through Success until Perfection*.

Try to write specs by yourself. When done, compare them with the solution in this book. Repeat the same process with the code that implements specs. Try to write it by yourself and, once done, compare it with the solution we're proposing.

Specification – keeping position and direction in memory

The specification for this requirement can be the following:

```
@Test
public class ShipSpec {
  public void whenInstantiatedThenLocationIsSet() {
    Location location = new Location(new Point(21, 13), Direction.NORTH);
    Ship ship = new Ship(location);
```

```
            assertEquals(ship.getLocation(), location);
    }
}
```

This was an easy one. We're just checking whether the `Location` object we're passing as the `Ship` constructor is stored and can be accessed through the `location` getter.

 The `@Test` annotation—When TestNG has the `@Test` annotation set on the class level, there is no need to specify which methods should be used as tests. In this case, all public methods are considered to be TestNG tests.

Implementation

The implementation of this specification should be fairly easy. All we need to do is set the constructor argument to the `location` variable:

```
public class Ship {
  private final Location location;
  public Ship(Location location) {
    this.location = location;
  }

  public Location getLocation() {
    return location;
  }
}
```

The full source can be found in the `req01-location` branch of the `tdd-java-ch04-ship` repository (https://bitbucket.org/vfarcic/tdd-java-ch04-ship/branch/req01-location).

Refactoring

We know that we'll need to instantiate `Ship` for every spec, so we might as well refactor the specification class by adding the `@BeforeMethod` annotation. The code can be the following:

```
@Test
public class ShipSpec {

  private Ship ship;
  private Location location;
```

```
    @BeforeMethod
    public void beforeTest() {
        Location location = new Location(new Point(21, 13),
Direction.NORTH);
        ship = new Ship(location);
    }

    public void whenInstantiatedThenLocationIsSet() {
        // Location location = new Location(new Point(21, 13),
Direction.NORTH);
        // Ship ship = new Ship(location);
        assertEquals(ship.getLocation(), location);
    }
}
```

No new behavior has been introduced. We just moved part of the code to the `@BeforeMethod` annotation in order to avoid duplication, which would be produced by the rest of the specifications that we are about to write. Now, every time a test is run, the `ship` object will be instantiated with `location` as the argument.

Requirement – forward and backward moves

Now that we know where our ship is, let's try to move it. To begin with, we should be able to go both forwards and backwards.

Implement commands that move the ship forwards and backwards (*f* and *b*).

The `Location` helper class already has the `forward` and `backward` methods that implement this functionality:

```
public boolean forward() {
    ...
}
```

Specification – moving forward

What should happen when, for example, we are facing north and we move the ship forwards? Its location on the *y*-axis should decrease. Another example would be that when the ship is facing east, it should increase its *x*-axis location by 1.

Chapter 4

The first reaction can be to write specifications similar to the following two:

```
public void givenNorthWhenMoveForwardThenYDecreases() {
  ship.moveForward();
  assertEquals(ship.getLocation().getPoint().getY(), 12);
}

public void givenEastWhenMoveForwardThenXIncreases() {
  ship.getLocation().setDirection(Direction.EAST);
  ship.moveForward();
  assertEquals(ship.getLocation().getPoint().getX(), 22);
}
```

We should create at least two more specifications related to cases where a ship is facing south and west.

However, this is not how unit tests should be written. Most people new to unit testing fall into the trap of specifying the end result that requires the knowledge of the inner workings of methods, classes, and libraries used by the method that is being specified. This approach is problematic on many levels.

When including external code in the unit that is being specified, we should take into account, at least in our case, the fact that the external code is already tested. We know that it is working since we're running all the tests every time any change to the code is made.

> Rerun all the tests every time the implementation code changes.
>
> This ensures that there is no unexpected side-effect caused by code changes.

Every time any part of the implementation code changes, all tests should be run. Ideally, tests are fast to execute and can be run by a developer locally. Once code is submitted to the version control, all tests should be run again to ensure that there was no problem due to code merges. This is especially important when more than one developer is working on the code. CI tools, such as Jenkins, Hudson, Travind, Bamboo, and Go-CD should be used to pull the code from the repository, compile it, and run tests.

Another problem with this approach is that if an external code changes, there will be many more specifications to change. Ideally, we should be forced to change only specifications directly related to the unit that will be modified. Searching for all other places where that unit is called from might be very time-consuming and error-prone.

A much easier, faster, and better way to write specifications for this requirement would be the following:

```
public void whenMoveForwardThenForward() {
  Location expected = location.copy();
  expected.forward();
  ship.moveForward();
  assertEquals(ship.getLocation(), expected);
}
```

Since `Location` already has the `forward` method, all we'd need to do is to make sure that the proper invocation of that method is performed. We created a new `Location` object called `expected`, invoked the `forward` method, and compared that object with the location of the ship after its `moveForward` method is called.

Note that specifications are not only used to validate the code, but are also used as executable documentation and, most importantly, as a way to think and design. This second attempt specifies more clearly what the intent is behind it. We should create a `moveForward` method inside the `Ship` class and make sure that the `location.forward` is called.

Implementation

With such a small and clearly defined specification, it should be fairly easy to write the code that implements it:

```
public boolean moveForward() {
  return location.forward();
}
```

Specification – moving backward

Now that we have a forward movement specified and implemented, the backward movement should almost be the same:

```
public void whenMoveBackwardThenBackward() {
  Location expected = location.copy();
  expected.backward();
  ship.moveBackward();
  assertEquals(ship.getLocation(), expected);
}
```

Implementation

Just like the specification, the backward movement implementation is just as easy:

```
public boolean moveBackward() {
  return location.backward();
}
```

The full source code for this requirement can be found in the `req02-forward-backward` branch of the `tdd-java-ch04-ship` repository (https://bitbucket.org/vfarcic/tdd-java-ch04-ship/branch/req02-forward-backward).

Requirement – rotating the ship

Moving the ship only back and forth won't get us far. We should be able to change the direction by rotating the ship to the left or right as well.

Implement commands that turn the ship left and right (*l* and *r*).

After implementing the previous requirement, this one should be very easy since it can follow the same logic. The `Location` helper class already contains the `turnLeft` and `turnRight` methods that perform exactly what is required by this requirement. All we need to do is integrate them into the `Ship` class.

Specification – turning left

Using the same guidelines as those we have used so far, the specification for turning left can be the following:

```
public void whenTurnLeftThenLeft() {
  Location expected = location.copy();
  expected.turnLeft();
  ship.turnLeft();
  assertEquals(ship.getLocation(), expected);
}
```

Implementation

You probably did not have a problem writing the code to pass the previous specification:

```
public void turnLeft() {
  location.turnLeft();
}
```

Specification – turning right

Turning right should be almost the same as turning left:

```
public void whenTurnRightThenRight() {
  Location expected = location.copy();
  expected.turnRight();
  ship.turnRight();
  assertEquals(ship.getLocation(), expected);
}
```

Implementation

Finally, let's finish this requirement by implementing the specification for turning right:

```
public void turnRight() {
  location.turnRight();
}
```

The full source for this requirement can be found in the req03-left-right branch of the tdd-java-ch04-ship repository (https://bitbucket.org/vfarcic/tdd-java-ch04-ship/branch/req03-left-right).

Requirement – commands

Everything we have done so far was fairly easy since there were helper classes that provided all the functionality. This exercise was to learn how to stop attempting to test the end outcome and focus on a unit we're working on. We are building trust; we had to trust the code done by others (the helper classes).

Starting from this requirement, you'll have to trust the code you wrote by yourself. We'll continue in the same fashion. We'll write specifications, run tests, and see them fail; we'll write implementations, run tests, and see them succeed; finally, we'll refactor if we think the code can be improved. Continue thinking how to test a unit (method) without going deeper into methods or classes that the unit will be invoking.

Now that we have individual commands (forwards, backwards, left, and right) implemented, it's time to tie it all together. We should create a method that will allow us to pass any number of commands as a single string. Each command should be a character with *f* meaning forwards, *b* being backwards, *l* for turning left, and *r* for turning right.

 The ship can receive a string with commands (lrfb, which are equivalent to left, right, forwards, and backwards).

Specification – single commands

Let's start with the command argument, that only has the f (forwards) character:

```
public void whenReceiveCommandsFThenForward() {
  Location expected = location.copy();
  expected.forward();
  ship.receiveCommands("f");
  assertEquals(ship.getLocation(), expected);
}
```

This specification is almost the same as the `whenMoveForwardThenForward` specification except that, this time, we're invoking the `ship.receiveCommands("f")` method.

Implementation

We already spoke about the importance of writing the simplest possible code that passes the specification.

Write the simplest code to pass the test. This ensures a cleaner and clearer design and avoids unnecessary features

The idea is that the simpler the implementation, the better and easier it is to maintain the product. The idea adheres to the KISS principle. It states that most systems work best if they are kept simple rather than made complex; therefore, simplicity should be a key goal in design and unnecessary complexity should be avoided.

This is a good opportunity to apply this rule. You might be inclined to write a piece of code similar to the following:

```
public void receiveCommands(String commands) {
  if (commands.charAt(0) == 'f') {
    moveForward();
  }
}
```

In this example code, we are verifying whether the first character is f and, if it is, invoking the moveForward method. There are many other variations that we can do. However, if we stick to the simplicity principle, a better solution would be the following:

```
public void receiveCommands(String command) {
  moveForward();
}
```

This is the simplest and shortest possible code that will make the specification pass. Later on, we might end up with something closer to the first version of the code; we might use some kind of a loop or come up with some other solution when things become more complicated. As for now, we are concentrating on one specification at a time and trying to make things simple. We are attempting to clear our mind by focusing only on the task at hand.

For brevity, the rest of the combinations (b, l, and r) are not presented here (continue to implement them by yourself). Instead, we'll jump to the last specification for this requirement.

Specification – combined commands

Now that we are able to process one command (whatever that the command is), it is time to add the option to send a string of commands. The specification can be the following:

```
public void whenReceiveCommandsThenAllAreExecuted() {
  Location expected = location.copy();
  expected.turnRight();
  expected.forward();
  expected.turnLeft();
  expected.backward();
  ship.receiveCommands("rflb");
  assertEquals(ship.getLocation(), expected);
}
```

This is a bit longer, but is still not an overly complicated specification. We're passing commands `rflb` (right, forwards, left, and backwards) and expecting that the `Location` changes accordingly. As before, we're not verifying the end result (seeing whether the if coordinates have changed), but checking whether we are invoking the correct calls to helper methods.

Implementation

The end result can be the following:

```
public void receiveCommands(String commands) {
  for (char command : commands.toCharArray()) {
    switch(command) {
      case 'f':
        moveForward();
        break;
      case 'b':
        moveBackward();
        break;
      case 'l':
        turnLeft();
        break;
      case 'r':
        turnRight();
        break;
    }
  }
}
```

If you tried to write specifications and the implementation by yourself and if you followed the simplicity rule, you probably had to refactor your code a couple of times in order to get to the final solution. Simplicity is the key and refactoring is often a welcome necessity. When refactoring, remember that all specifications must be passing all the time.

Refactor only after all the tests have passed.

Benefits: refactoring is safe.

If all the implementation code that can be affected has tests and if they are all passing, it is relatively safe to refactor. In most cases, there is no need for new tests; small modifications to existing tests should be enough. The expected outcome of refactoring is to have all the tests passing both before and after the code is modified.

The full source for this requirement can be found in the req04-commands branch of the tdd-java-ch04-ship repository (https://bitbucket.org/vfarcic/tdd-java-ch04-ship/branch/req04-commands).

Requirement – representing spheric maps

Earth is a sphere, as is any other planet. When Earth is presented as a map, reaching one edge wraps us to another; for example, when we move east and reach the furthest point in the Pacific Ocean, we are wrapped to the west side of the map and we continue moving towards America. Furthermore, to make the movement easier, we can define the map as a grid. That grid should have length and height expressed as an *x*-axis and *y*-axis. That grid should have maximum length (x) and height (y).

Implement wrapping from one edge of the grid to another.

Specification – planet information

The first thing we can do is pass the `Planet` object with the maximum X and Y axis coordinates to the `Ship` constructor. Fortunately, `Planet` is one more of the helper classes that have already been made (and tested). All we need to do is instantiate it and pass it to the `Ship` constructor:

```
public void whenInstantiatedThenPlanetIsStored() {
  Point max = new Point(50, 50);
  Planet planet = new Planet(max);
  ship = new Ship(location, planet);
  assertEquals(ship.getPlanet(), planet);
}
```

We're defining the size of the planet as 50 x 50 and passing that to the `Planet` class. In turn, that class is afterwards passed to the `Ship` constructor. You might have noticed that the constructor needs an extra argument. In the current code, our constructor requires only `location`. To implement this specification, it should accept `planet`, as well.

How would you implement this specification without breaking any of the existing specifications?

Implementation

Let's take a bottom-up approach. An `assert` requires us to have a `planet` getter:

```
private Planet planet;
public Planet getPlanet() {
  return planet;
}
```

Next, the constructor should accept `Planet` as a second argument and assign it to the previously added `planet` variable. The first attempt might be to add it to the existing constructor, but that would break many existing specifications that are using a single argument constructor. This leaves us with only one option—a second constructor:

```
public Ship(Location location) {
  this.location = location;
}
public Ship(Location location, Planet planet) {
  this.location = location;
  this.planet = planet;
}
```

Run all the specifications and confirm that they are all successful.

Refactoring

Our specifications forced us to create the second constructor, since changing the original one would break the existing tests. However, now that everything is green, we can do some refactoring and get rid of the single argument constructor. The specification class already has the `beforeTest` method that is run before each test. We can move everything, but the `assert` itself to this method:

```
public class ShipSpec {
...
  private Planet planet;

  @BeforeMethod
  public void beforeTest() {
    Point max = new Point(50, 50);
    location = new Location(new Point(21, 13), Direction.NORTH);
    planet = new Planet(max);
    // ship = new Ship(location);
    ship = new Ship(location, planet);
  }

  public void whenInstantiatedThenPlanetIsStored() {
    // Point max = new Point(50, 50);
    // Planet planet = new Planet(max);
    // ship = new Ship(location, planet);
    assertEquals(ship.getPlanet(), planet);
  }
}
```

With this change, we effectively removed the usage of the Ship single argument constructor. By running all specifications, we should confirm that this change worked.

Now, with a single argument constructor that is not in use anymore, we can remove it from the implementation class, as well:

```
public class Ship {
...
  // public Ship(Location location) {
  //   this.location = location;
  // }
  public Ship(Location location, Planet planet) {
    this.location = location;
    this.planet = planet;
```

```
    }
    ...
}
```

By using this approach, all specifications were green all the time. Refactoring did not change any existing functionality, nothing got broken, and the whole process was done quickly.

Now, let's move into wrapping itself.

Specification – dealing with map boundaries

Like in other cases, the helper classes already provide all the functionality that we need. So far, we used the `location.forward` method without arguments. To implement wrapping, there is the overloaded `location.forward(Point max)` method that will wrap the location when we reach the end of the grid. With the previous specification, we made sure that `Planet` is passed to the `Ship` class and that it contains `Point max`. Our job is to make sure that `max` is used when moving forward. The specification can be the following:

```
public void whenOverpassingEastBoundaryThenPositionIsReset() {
    location.setDirection(Direction.EAST);
    location.getPoint().setX(planet.getMax().getX());
    ship.receiveCommands("f");
    assertEquals(location.getX(), 1);
}
```

Implementation

By now, you should be getting used to focusing on one unit at a time and to trust that those that were done before are working as expected. This implementation should be no different. We just need to make sure that the maximum coordinates are used when the `location.forward` method is called:

```
public boolean moveForward() {
    // return location.forward();
    return location.forward(planet.getMax());
}
```

The same specification and implementation should be done for the `backward` method. For brevity, it is excluded from this book, but it can be found in the source code.

The full source for this requirement can be found in the `req05-wrap` branch of the `tdd-java-ch04-ship` repository (https://bitbucket.org/vfarcic/tdd-java-ch04-ship/branch/req05-wrap).

Requirement – detecting obstacles

We're almost done. This is the last requirement.

Even though most of the Earth is covered in water (approximately 70%), there are continents and islands that can be considered as obstacles for our remotely-controlled ship. We should have a way to detect whether our next move would hit one of those obstacles. If such a thing happens, the move should be aborted and the ship should stay on the current position and report the obstacle.

Implement surface detection before each move to a new position. If a command encounters a surface, the ship aborts the move, stays on the current position, and reports the obstacle.

The specifications and the implementation of this requirement are very similar to those we did previously, and we'll leave that to you.

Here are a few tips that can be useful:

- The `Planet` object has the constructor that accepts a list of obstacles. Each obstacle is an instance of the `Point` class.
- The `location.foward` and `location.backward` methods have overloaded versions that accept a list of obstacles. They return `true` if a move was successful and `false` if it failed. Use this Boolean to construct a status report required for the `Ship.receiveCommands` method.
- The `receiveCommands` method should return a string with the status of each command. `O` can represent OK and `X` can be for a failure to move (`OOXO` = OK, OK, Failure, OK).

The full source for this requirement can be found in the `req06-obstacles` branch of the `tdd-java-ch04-ship` repository (https://bitbucket.org/vfarcic/tdd-java-ch04-ship/branch/req06-obstacles).

Summary

In this chapter, we used TestNG as our testing framework of choice. There wasn't much difference when compared to JUnit, simply because we didn't use any of the more advanced features of TestNG (for example, data providers, factories, and so on). With TDD, it is questionable whether we'll ever have a need for those features.

Visit http://testng.org/, explore it, and decide for yourself which framework best suits your needs.

The main objective of this chapter was to learn how to focus on one unit at a time. We already had a lot of helper classes and we tried our best to ignore their internal workings. In many cases, we did not write specifications that verified that the end result was correct, but we checked whether the method we were working on invoked the correct method from those helper classes. In the real-world, you will be working on projects together with other team members, and it is important to learn how to focus on your tasks and trust that what others do works as expected. The same can be said for third-party libraries. It would be too expensive to test all inner processes that can happen when we invoke them. There are other types of tests that will try to cover those possibilities. When working with unit tests, the focus should only be on the unit we're currently working on.

Now that you have a better grasp of how to use unit tests effectively in the context of TDD, it is time to dive into some other advantages that TDD provides. Specifically, we'll explore how to design our applications better.

5
Design – If It's Not Testable, It's Not Designed Well

"Simplicity is the ultimate sophistication."

– Leonardo da Vinci

In the past, the software industry was focused on developing software at high speed, with nothing in mind but cost and time. Quality was a secondary goal, with the false feeling that customers were not interested in it.

Nowadays, with the increasing connectivity of all kinds of platforms and devices, quality has become a first-class citizen in customer's requirements. Good applications offer a good service with a reasonable response-time, without being affected by a multitude of concurrent requests from many users.

Good applications in terms of quality are those that have been well designed. A good design means scalability, security, maintainability, and many other desired attributes.

In this chapter, we will explore how TDD leads developers to good design and best practices by implementing the same application using both the traditional and TDD approaches.

The following topics will be covered in this chapter:

- Why should we care about design?
- Design considerations and principles
- The traditional development process
- The TDD approach using Hamcrest

Why should we care about design?

In software development, whether you are an expert or a beginner, there are some situations where code seems to be unnatural. You can't avoid the feeling that something is wrong with that code when reading it. Occasionally, you even wonder why the previous programmer implemented a specific method or a class in such a twisted manner. This is because the same functionality can be implemented in a vast number of different ways, each of them unique. With this huge number of possibilities, which is the best one? What defines a good solution? Why is one better than the others? The fact is, all of them are valid so long as the goal is achieved. However, it is true that some aspects should be considered when choosing the right solution. This is where the design of the solution becomes relevant.

Design principles

A **software design principle** is a rule or set of rules that work as a guide for software developers and push them towards smart and maintainable solutions. In other words, design principles are conditions that code must fulfill to be considered objectively well designed.

Most senior developers and experienced programmers know about software design principles and it's very likely that, independently of whether they practice TDD, they are applying them to their daily work. The TDD philosophy encourages programmers—even beginners—to follow some principles and good practices that make code cleaner and more readable. Those practices are enforced by the Red-Green-Refactor cycle.

The Red-Green-Refactor cycle advocates for small feature increments by introducing one test that fails at a time. Programmers add code fragments, as concise and short as possible, so neither the new test or the old ones do not fail anymore. And ultimately, they refactor the code, which consists of cleanup and improvement tasks such as duplication removal or code optimization.

As a result of the process, the code becomes easier to understand and safer to modify in the future. Let's take a look at some of the most popular software design principles.

You Ain't Gonna Need It

YAGNI is the acronym for the **You Ain't Gonna Need It** principle. It aims to erase all unnecessary code and focuses on the current functionalities, not the future ones. The less code you have, the less code you're going to maintain and the lower the probability that bugs will be introduced.

For more information on YAGNI, visit Martin Fowler's article available at `http://martinfowler.com/bliki/Yagni.html`.

Don't Repeat Yourself

The idea behind the **Don't Repeat Yourself** (**DRY**) principle is to reuse the code you previously wrote instead of repeating it. The benefits are less code to maintain and the use of code that you know that already works, which is a great thing. It helps you to discover new abstraction levels inside your code.

For additional information, visit `http://en.wikipedia.org/wiki/Don%27t_repeat_yourself`.

Keep it simple, stupid

This principle has the confusing acronym of **keep it simple, stupid** (**KISS**) and states that things perform their function better if they are kept simple rather than complicated. It was coined by Kelly Johnson.

To read about the story behind this principle, visit `http://en.wikipedia.org/wiki/KISS_principle`.

Occam's razor

Although **Occam's razor** is a philosophical principle, not a software engineering one, it is still applicable to what we do. It is very similar to the previous principle, with the main statement being as follows:

> "When you have two competing solutions to the same problem, the simpler one is the better."

> – William of Ockham

For more information on Occam's razor, visit `http://en.wikipedia.org/wiki/Occam%27s_razor`.

SOLID principles

The word **SOLID** is an acronym invented by Robert C. Martin for the five basic principles of object-oriented programming. By following these five principles, a developer is more likely to create a great, durable, and maintainable application:

- **Single Responsibility Principle**: A class should have only a single reason to change.
- **Open-Closed Principle**: A class should be open for extension and closed for modification. This is attributed to Bertrand Meyer.
- **Liskov Substitution Principle**: This was created by Barbara Liskov, and she says *a class should be replaceable by others that extend that class*.
- **Interface Segregation Principle**: A few specific interfaces are preferable to one general-purpose interface.
- **Dependency Inversion Principle**: A class should depend on abstraction instead of implementation. This means that class dependencies must be focused on what is done and forget about how it is done.

For further information on SOLID or other related principles, visit `http://butunclebob.com/ArticleS.UncleBob.PrinciplesOfOod`.

The first four principles are part of the core of TDD thinking, since they aim to simplify the code we write. The last one is focused on classes construction and dependency relationships in the application assembly process.

All of these principles are applicable and desirable in both test and non-test driven development, because, apart from other benefits, they make our code more maintainable. The proper practical application of them is worth a whole book by itself. While we won't have time to go deep into it, we encourage you to investigate further.

In this chapter, we will see how TDD induces developers to put some of these principles into practice effortlessly. We will implement a small but fully functional version of the famous game Connect 4 with both the TDD and non-TDD approaches. Note that repetitive parts, such as Gradle project creation and so on, are omitted, as they are not considered relevant for the purpose of this chapter.

Chapter 5

Connect 4

Connect 4 is a popular, very easy-to-play board game. The rules are limited and simple.

Connect 4 is a two-player connection game in which the players first choose a color and then take turns dropping colored discs from the top into a seven column, six row, vertically suspended grid. The pieces fall straight down, occupying the next available space within the column. The objective of the game is to connect four of your own discs of the same color next to one another vertically, horizontally, or diagonally, before your opponent connects four of theirs.

For further information on the game, visit Wikipedia (http://en.wikipedia.org/wiki/Connect_Four).

Requirements

To code the two implementations of Connect 4, the game rules are transcribed as follows in the form of requirements. These requirements are the starting point for both the developments. We will go through the code with some explanations and compare both implementations at the end:

1. The board is composed of seven columns and six rows; all positions are empty.
2. Players introduce discs on the top of the columns. The introduced disc drops down the board if the column is empty. Future discs introduced in the same column will stack over the previous ones.
3. It is a two-person game, so there is one color for each player. One player uses red (R) and the other one uses green (G). Players alternate turns, inserting one disc every time.
4. We want feedback when either an event or an error occurs within the game. The output shows the status of the board after every move.
5. When no more discs can be inserted, the game finishes, and it is considered a draw.
6. If a player inserts a disc and connects more than three discs of his color in a straight vertical line, then that player wins.
7. The same happens in a horizontal line direction.
8. The same happens in a diagonal line direction.

Test-last implementation of Connect 4

This is the traditional approach, focusing on problem-solving code rather than tests. Some people and companies forget about the value of automated testing and rely on users in what are called **user acceptance tests**.

This kind of user acceptance test consists of recreating real-world scenarios in a controlled environment, ideally identical to production. Some users perform a lot of different tasks to verify the correctness of the application. If any of these actions fail, then the code is not accepted, as it is breaking some functionality or it is not working as expected.

Moreover, a great number of these companies also use unit testing as a way to perform early regression checks. These unit tests are created after the development process and they try to cover as much code as possible. Last of all, code coverage analysis is executed to get a trace of what is actually covered by those unit tests. These companies follow a single rule of thumb: the bigger the code coverage, the better the quality delivered.

The main problem of this approach is that writing tests afterwards does nothing but demonstrates that the code behaves the way it has been programmed, which is not necessarily the way code is expected to behave. Also, focusing on code coverage leads to bad tests that turn our production code into immutable entities. Every modification we may want to add may cause several tests from different, unrelated parts of the code to fail. That fact means the cost of introducing changes becomes really high and performing any slight modification could end up being a nightmare and very expensive.

To demonstrate some points described earlier, let's implement the Connect 4 game using a TDD and not-TDD approach. The relevant code for each of the identified requirements is presented as we proceed further. This code isn't written incrementally, so some code snippets might contain a few code lines unrelated to the mentioned requirement.

Requirement 1 – the game's board

Let us start with the first requirement.

 The board is composed of seven horizontal and six vertical empty positions.

The implementation of this requirement is pretty straightforward. We just need the representation of an empty position and the data structure to hold the game. Note that the colors used by the players are also defined:

```
public class Connect4 {
  public enum Color {
    RED('R'), GREEN('G'), EMPTY(' ');

    private final char value;

    Color(char value) { this.value = value; }

    @Override
    public String toString() {
      return String.valueOf(value);
    }
  }

  public static final int COLUMNS = 7;

  public static final int ROWS = 6;

  private Color[][] board = new Color[COLUMNS][ROWS];

  public Connect4() {
    for (Color[] column : board) {
      Arrays.fill(column, Color.EMPTY);
    }
  }
}
```

Requirement 2 – introducing discs

This requirement introduces part of the logic of the game.

Players introduce discs on the top of the columns. The introduced disc drops down the board if the column is empty. Future discs introduced in the same column will stack over the previous ones.

In this part, board bounds become relevant. We need to mark what positions are already taken, using Color.RED to indicate them. Finally, the first private method is created. It is a helper method that calculates the number of discs introduced in a given column:

```
public void putDisc(int column) {
  if (column > 0 && column <= COLUMNS) {
    int numOfDiscs = getNumberOfDiscsInColumn(column - 1);
    if (numOfDiscs < ROWS) {
      board[column - 1][numOfDiscs] = Color.RED;
    }
  }
}

private int getNumberOfDiscsInColumn(int column) {
  if (column >= 0 && column < COLUMNS) {
    int row;
    for (row = 0; row < ROWS; row++) {
      if (Color.EMPTY == board[column][row]) {
        return row;
      }
    }
    return row;
  }
  return -1;
}
```

Requirement 3 – player shifts

More game logic is introduced with this requirement.

It is a two-person game, so there is one colour for each player. One player uses red (R) and the other one uses green (G). Players alternate turns, inserting one disc every time.

We need to save the current player to determine which player is playing this turn. We also need a function to switch the players to recreate the logic of turns. Some lines of code become relevant in the putDisc function. Specifically, the board position assignment is made using the current player, and it is switched after every move, as the game rules say:

```
...
private Color currentPlayer = Color.RED;

private void switchPlayer() {
```

```java
      if (Color.RED == currentPlayer) {
        currentPlayer = Color.GREEN;
      } else {
        currentPlayer = Color.RED;
      }
    }

    public void putDisc(int column) {
      if (column > 0 && column <= COLUMNS) {
        int numOfDiscs = getNumberOfDiscsInColumn(column - 1);
        if (numOfDiscs < ROWS) {
          board[column - 1][numOfDiscs] = currentPlayer;
          switchPlayer();
        }
      }
    }
    ...
```

Requirement 4 – the game's output

A few outputs should be added to let the players know the current status of the game.

We want feedback when either an event or an error occurs within the game. The output shows the status of the board after every move.

No output channel is specified. To make it easier, we decided to use the system standard output to print an event when it occurs. A few lines have been added on every action to let the user know about the status of the game:

```java
    ...
    private static final String DELIMITER = "|";

    private void switchPlayer() {
      if (Color.RED == currentPlayer) {
        currentPlayer = Color.GREEN;
      } else {
        currentPlayer = Color.RED;
      }
      System.out.println("Current turn: " + currentPlayer);
    }

    public void printBoard() {
      for (int row = ROWS - 1; row >= 0; --row) {
```

```
      StringJoiner stringJoiner =
        new StringJoiner(DELIMITER, DELIMITER, DELIMITER);
      for (int col = 0; col < COLUMNS; ++col) {
        stringJoiner.add(board[col][row].toString());
      }
      System.out.println(stringJoiner.toString());
    }
  }

  public void putDisc(int column) {
    if (column > 0 && column <= COLUMNS) {
      int numOfDiscs = getNumberOfDiscsInColumn(column - 1);
      if (numOfDiscs < ROWS) {
        board[column - 1][numOfDiscs] = currentPlayer;
        printBoard();
        switchPlayer();
      } else {
        System.out.println(numOfDiscs);
        System.out.println("There's no room " +
          "for a new disc in this column");
        printBoard();
      }
    } else {
      System.out.println("Column out of bounds");
      printBoard();
    }
  }
...
```

Requirement 5 – win conditions (I)

The first game has a finished condition.

When no more discs can be inserted, the game finishes and it is considered a draw.

The following code shows one of the possible implementations:

```
...
public boolean isFinished() {
  int numOfDiscs = 0;
  for (int col = 0; col < COLUMNS; ++col) {
    numOfDiscs += getNumberOfDiscsInColumn(col);
```

```
    }
    if (numOfDiscs >= COLUMNS * ROWS) {
      System.out.println("It's a draw");
      return true;
    }
    return false;
  }
  ...
```

Requirement 6 – win condition (II)

The first win condition.

If a player inserts a disc and connects more than three discs of his colour in a straight vertical line, then that player wins.

The `checkWinCondition` private method implements this rule by scanning whether or not the last move is a winning one:

```
...
private Color winner;

public static final int DISCS_FOR_WIN = 4;

public void putDisc(int column) {
  ...
  if (numOfDiscs < ROWS) {
    board[column - 1][numOfDiscs] = currentPlayer;
    printBoard();
    checkWinCondition(column - 1, numOfDiscs);
    switchPlayer();
    ...
}

private void checkWinCondition(int col, int row) {
  Pattern winPattern = Pattern.compile(".*" +
    currentPlayer + "{" + DISCS_FOR_WIN + "}.*");

  // Vertical check
  StringJoiner stringJoiner = new StringJoiner("");
  for (int auxRow = 0; auxRow < ROWS; ++auxRow) {
    stringJoiner.add(board[col][auxRow].toString());
  }
```

```
      if (winPattern.matcher(stringJoiner.toString()).matches()) {
        winner = currentPlayer;
        System.out.println(currentPlayer + " wins");
      }
  }

  public boolean isFinished() {
    if (winner != null) return true;
    ...
  }
  ...
```

Requirement 7 – win condition (III)

This is the same win condition, but in a different direction.

If a player inserts a disc and connects more than three discs of his color in a straight horizontal line, then that player wins.

A few lines to implement this rule are as follows:

```
...
private void checkWinCondition(int col, int row) {
  ...
  // Horizontal check
  stringJoiner = new StringJoiner("");
  for (int column = 0; column < COLUMNS; ++column) {
    stringJoiner.add(board[column][row].toString());
  }
  if (winPattern.matcher(stringJoiner.toString()).matches()) {
    winner = currentPlayer;
    System.out.println(currentPlayer + " wins");
    return;
  }
  ...
}
...
```

Requirement 8 – win condition (IV)

The last requirement is the last win condition. It is pretty similar to the last two; in this case, in a diagonal direction.

If a player inserts a disc and connects more than three discs of his color in a straight diagonal line, then that player wins.

This is a possible implementation for this last requirement. The code is very similar to the other win conditions because the same statement must be fulfilled:

```
...
private void checkWinCondition(int col, int row) {
  ...
  // Diagonal checks
  int startOffset = Math.min(col, row);
  int column = col - startOffset, auxRow = row - startOffset;
  stringJoiner = new StringJoiner("");
  do {
    stringJoiner.add(board[column++][auxRow++].toString());
  } while (column < COLUMNS && auxRow < ROWS);

  if (winPattern.matcher(stringJoiner.toString()).matches()) {
    winner = currentPlayer;
    System.out.println(currentPlayer + " wins");
    return;
  }

  startOffset = Math.min(col, ROWS - 1 - row);
  column = col - startOffset;
  auxRow = row + startOffset;
  stringJoiner = new StringJoiner("");
  do {
    stringJoiner.add(board[column++][auxRow--].toString());
  } while (column < COLUMNS && auxRow >= 0);

  if (winPattern.matcher(stringJoiner.toString()).matches()) {
    winner = currentPlayer;
    System.out.println(currentPlayer + " wins");
  }
}
...
```

Design – If It's Not Testable, It's Not Designed Well

What we have got is a class with one constructor, three public methods, and three private methods. The logic of the application is distributed among all methods. The biggest flaw here is that this class is very difficult to maintain. The crucial methods, such as `checkWinCondition`, are non-trivial, with potential for bug entries in future modifications.

If you want to take a look at the full code, you can find it in the `https://bitbucket.org/vfarcic/tdd-java-ch05-design.git` repository.

We made this small example to demonstrate the common problems with this approach. Topics such as the SOLID principle requires a bigger project to become more illustrative.

In large projects with hundreds of classes, the problems become hours wasted in a sort of surgical development. Developers spend a lot of their time investigating tricky code and understanding how it works, instead of creating new features.

The TDD or test-first implementation

At this time, we know how TDD works—writing tests before, implementation after tests, and refactoring later on. We are going to pass through the process and only show the final result for each requirement. It is left to you to figure out the iterative Red-Green-Refactor process. Let's make this more interesting, if possible, by using a Hamcrest framework in our tests.

Hamcrest

As described in `Chapter 2`, *Tools, Frameworks, and Environment*, Hamcrest improves our test's readability. It makes assertions more semantic and comprehensive when complexity is reduced by using **matchers**. When a test fails, the error shown becomes more expressive by interpreting the matchers used in the assertion. A message could also be added by the developer.

The `Hamcrest` library is full of different matchers for different object types and collections. Let's start coding and get a taste of it.

Requirement 1 – the game's board

We will start with the first requirement.

The board is composed of seven horizontal and six vertical empty positions.

There is no big challenge with this requirement. The board bounds are specified, but there's no described behavior in it; just the consideration of an empty board when the game starts. That means zero discs when the game begins. However, this requirement must be taken into account later on.

This is how the test class looks for this requirement. There's a method to initialize the `tested` class to use a completely fresh object in each test. There's also the first test to verify that there's no disc when we start the game, meaning that all board positions are empty:

```
public class Connect4TDDSpec {
  private Connect4TDD tested;

  @Before
  public void beforeEachTest() {
    tested = new Connect4TDD();
  }
  @Test
  public void whenTheGameIsStartedTheBoardIsEmpty() {
    assertThat(tested.getNumberOfDiscs(), is(0));
  }
}
```

This is the TDD implementation of the previous specification. Observe the simplicity of the given solution for this first requirement; a simple method returning the result in a single line:

```
public class Connect4TDD {
  public int getNumberOfDiscs() {
    return 0;
  }
}
```

Requirement 2 – introducing discs

This is the implementation for the second requirement.

Players introduce discs on the top of the columns. An introduced disc drops down the board if the column is empty. Future discs introduced in the same column will stack over the previous ones.

We can split this requirement into the following tests:

- When a disc is inserted into an empty column, its position is 0
- When a second disc is inserted into the same column, its position is 1
- When a disc is inserted into the board, the total number of discs increases
- When a disc is put outside the boundaries, a `Runtime Exception` is thrown
- When a disc is inserted into a column and there's no room available for it, then a `Runtime Exception` is thrown

Also, these other tests are derived from the first requirement. They are related to the board limits or board behavior.

The Java implementation of the aforementioned tests is as follows:

```
@Test
public void whenDiscOutsideBoardThenRuntimeException() {
  int column = -1;
  exception.expect(RuntimeException.class);
  exception.expectMessage("Invalid column " + column);
  tested.putDiscInColumn(column);
}

@Test
public void whenFirstDiscInsertedInColumnThenPositionIsZero() {
  int column = 1;
  assertThat(tested.putDiscInColumn(column),  is(0));
}

@Test
public void whenSecondDiscInsertedInColumnThenPositionIsOne() {
  int column = 1;
  tested.putDiscInColumn(column);
  assertThat(tested.putDiscInColumn(column), is(1));
}
```

```
@Test
public void whenDiscInsertedThenNumberOfDiscsIncreases() {
  int column = 1;
  tested.putDiscInColumn(column);
  assertThat(tested.getNumberOfDiscs(), is(1));
}

@Test
public void whenNoMoreRoomInColumnThenRuntimeException() {
  int column = 1;
  int maxDiscsInColumn = 6; // the number of rows
  for (int times = 0; times < maxDiscsInColumn; ++times) {
    tested.putDiscInColumn(column);
  }
  exception.expect(RuntimeException.class);
  exception.expectMessage("No more room in column " + column);
  tested.putDiscInColumn(column);
}
```

This is the necessary code to satisfy the tests:

```
private static final int ROWS = 6;

private static final int COLUMNS = 7;

private static final String EMPTY = " ";

private String[][] board = new String[ROWS][COLUMNS];

public Connect4TDD() {
  for (String[] row : board) Arrays.fill(row, EMPTY);
}

public int getNumberOfDiscs() {
  return IntStream
          .range(0, COLUMNS)
          .map(this::getNumberOfDiscsInColumn)
          .sum();
}

private int getNumberOfDiscsInColumn(int column) {
  return (int) IntStream
              .range(0, ROWS)
              .filter(row -> !EMPTY.equals(board[row][column]))
              .count();
}

public int putDiscInColumn(int column) {
```

```
    checkColumn(column);
    int row = getNumberOfDiscsInColumn(column);
    checkPositionToInsert(row, column);
    board[row][column] = "X";
    return row;
}

private void checkColumn(int column) {
  if (column < 0 || column >= COLUMNS)
    throw new RuntimeException("Invalid column " + column);
}

private void checkPositionToInsert(int row, int column) {
  if (row == ROWS)
    throw new RuntimeException("No more room in column " + column);
}
```

Requirement 3 – player shifts

The third requirement relates to the game logic.

It is a two-person game, so there is one colour for each player. One player uses red (R) and the other one uses green (G). Players alternate turns, inserting one disc every time.

These tests cover the verification of the new functionality. For the sake of simplicity, the red player will always start the game:

```
@Test
public void whenFirstPlayerPlaysThenDiscColorIsRed() {
  assertThat(tested.getCurrentPlayer(), is("R"));
}

@Test
public void whenSecondPlayerPlaysThenDiscColorIsRed() {
  int column = 1;
  tested.putDiscInColumn(column);
  assertThat(tested.getCurrentPlayer(), is("G"));
}
```

A couple of methods need to be created to cover this functionality. The `switchPlayer` method is called before returning the row in the `putDiscInColumn` method:

```
private static final String RED = "R";

private static final String GREEN = "G";

private String currentPlayer = RED;

public Connect4TDD() {
   for (String[] row : board) Arrays.fill(row, EMPTY);
}

public String getCurrentPlayer() {
   return currentPlayer;
}

private void switchPlayer() {
   if (RED.equals(currentPlayer)) currentPlayer = GREEN;
   else currentPlayer = RED;
}

public int putDiscInColumn(int column) {
   ...
   switchPlayer();
   return row;
}
```

Requirement 4 – the game's output

Next, we should let the player know the status of the game.

We want feedback when either an event or an error occurs within the game. The output shows the status of the board on every move.

As we are throwing exceptions when an error occurs, this is already covered, so we only need to implement these two tests. Furthermore, for the sake of testability, we need to introduce a parameter within the constructor. By introducing this parameter, the output becomes easier to test:

```
private OutputStream output;

@Before
```

Design – If It's Not Testable, It's Not Designed Well

```java
public void beforeEachTest() {
  output = new ByteArrayOutputStream();
  tested = new Connect4TDD(new PrintStream(output));
}

@Test
public void whenAskedForCurrentPlayerTheOutputNotice() {
  tested.getCurrentPlayer();
  assertThat(output.toString(), containsString("Player R turn"));
}

@Test
public void whenADiscIsIntroducedTheBoardIsPrinted() {
  int column = 1;
  tested.putDiscInColumn(column);
  assertThat(output.toString(), containsString("| |R| | | | | |"));
}
```

One possible implementation is to pass the preceding tests. As you can see, the class constructor now has one parameter. This parameter is used in several methods to print the event or action description:

```java
private static final String DELIMITER = "|";

public Connect4TDD(PrintStream out) {
  outputChannel = out;
  for (String[] row : board) Arrays.fill(row, EMPTY);
}

public String getCurrentPlayer() {
  outputChannel.printf("Player %s turn%n", currentPlayer);
  return currentPlayer;
}

private void printBoard() {
  for (int row = ROWS - 1; row >= 0; row--) {
    StringJoiner stringJoiner = new StringJoiner(DELIMITER,
DELIMITER, DELIMITER);
    Stream.of(board[row]).forEachOrdered(stringJoiner::add);
    outputChannel.println(stringJoiner.toString());
  }
}

public int putDiscInColumn(int column) {
  ...
  printBoard();
  switchPlayer();
```

```
    return row;
}
```

Requirement 5 – win condition (I)

This requirement tells the system whether the game is finished.

When no more discs can be inserted, the game finishes and it is considered a draw.

There are two conditions to test. The first condition is that new game must be unfinished; the second condition is that full board games must be finished:

```
@Test
public void whenTheGameStartsItIsNotFinished() {
  assertFalse("The game must not be finished",
tested.isFinished());
}

@Test
public void whenNoDiscCanBeIntroducedTheGamesIsFinished() {
  for (int row = 0; row < 6; row++)
    for (int column = 0; column < 7; column++)
      tested.putDiscInColumn(column);
    assertTrue("The game must be finished", tested.isFinished());
}
```

An easy and simple solution to these two tests is as follows:

```
public boolean isFinished() {
  return getNumberOfDiscs() == ROWS * COLUMNS;
}
```

Requirement 6 – win condition (II)

This is the first win condition requirement for players.

If a player inserts a disc and connects more than three discs of his color in a straight vertical line, then that player wins.

Design – If It's Not Testable, It's Not Designed Well

In fact, this requires one single check. If the current inserted disc connects other three discs in a vertical line, the current player wins the game:

```
@Test
public void when4VerticalDiscsAreConnectedThenPlayerWins() {
  for (int row = 0; row < 3; row++) {
    tested.putDiscInColumn(1); // R
    tested.putDiscInColumn(2); // G
  }
  assertThat(tested.getWinner(), isEmptyString());
  tested.putDiscInColumn(1); // R
  assertThat(tested.getWinner(), is("R"));
}
```

There are a couple of changes to the `putDiscInColumn` method. Also, a new method called `checkWinner` has been created:

```
private static final int DISCS_TO_WIN = 4;

private String winner = "";

private void checkWinner(int row, int column) {
  if (winner.isEmpty()) {
    String colour = board[row][column];
    Pattern winPattern =
      Pattern.compile(".*" + colour + "{" +
          DISCS_TO_WIN + "}.*");

    String vertical = IntStream
                      .range(0, ROWS)
                      .mapToObj(r -> board[r][column])
                      .reduce(String::concat).get();
    if (winPattern.matcher(vertical).matches())
      winner = colour;
  }
}
```

Requirement 7 – win condition (III)

This is the second win condition, which is pretty similar to the previous one.

If a player inserts a disc and connects more than three discs of his color in a straight horizontal line, then that player wins.

[138]

This time, we are trying to win the game by inserting discs into adjacent columns:

```
@Test
public void when4HorizontalDiscsAreConnectedThenPlayerWins() {
  int column;
  for (column = 0; column < 3; column++) {
    tested.putDiscInColumn(column); // R
    tested.putDiscInColumn(column); // G
  }
  assertThat(tested.getWinner(), isEmptyString());
  tested.putDiscInColumn(column); // R
  assertThat(tested.getWinner(), is("R"));
}
```

The code to pass this test is put into the `checkWinners` method:

```
if (winner.isEmpty()) {
  String horizontal = Stream
                        .of(board[row])
                        .reduce(String::concat).get();
  if (winPattern.matcher(horizontal).matches())
    winner = colour;
}
```

Requirement 8 – win condition (IV)

The last requirement is the last win condition.

If a player inserts a disc and connects more than three discs of his color in a straight diagonal line, then that player wins.

We need to perform valid game movements to achieve the condition. In this case, we need to test both diagonals across the board: from top-right to bottom-left and from bottom-right to top-left. The following tests use a list of columns to recreate a full game to reproduce the scenario under test:

```
@Test
public void when4Diagonal1DiscsAreConnectedThenThatPlayerWins() {
  int[] gameplay = new int[] {1, 2, 2, 3, 4, 3, 3, 4, 4, 5, 4};
  for (int column : gameplay) {
    tested.putDiscInColumn(column);
  }
  assertThat(tested.getWinner(), is("R"));
```

```
    }
    @Test
    public void when4Diagonal2DiscsAreConnectedThenThatPlayerWins() {
      int[] gameplay = new int[] {3, 4, 2, 3, 2, 2, 1, 1, 1, 1};
      for (int column : gameplay) {
        tested.putDiscInColumn(column);
      }
      assertThat(tested.getWinner(), is("G"));
    }
```

Again, the `checkWinner` method needs to be modified, adding new board verifications:

```
if (winner.isEmpty()) {
  int startOffset = Math.min(column, row);
  int myColumn = column - startOffset,
    myRow = row - startOffset;
  StringJoiner stringJoiner = new StringJoiner("");
  do {
    stringJoiner .add(board[myRow++][myColumn++]);
  } while (myColumn < COLUMNS && myRow < ROWS);
  if (winPattern .matcher(stringJoiner.toString()).matches())
    winner = currentPlayer;
}

if (winner.isEmpty()) {
  int startOffset = Math.min(column, ROWS - 1 - row);
  int myColumn = column - startOffset,
    myRow = row + startOffset;
  StringJoiner stringJoiner = new StringJoiner("");
  do {
    stringJoiner.add(board[myRow--][myColumn++]);
  } while (myColumn < COLUMNS && myRow >= 0);
  if (winPattern.matcher(stringJoiner.toString()).matches())
    winner = currentPlayer;
}
```

Final considerations

Using TDD, we got a class with a constructor, five public methods, and six private methods. In general, all methods look pretty simple and easy to understand. In this approach, we also got a big method to check winner conditions: `checkWinner`. The advantage is that with this approach we got a bunch of useful tests to guarantee that future modifications do not alter the behavior of the method accidentally, allowing for the introduction of new changes painlessly. Code coverage wasn't the goal, but we got a really high percentage.

Additionally, for testing purposes, we refactored the constructor of the class to accept the output channel as a parameter (**dependency injection**). If we need to modify the way the game status is printed, it will be easier that way than replacing all the uses in the traditional approach. Hence, it is more extensible. In the test-last approach, we have been abusing the `System.println` method and it will be really tedious task if we decide to change all the occurrences for any other thing.

In large projects, when you detect that a great number of tests must be created for a single class, this enables you to split the class following the Single Responsibility Principle. As the output printing was delegated to an external class passed in a parameter in initialization, a more elegant solution would be to create a class with high-level printing methods. That would keep the printing logic separated from the game logic. Like the huge code coverage shown in the following image, these are a few examples of the benefits of good design using TDD:

Connect4TDD

Element	Missed Instructions	Cov.	Missed Branches	Cov.	Missed	Cxty	Missed	Lines	Missed	Methods
checkWinner(int, int)		100%		100%	0	13	0	29	0	1
Connect4TDD(PrintStream)		100%		100%	0	2	0	8	0	1
printBoard()		100%		100%	0	2	0	5	0	1
putDiscInColumn(int)		100%		n/a	0	1	0	8	0	1
checkColumn(int)		100%		75%	1	3	0	3	0	1
checkPositionToInsert(int, int)		100%		100%	0	2	0	3	0	1
getCurrentPlayer()		100%		n/a	0	1	0	2	0	1
switchPlayer()		100%		100%	0	2	0	4	0	1
getNumberOfDiscsInColumn(int)		100%		n/a	0	1	0	3	0	1
getNumberOfDiscs()		100%		n/a	0	1	0	2	0	1
isFinished()		100%		100%	0	2	0	1	0	1
getWinner()		100%		n/a	0	1	0	1	0	1
Total	0 of 356	100%	1 of 38	97%	1	31	0	69	0	12

The code of this approach is available at `https://bitbucket.org/vfarcic/tdd-java-ch05-design.git`.

Summary

In this chapter, we briefly talked about software design and a few basic design principles. We implemented a fully functional version of the board game Connect 4 using two approaches—traditional and TDD.

We analyzed both solutions in terms of pros and cons, and used a Hamcrest framework to empower our tests.

Finally, we concluded that good design and good practices can be performed by both approaches, but TDD is a better approach.

For further information about the topics that this chapter covers, refer to two highly recommended books written by Robert C. Martin: *Clean Code: A Handbook of Agile Software Craftsmanship* and *Agile Software Development: Principles, Patterns, and Practices*.

6
Mocking – Removing External Dependencies

"Talk is cheap. Show me the code."

– Linus Torvalds

TDD is about speed. We want to quickly demonstrate whether an idea, concept, or implementation is valid or not. Further on, we want to run all tests quickly. A major bottleneck to this speed is external dependencies. Setting up the DB data required by tests can be time-consuming. The execution of tests that verify code that uses third-party APIs can be slow. Most importantly, writing tests that satisfy all external dependencies can become too complicated to be worthwhile. Mocking both external and internal dependencies helps us solve these problems.

We'll build on what we did in `Chapter 3`, *Red-Green-Refactor – From Failure Through Success until Perfection*. We'll extend Tic-Tac-Toe to use MongoDB as data storage. None of our unit tests will actually use MongoDB since all communications will be mocked. At the end, we'll create an integration test that will verify that our code and MongoDB are indeed integrated.

The following topics will be covered in this chapter:

- Mocking
- Mockito
- Tic-Tac-Toe v2 requirements
- Developing Tic-Tac-Toe v2
- Integration tests

Mocking

Everyone who has done any of the applications more complicated than *Hello World* knows that Java code is full of dependencies. There can be classes and methods written by other members of the team, third-party libraries, or external systems that we communicate with. Even libraries found inside JDK are dependencies. We might have a business layer that communicates with the data access layer which, in turn, uses database drivers to fetch data. When working with unit tests, we take dependencies even further and often consider all public and protected methods (even those inside the class we are working on) as dependencies that should be isolated.

When doing TDD on the unit tests level, creating specifications that contemplate all those dependencies can be so complex that the tests themselves would become bottlenecks. Their development time can increase so much that the benefits gained with TDD quickly become overshadowed by the ever-increasing cost. More importantly, those same dependencies tend to create such complex tests that they contain more bugs than the implementation itself.

The idea of unit testing (especially when tied to TDD) is to write specifications that validate whether the code of a single unit works regardless of dependencies. When dependencies are internal, they are already tested, and we know that they do what we expect them to do. On the other hand, external dependencies require trust. We must believe that they work correctly. Even if we don't, the task of performing deep testing of, let's say, the JDK `java.nio` classes is too big for most of us. Besides, those potential problems will surface when we run functional and integration tests.

While focused on units, we must try to remove all dependencies that a unit may use. Removal of those dependencies is accomplished through a combination of design and mocking.

> The benefits of using mocks include reduced code dependency and faster text execution.

> Mocks are prerequisites for the fast execution of tests and the ability to concentrate on a single unit of functionality. By mocking dependencies external to the method that is being tested, the developer is able to focus on the task at hand without spending time setting them up. In a case of bigger or multiple teams working together, those dependencies may not even be developed. Also, the execution of tests without mocks tends to be slow. Good candidates for mocks are databases, other products, services, and so on.

Before we go deeper into mocks, let us go through reasons why one would employ them in the first place.

Why mocks?

The following list represents some of the reasons why we employ mock objects:

- The object generates nondeterministic results. For example, `java.util.Date()` provides a different result every time we instantiate it. We cannot test that its result is as expected:

    ```
    java.util.Date date = new java.util.Date();
    date.getTime(); // What is the result this method returns?
    ```

- The object does not yet exist. For example, we might create an interface and test against it. The object that implements that interface might not have been written at the time we test code that uses that interface.
- The object is slow and requires time to process. The most common example would be databases. We might have a code that retrieves all records and generates a report. This operation can last minutes, hours, or, in some cases, even days.

The preceding reasons in the support of mock objects apply to any type of testing. However, in the case of unit tests and, especially, in the context of TDD, there is one more reason, perhaps more important than others. Mocking allows us to isolate all dependencies used by the method we are currently working on. This empowers us to concentrate on a single unit and ignore the inner workings of the code that the unit invokes.

Terminology

Terminology can be a bit confusing, especially since different people use different names for the same thing. To make things even more complicated, mocking frameworks tend not to be consistent when naming their methods.

Before we proceed, let us briefly go through terminology.

Test doubles is a generic name for all of the following types:

- Dummy object's purpose is to act as a substitute for a real method argument
- Test stub can be used to replace a real object with a test-specific object that feeds the desired indirect inputs into the system under test
- **Test Spy** captures the indirect output calls made to another component by the **System Under Test (SUT)** for later verification by the test
- Mock object replaces an object the SUT depends on, with a test-specific object that verifies that it is being used correctly by the SUT
- Fake object replaces a component that the SUT depends on with a much lighter-weight implementation

If you are confused, it may help you to know that you are not the only one. Things are even more complicated than this, since there is no clear agreement, nor a naming standard, between frameworks or authors. Terminology is confusing and inconsistent, and the terms mentioned earlier are by no means accepted by everyone.

To simplify things, throughout this book we'll use the same naming used by Mockito (our framework of choice). This way, methods that you'll be using will correspond with the terminology that you'll be reading further on. We'll continue using mocking as a general term for what others might call **test doubles**. Furthermore, we'll use a mock or spy term to refer to `Mockito` methods.

Mock objects

Mock objects simulate the behavior of real (often complex) objects. They allow us to create an object that will replace the real one used in the implementation code. A mocked object will expect a defined method with defined arguments to return the expected result. It knows in advance what is supposed to happen and how we expect it to react.

Let's take a look at one simple example:

```
TicTacToeCollection collection = mock(TicTacToeCollection.class);
assertThat(collection.drop()).isFalse();
doReturn(true).when(collection).drop();

assertThat(collection.drop()).isTrue();
```

First, we defined `collection` to be a mock of `TicTacToeCollection`. At this moment, all methods from this mocked object are fake and, in the case of Mockito, return default values. This is confirmed in the second line, where we `assert` that the `drop` method returns `false`. Further on, we specify that our mocked object collection should return `true` when the `drop` method is invoked. Finally, we `assert` that the `drop` method returns `true`.

We created a mock object that returns default values and, for one of its methods, defined what should be the return value. At no point was a real object used.

Later on, we'll work with spies that have this logic inverted; an object uses real methods unless specified otherwise. We'll see and learn more about mocking soon when we start extending our Tic-Tac-Toe application. Right now, we'll take a look at one of the Java mocking frameworks called Mockito.

Mockito

Mockito is a mocking framework with a clean and simple API. Tests produced with Mockito are readable, easy to write, and intuitive. It contains three major static methods:

- `mock()`: This is used to create mocks. Optionally, we can specify how those mocks behave with `when()` and `given()`.
- `spy()`: This can be used for partial mocking. Spied objects invoke real methods unless we specify otherwise. As with `mock()`, behavior can be set for every public or protected method (excluding static). The major difference is that `mock()` creates a fake of the whole object, while `spy()` uses the real object.
- `verify()`: This is used to check whether methods were called with given arguments. It is a form of assert.

We'll go deeper into Mockito once we start coding our Tic-Tac-Toe v2 application. First, however, let us quickly go through a new set of requirements.

Tic-Tac-Toe v2 requirements

The requirements of our Tic-Tac-Toe v2 application are simple. We should add a persistent storage so that players can continue playing the game at some later time. We'll use MongoDB for this purpose.

Add MongoDB persistent storage to the application.

Developing Tic-Tac-Toe v2

We'll continue where we left off with Tic-Tac-Toe in Chapter 3, *Red-Green-Refactor – From Failure Through Success until Perfection*. The complete source code of the application developed so far can be found at https://bitbucket.org/vfarcic/tdd-java-ch06-tic-tac-toe-mongo.git. Use the **VCS**|**Checkout from Version Control**|**Git** option from the **IntelliJ IDEA** to clone the code. As with any other project, the first thing we need to do is add the dependencies to build.gradle:

```
dependencies {
    compile 'org.jongo:jongo:1.1'
    compile 'org.mongodb:mongo-java-driver:2.+'
    testCompile 'junit:junit:4.12'
    testCompile 'org.mockito:mockito-all:1.+'
}
```

Importing the MongoDB driver should be self-explanatory. Jongo is a very helpful set of utility methods that make working with Java code much more similar to the Mongo query language. For the testing part, we'll continue using JUnit with the addition of Mockito mocks, spies, and validations.

You'll notice that we won't install MongoDB until the very end. With Mockito, we will not need it, since all our Mongo dependencies will be mocked.

Once dependencies are specified, remember to refresh them in the IDEA **Gradle Projects** dialogue.

The source code can be found in the 00-prerequisites branch of the tdd-java-ch06-tic-tac-toe-mongo Git repository (https://bitbucket.org/vfarcic/tdd-java-ch06-tic-tac-toe-mongo/branch/00-prerequisites).

Now that we have prerequisites set, let's start working on the first requirement.

Requirement 1 – store moves

We should be able to save each move to the DB. Since we already have all the game logic implemented, this should be trivial to do. Nonetheless, this will be a very good example of mock usage.

 Implement an option to save a single move with the turn number, the *x* and *y* axis positions, and the player (X or O).

We should start by defining the Java bean that will represent our data storage schema. There's nothing special about it, so we'll skip this part with only one note.

Do not spend too much time defining specifications for Java boilerplate code. Our implementation of the bean contains overwritten `equals` and `hashCode`. Both are generated automatically by IDEA and do not provide a real value, except to satisfy the need to compare two objects of the same type (we'll use that comparison later on in specifications). TDD is supposed to help us design better and write better code. Writing 15-20 specifications to define boilerplate code that could be written automatically by IDE (as is the case with the `equals` method) does not help us meet these objectives. Mastering TDD means not only learning how to write specifications, but also knowing when it's not worth it.

That being said, consult the source code to see the bean specification and implementation in it's entirety.

The source code can be found in the `01-bean` branch of the `tdd-java-ch06-tic-tac-toe-mongo` Git repository (https://bitbucket.org/vfarcic/tdd-java-ch06-tic-tac-toe-mongo/branch/01-bean). The particular classes are `TicTacToeBeanSpec` and `TicTacToeBean`.

Now, let's go to a more interesting part (but still without mocks, spies, and validations). Let's write specifications related to saving data to MongoDB.

For this requirement, we'll create two new classes inside the `com.packtpublishing.tddjava.ch03tictactoe.mongo` package:

- `TicTacToeCollectionSpec` (inside `src/test/java`)
- `TicTacToeCollection` (inside `src/main/java`)

Specification – DB name

We should specify what the name of the DB that we'll use will be:

```
@Test
public void whenInstantiatedThenMongoHasDbNameTicTacToe() {
  TicTacToeCollection collection = new TicTacToeCollection();
  assertEquals(
      "tic-tac-toe",
collection.getMongoCollection().getDBCollection().getDB().getName()
  );
}
```

We are instantiating a new `TicTacToeCollection` class and verifying that the DB name is what we expect.

Implementation

The implementation is very straightforward, as follows:

```
private MongoCollection mongoCollection;
protected MongoCollection getMongoCollection() {
  return mongoCollection;
}
public TicTacToeCollection() throws UnknownHostException {
  DB db = new MongoClient().getDB("tic-tac-toe");
  mongoCollection = new Jongo(db).getCollection("bla");
}
```

When instantiating the `TicTacToeCollection` class, we're creating a new `MongoCollection` with the specified DB name (`tic-tac-toe`) and assigning it to the local variable.

Bear with us. There's only one more specification left until we get to the interesting part where we'll use mocks and spies.

Specification – a name for the Mongo collection

In the previous implementation, we used `bla` as the name of the collection because Jongo forced us to put some string. Let's create a specification that will define the name of the Mongo collection that we'll use:

```
@Test
public void whenInstantiatedThenMongoCollectionHasNameGame() {
  TicTacToeCollection collection = new TicTacToeCollection();
  assertEquals(
          "game",
          collection.getMongoCollection().getName());
}
```

This specification is almost identical to the previous one and probably self explanatory.

Implementation

All we have to do to implement this specification is change the string we used to set the collection name:

```
public TicTacToeCollection() throws UnknownHostException {
  DB db = new MongoClient().getDB("tic-tac-toe");
  mongoCollection = new Jongo(db).getCollection("game");
}
```

Refactoring

You might have got the impression that refactoring is reserved only for the implementation code. However, when we look the objectives behind refactoring (more readable, optimal, and faster code), they apply as much to specifications as to the implementation code.

The last two specifications have the instantiation of the `TicTacToeCollection` class repeated. We can move it to a method annotated with `@Before`. The effect will be the same (the class will be instantiated before each method annotated with `@Test` is run) and we'll remove the duplicated code. Since the same instantiation will be needed in further specs, removing duplication now will provide even more benefits later on. At the same time, we'll save ourselves from throwing `UnknownHostException` over and over again:

```
TicTacToeCollection collection;

@Before
public void before() throws UnknownHostException {
```

```
        collection = new TicTacToeCollection();
}
@Test
public void whenInstantiatedThenMongoHasDbNameTicTacToe() {
//          throws UnknownHostException {
//    TicTacToeCollection collection = new TicTacToeCollection();
    assertEquals(
        "tic-tac-toe",
collection.getMongoCollection().getDBCollection().getDB().getName()
    );
}

@Test
public void whenInstantiatedThenMongoHasNameGame() {
//          throws UnknownHostException {
//    TicTacToeCollection collection = new TicTacToeCollection();
    assertEquals(
        "game",
        collection.getMongoCollection().getName());
}
```

Use setup and teardown methods. The benefits of these allow preparation or setup and disposal or teardown code to be executed before and after the class or each test method.

In many cases, some code needs to be executed before the test class or each method in a class. For this purpose, JUnit has the @BeforeClass and @Before annotations that should be used in the setup phase. The @BeforeClass executes the associated method before the class is loaded (before the first test method is run). @Before executes the associated method before each test is run. Both should be used when there are certain preconditions required by tests. The most common example is setting up test data in the (hopefully in-memory) database. On the opposite end are the @After and @AfterClass annotations, which should be used as the teardown phase. Their main purpose is to destroy the data or state created during the setup phase or by tests themselves. Each test should be independent from others. Moreover, no test should be affected by the others. The teardown phase helps maintain the system as if no test were previously executed.

Now let's do some mocking, spying, and verifying!

Specification – adding items to the Mongo collection

We should create a method that saves data to MongoDB. After studying Jongo documentation, we discovered that there is the `MongoCollection.save` method, which does exactly that. It accepts any object as a method argument and transforms it (using Jackson) into JSON, which is natively used in MongoDB. The point is that after playing around with Jongo, we decided to use and, more importantly, trust this library.

We can write Mongo specifications in two ways. One more traditional and appropriate for **End2End** (**E2E**) or integration tests would be to bring up a MongoDB instance, invoke the Jongo's save method, query the database, and confirm that data has indeed been saved. It does not end here, as we would need to clean up the database before each test to always guarantee that the same state is unpolluted by the execution of previous tests. Finally, once all tests are finished executing, we might want to stop the MongoDB instance and free server resources for some other tasks.

As you might have guessed, there is quite a lot of work involved for a single test written in this way. Also, it's not only about work that needs to be invested into writing such tests. The execution time would be increased quite a lot. Running one test that communicates with a DB does not take long. Running ten tests is usually still fast. Running hundreds or thousands can take quite a lot of time. What happens when it takes a lot of time to run all unit tests? People lose patience and start dividing them into groups or give up on TDD all together. Dividing tests into groups means that we lose confidence in the fact that nothing got broken, since we are continuously testing only parts of it. Giving up on TDD... Well, that's not the objective we're trying to accomplish. However, if it takes a lot of time to run tests, it's reasonable to expect developers to not want to wait until they are finished running before they move to the next specification, and that is the point when we stop doing TDD. What is a reasonable amount of time to allow our unit tests to run? There is no one-fits-all rule that defines this; however, as a rule of thumb, if the time is longer than 10-15 seconds, we should start worrying, and dedicate time to optimizing them.

> Tests should run quickly. The benefits are that the tests are used often.

If it takes a lot of time to run tests, developers will stop using them or run only a small subset related to the changes they are making. One benefit of fast tests, besides fostering their usage, is fast feedback. The sooner the problem is detected, the easier it is to fix it. Knowledge about the code that produced the problem is still fresh. If a developer has already started working on the next feature while waiting for the completion of the execution of tests, they might decide to postpone fixing the problem until that new feature is developed. On the other hand, if they drops their current work to fix the bug, time is lost in context switching.

If using live DB to run unit tests is not a good option, then what is the alternative? Mocking and spying! In our example, we know which method of a third-party library should be invoked. We also invested enough time to trust this library (besides integration tests that will be performed later on). Once we know how to use the library, we can limit our job to verifying that correct invocations of that library have been made.

Let us give it a try.

First, we should modify our existing code and convert our instantiation of the TicTacToeCollection into a spy:

```
import static org.mockito.Mockito.*;
...
@Before
public void before() throws UnknownHostException {
  collection = spy(new TicTacToeCollection());
}
```

Spying on a class is called **partial** mocking. When applied, the class will behave exactly the same as it would if it was instantiated normally. The major difference is that we can apply partial mocking and substitute one or more methods with mocks. As a general rule, we tend to use spies mostly on classes that we're working on. We want to retain all the functionality of a class that we're writing specifications for, but with an additional option to, when needed, mock a part of it.

Now let us write the specification itself. It could be the following:

```
@Test
public void whenSaveMoveThenInvokeMongoCollectionSave() {
  TicTacToeBean bean = new TicTacToeBean(3, 2, 1, 'Y');
  MongoCollection mongoCollection = mock(MongoCollection.class);
  doReturn(mongoCollection).when(collection).getMongoCollection();
  collection.saveMove(bean);

  verify(mongoCollection, times(1)).save(bean);
}
```

Static methods, such as mock, doReturn, and verify, are all from the org.mockito.Mockito class.

First, we're creating a new `TicTacToeBean`. There's nothing special there. Next, we are creating a `mock` object out of the `MongoCollection`. Since we already established that, when working on a unit level, we want to avoid direct communication with the DB, mocking this dependency will provide this for us. It will convert a real class into a mocked one. For the class using `mongoCollection`, it'll look like a real one; however, behind the scenes, all its methods are shallow and do not actually do anything. It's like overwriting that class and replacing all the methods with empty ones:

```
MongoCollection mongoCollection = mock(MongoCollection.class);
```

Next, we're telling that a mocked `mongoCollection` should be returned whenever we call the `getMongoCollection` method of the collection spied class. In other words, we're telling our class to use a fake collection instead of the real one:

```
doReturn(mongoCollection).when(collection).getMongoCollection();
```

Then, we're calling the method that we are working on:

```
collection.saveMove(bean);
```

Finally, we should verify that the correct invocation of the `Jongo` library is performed once:

```
verify(mongoCollection, times(1)).save(bean);
```

Let's try to implement this specification.

Implementation

To better understand the specification we just wrote, let us do only a partial implementation. We'll create an empty method, `saveMove`. This will allow our code to compile without implementing the specification yet:

```java
public void saveMove(TicTacToeBean bean) {
}
```

When we run our specifications (`gradle test`), the result is the following:

```
Wanted but not invoked:
mongoCollection.save(Turn: 3; X: 2; Y: 1; Player: Y);
```

Mocking – Removing External Dependencies

Mockito tells us that, according to our specification, we expect the `mongoCollection.save` method to be invoked, and that the expectation was not fulfilled. Since the test is still failing, we need to go back and finish the implementation. One of the biggest sins in TDD is to have a failing test and move onto something else.

> All tests should pass before a new test is written. The benefits of this are that the focus is maintained on a small unit of work, and implementation code is (almost) always in a working condition.

> It is sometimes tempting to write multiple tests before the actual implementation. In other cases, developers ignore problems detected by the existing tests and move towards new features. This should be avoided whenever possible. In most cases, breaking this rule will only introduce technical debt that will need to be paid with interest. One of the goals of TDD is ensuring that the implementation code is (almost) always working as expected. Some projects, due to pressures to reach the delivery date or maintain the budget, break this rule and dedicate time to new features, leaving the fixing of the code associated with failed tests for later. Those projects usually end up postponing the inevitable.

Let's modify the implementation too, for example, the following:

```
public void saveMove(TicTacToeBean bean) {
  getMongoCollection().save(null);
}
```

If we run our specifications again, the result is the following:

```
Argument(s) are different! Wanted:
mongoCollection.save(Turn: 3; X: 2; Y: 1; Player: Y);
```

This time we are invoking the expected method, but the arguments we are passing to it are not what we hoped for. In the specification, we set the expectation to a bean (new `TicTacToeBean(3, 2, 1, 'Y')`) and in the implementation, we passed null. Not only that, Mockito verifications can tell us whether a correct method was invoked, and also whether the arguments passed to that method are correct.

The correct implementation of the specification is the following:

```
public void saveMove(TicTacToeBean bean) {
  getMongoCollection().save(bean);
}
```

This time all specifications should pass, and we can, happily, proceed to the next one.

Specification – adding operation feedback

Let us change the return type of our `saveMove` method to `boolean`:

```
@Test
public void whenSaveMoveThenReturnTrue() {
  TicTacToeBean bean = new TicTacToeBean(3, 2, 1, 'Y');
  MongoCollection mongoCollection = mock(MongoCollection.class);
  doReturn(mongoCollection).when(collection).getMongoCollection();
  assertTrue(collection.saveMove(bean));
}
```

Implementation

This implementation is very straightforward. We should change the method return type. Remember that one of the rules of TDD is to use the simplest possible solution. The simplest solution is to return `true` as in the following example:

```
public boolean saveMove(TicTacToeBean bean) {
  getMongoCollection().save(bean);
  return true;
}
```

Refactoring

You have probably noticed that the last two specifications have the first two lines duplicated. We can refactor the specifications code by moving them to the method annotated with `@Before`:

```
TicTacToeCollection collection;
TicTacToeBean bean;
MongoCollection mongoCollection;

@Before
public void before() throws UnknownHostException {
  collection = spy(new TicTacToeCollection());
  bean = new TicTacToeBean(3, 2, 1, 'Y');
  mongoCollection = mock(MongoCollection.class);
}
...
@Test
public void whenSaveMoveThenInvokeMongoCollectionSave() {
  // TicTacToeBean bean = new TicTacToeBean(3, 2, 1, 'Y');
  // MongoCollection mongoCollection = mock(MongoCollection.class);
```

```
    doReturn(mongoCollection).when(collection).getMongoCollection();
    collection.saveMove(bean);
    verify(mongoCollection, times(1)).save(bean);
}

@Test
public void whenSaveMoveThenReturnTrue() {
// TicTacToeBean bean = new TicTacToeBean(3, 2, 1, 'Y');
// MongoCollection mongoCollection = mock(MongoCollection.class);
    doReturn(mongoCollection).when(collection).getMongoCollection();
    assertTrue(collection.saveMove(bean));
}
```

Specification – error handling

Now let us contemplate the option that something might go wrong when using MongoDB. When, for example, an exception is thrown, we might want to return `false` from our `saveMove` method:

```
@Test
public void givenExceptionWhenSaveMoveThenReturnFalse() {
    doThrow(new MongoException("Bla"))
      .when(mongoCollection).save(any(TicTacToeBean.class));
    doReturn(mongoCollection).when(collection).getMongoCollection();
    assertFalse(collection.saveMove(bean));
}
```

Here, we introduce to another Mockito method: `doThrow`. It acts in a similar way to `doReturn` and throws an `Exception` when set conditions are fulfilled. The specification will throw the `MongoException` when the save method inside the `mongoCollection` class is invoked. This allows us to `assert` that our `saveMove` method returns `false` when an exception is thrown.

Implementation

The implementation can be as simple as adding a `try/catch` block:

```
public boolean saveMove(TicTacToeBean bean) {
  try {
    getMongoCollection().save(bean);
    return true;
  } catch (Exception e) {
    return false;
  }
}
```

Specification – clear state between games

This is a very simple application that, at least at this moment, can store only one game session. Whenever a new instance is created, we should start over and remove all data stored in the database. The easiest way to do this is to simply drop the MongoDB collection. Jongo has the `MongoCollection.drop()` method that can be used for that. We'll create a new method, `drop`, that will act in a similar way to `saveMove`.

If you haven't worked with Mockito, MongoDB, and/or Jongo, the chances are you were not able to do the exercises from this chapter by yourself, and just decided to follow the solutions we provided. If that's the case, this is the moment when you may want to switch gears and try to write the specifications and implementation by yourself.

We should verify that `MongoCollection.drop()` is invoked from our own method `drop()` inside the `TicTacToeCollection` class. Try it by yourself before looking at the following code. It should be almost the same as what we did with the `save` method:

```
@Test
public void whenDropThenInvokeMongoCollectionDrop() {
  doReturn(mongoCollection).when(collection).getMongoCollection();
  collection.drop();
  verify(mongoCollection).drop();
}
```

Implementation

Since this is a wrapper method, implementing this specification should be fairly easy:

```
public void drop() {
  getMongoCollection().drop();
}
```

Specification – drop operation feedback

We're almost done with this class. There are only two specifications left.

Let us make sure that, in normal circumstances, we return `true`:

```
@Test
public void whenDropThenReturnTrue() {
  doReturn(mongoCollection).when(collection).getMongoCollection();
  assertTrue(collection.drop());
}
```

Implementation

If things look too easy with TDD, then that is on purpose. We are splitting tasks into such small entities that, in most cases, implementing a specification is a piece of cake. This one is no exception:

```
public boolean drop() {
  getMongoCollection().drop();
  return true;
}
```

Specification – error handling

Finally, let us make sure that the `drop` method returns `false` in case of an `Exception`:

```
@Test
public void givenExceptionWhenDropThenReturnFalse() {
  doThrow(new MongoException("Bla")).when(mongoCollection).drop();
  doReturn(mongoCollection).when(collection).getMongoCollection();
  assertFalse(collection.drop());
}
```

Implementation

Let us just add a `try/catch` block:

```
public boolean drop() {
  try {
    getMongoCollection().drop();
    return true;
  } catch (Exception e) {
    return false;
  }
}
```

With this implementation, we are finished with the `TicTacToeCollection` class that acts as a layer between our `main` class and MongoDB.

The source code can be found in the `02-save-move` branch of the `tdd-java-ch06-tic-tac-toe-mongo` Git repository (https://bitbucket.org/vfarcic/tdd-java-ch06-tic-tac-toe-mongo/branch/02-save-move). The classes in particular are `TicTacToeCollectionSpec` and `TicTacToeCollection`.

Requirement 2 – store every turn

Let us employ the `TicTacToeCollection` methods inside our main class `TicTacToe`. Whenever a player plays a turn successfully, we should save it to the DB. Also, we should drop the collection whenever a new class is instantiated so that a new game does not overlap the old one. We could make it much more elaborate than this; however, for the purpose of this chapter and learning how to use mocking, this requirement should do for now.

Save each turn to the database and make sure that a new session cleans the old data.

Let's do some setup first.

[161]

Specification – creating new collection

Since all our methods that will be used to communicate with MongoDB are in the `TicTacToeCollection` class, we should make sure that it is instantiated. The specification could be the following:

```
@Test
public void whenInstantiatedThenSetCollection() {
  assertNotNull(ticTacToe.getTicTacToeCollection());
}
```

The instantiation of `TicTacToe` is already done in the method annotated with `@Before`. With this specification, we're making sure that the collection is instantiated as well.

Implementation

There is nothing special about this implementation. We should simply overwrite the default constructor and assign a new instance to the `ticTacToeCollection` variable.

To begin with, we should add a local variable and a getter for `TicTacToeCollection`:

```
private TicTacToeCollection ticTacToeCollection;

protected TicTacToeCollection getTicTacToeCollection() {
  return ticTacToeCollection;
}
```

Now all that's left is to instantiate a new `collection` and assign it to the variable when the `main` class is instantiated:

```
public TicTacToe() throws UnknownHostException {
  this(new TicTacToeCollection());
}
protected TicTacToe(TicTacToeCollection collection) {
  ticTacToeCollection = collection;
}
```

We also created another way to instantiate the class by passing `TicTacToeCollection` as an argument. This will come in handy inside specifications as an easy way to pass a mocked collection.

Now let us go back to the specifications class and make use of this new constructor.

Specification refactoring

To utilize a newly created `TicTacToe` constructor, we can do something such as the following:

```
private TicTacToeCollection collection;

@Before
public final void before() throws UnknownHostException {
  collection = mock(TicTacToeCollection.class);
// ticTacToe = new TicTacToe();
  ticTacToe = new TicTacToe(collection);
}
```

Now all our specifications will use a mocked version of the `TicTacToeCollection`. There are other ways to inject mocked dependencies (for example, with Spring); however, when possible, we feel that simplicity trumps complicated frameworks.

Specification – storing current move

Whenever we play a turn, it should be saved to the DB. The specification can be the following:

```
@Test
public void whenPlayThenSaveMoveIsInvoked() {
  TicTacToeBean move = new TicTacToeBean(1, 1, 3, 'X');
  ticTacToe.play(move.getX(), move.getY());
  verify(collection).saveMove(move);
}
```

By now, you should be familiar with Mockito, but let us go through the code as a refresher:

1. First, we are instantiating a `TicTacToeBean` since it contains the data that our collections expect:

   ```
   TicTacToeBean move = new TicTacToeBean(1, 1, 3, 'X');
   ```

2. Next, it is time to play an actual turn:

   ```
   ticTacToe.play(move.getX(), move.getY());
   ```

3. Finally, we need to verify that the `saveMove` method is really invoked:

   ```
   verify(collection, times(1)).saveMove(move);
   ```

As we have done throughout this chapter, we isolated all external invocations and focused only on the unit (`play`) that we're working on. Keep in mind that this isolation is limited only to the public and protected methods. When it comes to the actual implementation, we might choose to add the `saveMove` invocation to the `play` public method or one of the private methods that we wrote as a result of the refactoring we did earlier.

Implementation

This specification poses a couple of challenges. First, where should we place the invocation of the `saveMove` method? The `setBox` private method looks like a good place. That's where we are doing validations of if the turn is valid, and if it is, we can call the `saveMove` method. However, that method expects a `bean` instead of the variables x, y, and `lastPlayer` that are being used right now, so we might want to change the signature of the `setBox` method.

This is how the method looks now:

```
private void setBox(int x, int y, char lastPlayer) {
  if (board[x - 1][y - 1] != '\0') {
    throw new RuntimeException("Box is occupied");
  } else {
    board[x - 1][y - 1] = lastPlayer;
  }
}
```

This is how it looks after the necessary changes are applied:

```
private void setBox(TicTacToeBean bean) {
  if (board[bean.getX() - 1][bean.getY() - 1] != '\0') {
    throw new RuntimeException("Box is occupied");
  } else {
    board[bean.getX() - 1][bean.getY() - 1] = lastPlayer;
    getTicTacToeCollection().saveMove(bean);
  }
}
```

The change of the `setBox` signature triggers a few other changes. Since it is invoked from the `play` method, we'll need to instantiate the `bean` there:

```
public String play(int x, int y) {
  checkAxis(x);
  checkAxis(y);
  lastPlayer = nextPlayer();
// setBox(x, y, lastPlayer);
```

```
        setBox(new TicTacToeBean(1, x, y, lastPlayer));
        if (isWin(x, y)) {
          return lastPlayer + " is the winner";
        } else if (isDraw()) {
          return RESULT_DRAW;
        } else {
          return NO_WINNER;
        }
      }
```

You might have noticed that we used a constant value 1 as a turn. There is still no specification that says otherwise, so we took a shortcut. We'll deal with it later.

All those changes were still very simple, and it took a reasonably short period of time to implement them. If the changes were bigger, we might have chosen a different path; and made a simpler change to get to the final solution through refactoring. Remember that speed is the key. You don't want to get stuck with an implementation that does not pass tests for a long time.

Specification – error handling

What happens if a move could not be saved? Our helper method `saveMove` returns `true` or `false` depending on the MongoDB operation outcome. We might want to throw an exception when it returns `false`.

First things first: we should change the implementation of the `before` method and make sure that, by default, `saveMove` returns `true`:

```
@Before
public final void before() throws UnknownHostException {
  collection = mock(TicTacToeCollection.class);
doReturn(true).when(collection).saveMove(any(TicTacToeBean.class));
  ticTacToe = new TicTacToe(collection);
}
```

Now that we have stubbed the mocked collection with what we think is the default behavior (return `true` when `saveMove` is invoked), we can proceed and write the specification:

```
@Test
public void whenPlayAndSaveReturnsFalseThenThrowException() {
doReturn(false).when(collection).saveMove(any(TicTacToeBean.class));
  TicTacToeBean move = new TicTacToeBean(1, 1, 3, 'X');
```

```
        exception.expect(RuntimeException.class);
        ticTacToe.play(move.getX(), move.getY());
}
```

We're using Mockito to return `false` when `saveMove` is invoked. Since, in this case, we don't care about a specific invocation of `saveMove`, we used `any(TicTacToeBean.class)` as the method argument. This is another one of Mockito's static methods.

Once everything is set, we use a JUnit expectation in the same way as we did before throughout Chapter 3, *Red-Green-Refactor – From Failure Through Success until Perfection*.

Implementation

Let's do a simple `if` and throw a `RuntimeException` when the result is not expected:

```
private void setBox(TicTacToeBean bean) {
  if (board[bean.getX() - 1][bean.getY() - 1] != '\0') {
    throw new RuntimeException("Box is occupied");
  } else {
    board[bean.getX() - 1][bean.getY() - 1] = lastPlayer;
//    getTicTacToeCollection().saveMove(bean);
    if (!getTicTacToeCollection().saveMove(bean)) {
      throw new RuntimeException("Saving to DB failed");
    }
  }
}
```

Specification – alternate players

Do you remember the turn that we hard coded to be always 1? Let's fix that behavior.

We can invoke the `play` method twice and verify that the turn changes from 1 to 2:

```
@Test
public void whenPlayInvokedMultipleTimesThenTurnIncreases() {
  TicTacToeBean move1 = new TicTacToeBean(1, 1, 1, 'X');
  ticTacToe.play(move1.getX(), move1.getY());
  verify(collection, times(1)).saveMove(move1);
  TicTacToeBean move2 = new TicTacToeBean(2, 1, 2, 'O');
  ticTacToe.play(move2.getX(), move2.getY());
  verify(collection, times(1)).saveMove(move2);
}
```

Implementation

As with almost everything else done in the TDD fashion, implementation is fairly easy:

```
private int turn = 0;
...
public String play(int x, int y) {
  checkAxis(x);
  checkAxis(y);
  lastPlayer = nextPlayer();
  setBox(new TicTacToeBean(++turn, x, y, lastPlayer));
  if (isWin(x, y)) {
    return lastPlayer + " is the winner";
  } else if (isDraw()) {
    return RESULT_DRAW;
  } else {
    return NO_WINNER;
  }
}
```

Exercises

A few more specifications and their implementations are still missing. We should invoke the `drop()` method whenever our `TicTacToe` class is instantiated. We should also make sure that `RuntimeException` is thrown when `drop()` returns `false`. We'll leave those specifications and their implementations as an exercise for you.

The source code can be found in the `03-mongo` branch of the `tdd-java-ch06-tic-tac-toe-mongo` Git repository (https://bitbucket.org/vfarcic/tdd-java-ch06-tic-tac-toe-mongo/branch/03-mongo). The classes in particular are `TicTacToeSpec` and `TicTacToe`.

Integration tests

We did a lot of unit tests. We relied a lot on trust. Unit after unit was specified and implemented. While working on specifications, we isolated everything but the units we were working on, and verified that one invoked the other correctly. However, the time has come to validate that all those units are truly able to communicate with MongoDB. We might have made a mistake or, more importantly, we might not have MongoDB up and running. It would be a disaster to discover that, for example, we deployed our application, but forgot to bring up the DB, or that the configuration (IP, port, and so on) is not set correctly.

The integration test's objective is to validate, as you might have guessed, the integration of separate components, applications, systems, and so on. If you remember the testing pyramid, it states that unit tests are the easiest to write and fastest to run, so we should keep other types of tests limited to things that UTs did not cover.

We should isolate our integration tests in a way that they can be run occasionally (before we push our code to repository, or as a part of our **continuous integration** (**CI**) process) and keep unit test as a continuous feedback loop.

Tests separation

If we follow some kind of convention, it is fairly easy to separate tests in Gradle. We can have our tests in different directories and distinct packages or, for example, with different file suffixes. In this case, we choose the latter. All our specification classes are named with the Spec suffix (that is, TicTacToeSpec). We can make a rule that all integration tests have the Integ suffix.

With that in mind, let us modify our build.gradle file.

First, we'll tell Gradle that only classes ending with Spec should be used by the test task:

```
test {
    include '**/*Spec.class'
}
```

Next, we can create a new task, `testInteg`:

```
task testInteg(type: Test) {
    include '**/*Integ.class'
}
```

With those two additions to `build.gradle`, we continue having the test tasks that we used heavily throughout the book; however, this time, they are limited only to specifications (unit tests). In addition, all integration tests can be run by clicking the `testInteg` task from the Gradle projects IDEA window or running the following command from command prompt:

gradle testInteg

Let us write a simple integration test.

The integration test

We'll create a `TicTacToeInteg` class inside the `com.packtpublishing.tddjava.ch03tictactoe` package in the `src/test/java` directory. Since we know that Jongo throws an exception if it cannot connect to the database, a test class can be as simple as the following:

```
import org.junit.Test;
import java.net.UnknownHostException;
import static org.junit.Assert.*;

public class TicTacToeInteg {

  @Test
  public void givenMongoDbIsRunningWhenPlayThenNoException()
      throws UnknownHostException {
    TicTacToe ticTacToe = new TicTacToe();
    assertEquals(TicTacToe.NO_WINNER, ticTacToe.play(1, 1));
  }
}
```

Mocking – Removing External Dependencies

The invocation of `assertEquals` is just as a precaution. The real objective of this test is to make sure that no `Exception` is thrown. Since we did not start MongoDB (unless you are very proactive and did it yourself, in which case you should stop it), `test` should fail:

```
vfarcic@viktor:~/IdeaProjects/tdd-java-ch06-tic-tac-toe-mongo$ gradle testInteg
:compileJava UP-TO-DATE
:processResources UP-TO-DATE
:classes UP-TO-DATE
:compileTestJava UP-TO-DATE
:processTestResources UP-TO-DATE
:testClasses UP-TO-DATE
:testInteg

com.packtpublishing.tddjava.ch03tictactoe.TicTacToeInteg > givenMongoDbIsRunning
WhenPlayThenNoException FAILED
    java.lang.RuntimeException at TicTacToeInteg.java:12

1 test completed, 1 failed
:testInteg FAILED

FAILURE: Build failed with an exception.

* What went wrong:
Execution failed for task ':testInteg'.
> There were failing tests. See the report at: file:///home/vfarcic/IdeaProjects
/tdd-java-ch06-tic-tac-toe-mongo/build/reports/tests/index.html

* Try:
Run with --stacktrace option to get the stack trace. Run with --info or --debug
option to get more log output.

BUILD FAILED

Total time: 14.6 secs
vfarcic@viktor:~/IdeaProjects/tdd-java-ch06-tic-tac-toe-mongo$
```

Now that we know that the integration test works, or in other words, that it indeed fails when MongoDB is not up and running, let us try it again with the DB started. To bring up MongoDB, we'll use Vagrant to create a virtual machine with Ubuntu OS. MongoDB will be run as a Docker.

Make sure that the **04-integration** branch is checked out:

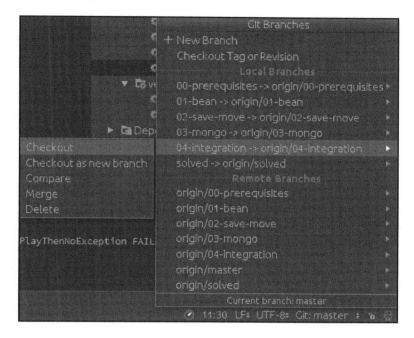

From the command prompt, run the following command:

```
$ vagrant up
```

Be patient until VM is up and running (it might take a while when executed for the first time, especially on a slower bandwidth). Once finished, rerun integration tests:

It worked, and now we're confident that we are indeed integrated with MongoDB.

This was a very simplistic integration test, and in the real-world, we would do a bit more than this single test. We could, for example, query the DB and confirm that data was stored correctly. However, the purpose of this chapter was to learn both how to mock and that we should not depend only on unit tests. The next chapter will explore integration and functional tests in more depth.

The source code can be found in the `04-integration` branch of the `tdd-java-ch06-tic-tac-toe-mongo` Git repository (https://bitbucket.org/vfarcic/tdd-java-ch06-tic-tac-toe-mongo/branch/04-integration).

Summary

Mocking and spying techniques are used to isolate different parts of code or third-party libraries. They are essential if we are to proceed with great speed, not only while coding, but also while running tests. Tests without mocks are often too complex to write and can be so slow that, with time, TDD tends to become close to impossible. Slow tests mean that we won't be able to run all of them every time we write a new specification. That in itself leads to deterioration in the confidence we have in the our tests, since only a part of them is run.

Mocking is not only useful as a way to isolate external dependencies, but also as a way to isolate our own code from a unit we're working on.

In this chapter, we presented Mockito as, in our opinion, the framework with the best balance between functionality and ease of use. We invite you to investigate its documentation in more detail (http://mockito.org/), as well as other Java frameworks dedicated to mocking. EasyMock (http://easymock.org/), JMock (http://www.jmock.org/), and PowerMock (https://code.google.com/p/powermock/) are a few of the most popular.

In the next chapter we are going to put some functional programming concepts as well as some TDD concepts applied to them. For that matter, part of the Java functional API is going to be presented.

7
TDD and Functional Programming – A Perfect Match

"Any sufficiently advanced technology is indistinguishable from magic."

– *Arthur C. Clarke*

All of the code examples that we have seen so far in this book follow a particular programming paradigm: **object-oriented programming** (**OOP**). This paradigm has monopolized the software industry for a long time and the majority of software companies have adopted OOP as the standard way of programming.

However the fact that OOP has become the most used paradigm does not mean it is the only one that exists. In fact, there are more that are worth mentioning, but this chapter is going to focus only on one of them: functional programming. Additionally, this book's language is Java, so all code snippets and examples will be based on the functional API that were included in version 8 of Java.

Topics covered in this chapter include:

- Optional class
- Functions revisited
- Streams
- Applying TDD to functional programming

Setting up the environment

In order to explore some of the goodies of Java Functional Programming in a test-driven fashion, we are going to set up a Java project with JUnit and AssertJ frameworks. The last one includes quite a few convenient methods for `Optional`.

Let's start a new Gradle project. This is how `build.gradle` looks:

```
apply plugin: 'java'

sourceCompatibility = 1.8
targetCompatibility = 1.8

repositories {
  mavenCentral()
}

dependencies {
  testCompile group: 'junit', name: 'junit', version: '4.12'
  testCompile group: 'org.assertj', name: 'assertj-core', version: '3.9.0'
}
```

In the following sections, we are going to explore some of the utilities and classes included in Java 8 that enhance the experience of programming. Most of them are not only for functional programming and can be used even in imperative-style programming.

Optional – dealing with uncertainty

Since it was created, `null` has been used and misused by developers innumerable times in innumerable programs. One of the common cases for `null` is, among others, to represent the absence of a value. That is not convenient at all; it could either represent the absence of a value or the abnormal execution of a piece of code.

Moreover, in order to access variables that can potentially be `null`, and mitigate undesired runtime exceptions like `NullPointerException`, developers tend to wrap variables with an `if` statement so those variables are accessed in safe mode. Although it works, this protection against nulls adds some boilerplate that has nothing to do with the functionality or the goal of the code:

```
if (name != null) {
  // do something with name
}
```

The preceding code overcomes the problems that the creator of `null` spotted in his famous quote during a conference in 2009:

> *"I call it my billion-dollar mistake. It was the invention of the null reference in 1965. At that time, I was designing the first comprehensive type system for references in an object oriented language (ALGOL W). My goal was to ensure that all use of references should be absolutely safe, with checking performed automatically by the compiler. But I couldn't resist the temptation to put in a null reference, simply because it was so easy to implement. This has led to innumerable errors, vulnerabilities, and system crashes, which have probably caused a billion dollars of pain and damage in the last forty years."*
>
> *– Tony Hoare*

With the release of Java 8, the utility class called `Optional` was included as an alternative to the preceding code block. Among other benefits, it brings compilation checks and zero boilerplate code. Let's see `Optional` in action with a simple example.

Example of Optional

As a demonstration of `Optional`, we are going to create an in-memory student repository. This repository has a method to find students by their `name`, which, for convenience, will be considered the ID. The value returned by the method is `Optional<Student>`; this means that the response might or might not contain a `Student`. This pattern is basically one of the common scenarios for `Optional`.

 At this point, the reader should be familiar with the TDD process. For the sake of brevity the complete Red-Green-Refactor process is skipped. Tests are going to be presented along with the implementation in a convenient order, which could not coincide with the order in a TDD iteration.

First of all, we need a `Student` class to represent students within our system. To keep it simple, our implementation is going to be very basic, with only two parameters: the student's `name` and `age`:

```
public class Student {
  public final String name;
  public final int age;
  public Student(String name, int age) {
    this.name = name;
    this.age = age;
```

        }
    }

The next test class verifies two scenarios: a successful lookup and an unsuccessful one. Note that AssertJ has some useful and meaningful assertion methods for Optional. That makes testing really fluent and readable:

```java
public class StudentRepositoryTest {

  private List<Student> studentList = Arrays.asList(
    new Student("Jane", 23),
    new Student("John", 21),
    new Student("Tom", 25)
  );

  private StudentRepository studentRepository =
    new StudentRepository(studentList);

  @Test
  public void whenStudentIsNotFoundThenReturnEmpty() {
    assertThat(studentRepository.findByName("Samantha"))
      .isNotPresent();
  }

  @Test
  public void whenStudentIsFoundThenReturnStudent() {
    assertThat(studentRepository.findByName("John"))
      .isPresent();
  }
}
```

In cases where verifying the existence of a student with that name is not enough, we can perform some assertions on the returned object. In the majority of scenarios, this is the way to go:

```java
@Test
public void whenStudentIsFoundThenReturnStudent() {
  assertThat(studentRepository.findByName("John"))
    .hasValueSatisfying(s -> {
      assertThat(s.name).isEqualTo("John");
      assertThat(s.age).isEqualTo(21);
    });
}
```

Now, it's time to focus on the `StudentRepository` class, which contains only one constructor and the method to perform student lookups. As shown in the following code, the lookup method `findByName` returns an `Optional` holding a `Student`. Note that this is a valid yet not functional implementation used as a starting point:

```
public class StudentRepository {
  StudentRepository(Collection<Student> students) { }

  public Optional<Student> findByName(String name) {
    return Optional.empty();
  }
}
```

If we run the tests against the preceding implementation we get one successful test, because the lookup method is returning by default an `Optional.empty()`. The other test throws an error, as follows:

```
java.lang.AssertionError:
Expecting Optional to contain a value but was empty.
```

For the sake of completeness, this is one of the possible implementations:

```
public class StudentRepository {
  private final Set<Student> studentSet;

  StudentRepository(Collection<Student> students) {
    studentSet = new HashSet<>(students);
  }

  public Optional<Student> findByName(String name) {
    for (Student student : this.studentSet) {
      if (student.name.equals(name))
        return Optional.of(student);
    }
    return Optional.empty();
  }
}
```

In the next section, we will see a different point of view on functions. In Java 8, some additional capabilities have been added to functions if they are used in a particular way. We are going to explore a few of them with some examples.

Functions revisited

Unlike object-oriented programs, those written in a functional way don't hold any mutable state. Instead, code is made up with functions that take arguments and return values. Because there is no internal state nor side-effects involved that can alter the execution, all functions are deterministic. This is a really good feature because it implies that different executions of the same function, with the same parameters, would produce the same outcome.

The following snippet illustrates a function that does not mutate any internal state:

```
public Integer add(Integer a, Integer b) {
  return a + b;
}
```

The following is the same function written using Java's functional API:

```
public final BinaryOperator<Integer> add =
  new BinaryOperator<Integer>() {

    @Override
    public Integer apply(Integer a, Integer b) {
      return a + b;
    }
};
```

The first example should be completely familiar to any Java developer; it follows the common syntax of a function that takes two integers as arguments and returns the sum of them. The second example, however, differs a bit from the traditional code we are used to. In this new version, the function is an object that counts as a value, and it can be assigned to a field. This is quite convenient in some scenarios because it can still be used as a function in some cases and in some others it can also be used as a return value, as an argument in a function or a field within a class.

One can argue that the first version of the function is more appropriated since it is shorter and does not require creating a new object. Well, it's true, but the fact that functions can also be objects enhances them with a bunch of new capabilities. Regarding code verbosity, it can be considerably reduced to a single line by using a lambda expression:

```
public final BinaryOperator<Integer> addLambda = (a, b) -> a + b;
```

In the next section, a possible solution to **Reverse Polish Notation** (**RPN**) kata is presented. We are going to use the power and expressiveness of functional programming, particularly the lambda notation, which becomes really handy when functions are required as arguments of some functions. Using lambdas makes our code very concise and elegant, increasing the readability.

Kata – Reverse Polish Notation

RPN is a notation used for representing mathematical expressions. It differs from the traditional and widely used infix notation in the order of operators and operands.

 In infix notation the operator is placed between the operands, whereas in RPN, operands are placed first and the operator is located at the end.

This is an expression written using infix notation:

        3 + 4

The same expression written using RPN:

        3 4 +

Requirements

We are going to obviate how the expressions are read so that we can focus on solving the problem. Furthermore, we are going to work only with positive integers to simplify the problem, although it shouldn't be very difficult to accept floats or doubles as well. In order to solve this kata, we are asked to fulfill only the following two requirements:

- On invalid input (not a RPN), an error message should be thrown
- It gets an arithmetic expression written using RPN and computes the result

The following code snippet is a small scaffold for us to start our project upon:

```
public class ReversePolishNotation {
  int compute(String expression) {
    return 0;
  }
}

public class NotReversePolishNotationError extends RuntimeException
{
  public NotReversePolishNotationError() {
    super("Not a Reverse Polish Notation");
  }
}
```

With the preceding code fragment as the starting point, we are going to proceed, breaking down the requirements into smaller specifications that can be tackled one by one.

Requirement – handling invalid input

Provided that our implementation is basically doing nothing, we are going to focus only on one thing—reading single operands. If the input is a single number (no operators) then it's a valid reverse notation and the value of the number is returned. Anything other than that is considered not a valid RPN for now.

This requirement is translated into these four tests:

```
public class ReversePolishNotationTest {
  private ReversePolishNotation reversePolishNotation =
    new ReversePolishNotation();

  @Test(expected = NotReversePolishNotationError.class)
  public void emptyInputThrowsError() {
    reversePolishNotation.compute("");
  }

  @Test(expected = NotReversePolishNotationError.class)
  public void notANumberThrowsError() {
    reversePolishNotation.compute("a");
  }

  @Test
  public void oneDigitReturnsNumber() {
    assertThat(reversePolishNotation.compute("7")).isEqualTo(7);
  }
```

```
@Test
public void moreThanOneDigitReturnsNumber() {
assertThat(reversePolishNotation.compute("120")).isEqualTo(120);
    }
}
```

Our `compute` method is now required to throw an `IllegalArgumentException` when an invalid input is provided. In any other case it returns the number as an integer value. This can be achieved with the following lines of code:

```
public class ReversePolishNotation {
  int compute(String expression) {
    try {
      return (Integer.parseInt(expression));
    } catch (NumberFormatException e) {
      throw new NotReversePolishNotationError();
    }
  }
}
```

This requirement has been fulfilled. The other requirement is a bit more complex, so we are going to divide it into two—single operations, which means only one operation, and complex operations, which involve more than one operation of any kind.

Requirement – single operations

So, the plan is to support add, subtract, multiply and divide operations. As explained in the kata presentation, in RPN the operator is located at the end of the expression.

That means *a - b* is represented as *a b -*, and the same applies to the other operators: addition +, multiplication *, and division /.

Let's add one of each of the supported operations to our tests:

```
@Test
public void addOperationReturnsCorrectValue() {
  assertThat(reversePolishNotation.compute("1 2 +")).isEqualTo(3);
}

@Test
public void subtractOperationReturnsCorrectValue() {
  assertThat(reversePolishNotation.compute("2 1 -")).isEqualTo(1);
}
```

```java
@Test
public void multiplyOperationReturnsCorrectValue() {
  assertThat(reversePolishNotation.compute("2 1 *")).isEqualTo(2);
}

@Test
public void divideOperationReturnsCorrectValue() {
  assertThat(reversePolishNotation.compute("2 2 /")).isEqualTo(1);
}
```

This also includes the necessary changes to make them pass successfully. The behavior is basically placing the operator between the expressions and performing the operation in case an expression is given as input. If there is only one element in the expression, then the former rules apply:

```java
int compute(String expression) {
  String[] elems = expression.trim().split(" ");
  if (elems.length != 1 && elems.length != 3)
    throw new NotReversePolishNotationError();
  if (elems.length == 1) {
    return parseInt(elems[0]);
  } else {
    if ("+".equals(elems[2]))
      return parseInt(elems[0]) + parseInt(elems[1]);
    else if ("-".equals(elems[2]))
      return parseInt(elems[0]) - parseInt(elems[1]);
    else if ("*".equals(elems[2]))
      return parseInt(elems[0]) * parseInt(elems[1]);
    else if ("/".equals(elems[2]))
      return parseInt(elems[0]) / parseInt(elems[1]);
    else
      throw new NotReversePolishNotationError();
  }
}
```

parseInt is a private method that parses the input and either returns the integer value or throws an exception:

```java
private int parseInt(String number) {
  try {
    return Integer.parseInt(number);
  } catch (NumberFormatException e) {
    throw new NotReversePolishNotationError();
  }
}
```

The next requirement is where the magic happens. We are going to support more than one operation within the `expression`.

Requirement – complex operations

Complex operations are difficult to address, because mixing operations makes it really difficult for the non-trained human eye to understand in which order the operations should take place. Also, different evaluation orders usually lead to different results. To solve that, the computation of reverse polish expressions is backed up by the implementation of a queue. These are some tests for our next functionality:

```
@Test
public void multipleAddOperationsReturnCorrectValue() {
  assertThat(reversePolishNotation.compute("1 2 5 + +"))
    .isEqualTo(8);
}

@Test
public void multipleDifferentOperationsReturnCorrectValue() {
  assertThat(reversePolishNotation.compute("5 12 + 3 -"))
    .isEqualTo(14);
}

@Test
public void aComplexTest() {
  assertThat(reversePolishNotation.compute("5 1 2 + 4 * + 3 -"))
    .isEqualTo(14);
}
```

The computation should pile up the numbers or operands in the expression sequentially, from left to right, in a queue or stack in Java. If at any point an operator is found then the pile replaces the two elements on top with the result of applying that operator to those values. For better comprehension, the logic is going to be separated in to different functions.

First of all, we are going to define a function that takes a stack and an operation and applies the function to the first two items on the top. Note that the second operand is retrieved in the first instance due to the implementation of stack:

```
private static void applyOperation(
    Stack<Integer> stack,
    BinaryOperator<Integer> operation
) {
  int b = stack.pop(), a = stack.pop();
  stack.push(operation.apply(a, b));
}
```

The next step is to create all the functions that our program must handle. For each operator a function is defined as an object. This has some advantages, such as better isolation for testing. In this case it might not make sense to test functions separately because they are trivial, but there are some other scenarios where testing the logic of these functions in isolation can be very useful:

```
static BinaryOperator<Integer> ADD = (a, b) -> a + b;
static BinaryOperator<Integer> SUBTRACT = (a, b) -> a - b;
static BinaryOperator<Integer> MULTIPLY = (a, b) -> a * b;
static BinaryOperator<Integer> DIVIDE = (a, b) -> a / b;
```

And now, putting all the pieces together. Depending on the operator we find, the proper operation is applied:

```
int compute(String expression) {
  Stack<Integer> stack = new Stack<>();
  for (String elem : expression.trim().split(" ")) {
    if ("+".equals(elem))
      applyOperation(stack, ADD);
    else if ("-".equals(elem))
      applyOperation(stack, SUBTRACT);
    else if ("*".equals(elem))
      applyOperation(stack, MULTIPLY);
    else if ("/".equals(elem))
      applyOperation(stack, DIVIDE);
    else {
      stack.push(parseInt(elem));
    }
  }
  if (stack.size() == 1) return stack.pop();
  else throw new NotReversePolishNotationError();
}
```

The code is readable and very easy to understand. Moreover, this design allows the extending of the functionality by adding support to other different operations with ease.

It can be a good exercise for readers to add a modulus (%) operation to the provided solution.

Another good example where lambdas fit perfectly is Streams API, since most functions have a self-explanatory name like `filter`, `map` or `reduce`, among others. Let's explore this more deeply in the next section.

Streams

One of the top utilities included in Java 8 are Streams. In this chapter we are going to use lambdas in combination with Streams in small code fragments, and create a test to verify them.

To better understand what Streams are, what to do, and what not to do with them, it is highly recommended to read Oracle's Stream pages. A good starting point is https://docs.oracle.com/javase/8/docs/api/java/util/stream/Stream.html.

To cut a long story short, Streams provide a bunch of facilities to deal with long computations that can be executed either in parallel or sequential order. Parallel programming is out of the scope of this book, so the next examples will be sequential only. Furthermore, in order to keep the chapter concise we are going to focus on:

- filter
- map
- flatMap
- reduce

filter

Let's start with the `filter` operation. Filters is a function with a self-explanatory name; it filters in/out elements in the stream depending on whether the value satisfies a condition, as shown in the following example:

```java
@Test
public void filterByNameReturnsCollectionFiltered() {
    List<String> names = Arrays.asList("Alex", "Paul", "Viktor",
            "Kobe", "Tom", "Andrea");
    List<String> filteredNames = Collections.emptyList();

    assertThat(filteredNames)
        .hasSize(2)
        .containsExactlyInAnyOrder("Alex", "Andrea");
}
```

One possibility for computing the list of `filteredNames` is the following:

```java
List<String> filteredNames = names.stream()
        .filter(name -> name.startsWith("A"))
        .collect(Collectors.toList());
```

That one is the easiest. In a few words, `filter` filters the input and returns a value without all the elements filtered out. Using lambdas makes the code elegant and really easy to read.

map

The `map` function transforms all the elements in the stream into another. The resultant object can share the type with the input, but it's also possible to return an object of a different type:

```java
@Test
public void mapToUppercaseTransformsAllElementsToUppercase() {
   List<String> names = Arrays.asList("Alex", "Paul", "Viktor");
   List<String> namesUppercase = Collections.emptyList();

   assertThat(namesUppercase)
       .hasSize(3)
       .containsExactly("ALEX", "PAUL", "VIKTOR");
}
```

The list `namesUppercase` should be computed as follows:

```java
List<String> namesUppercase = names.stream()
  .map(String::toUpperCase)
  .collect(Collectors.toList());
```

Note how the `toUpperCase` method is called. It belongs to the Java class `String` and can be used in that scenario only by referencing the function and the class that function belongs to. In Java, this is called **method reference**.

flatMap

The `flatMap` function is very similar to the `map` function, but it is used when the operation might return more than one value and we want to keep a stream of single elements. In the case of `map`, a stream of collections would be returned instead. Let's see `flatMap` in use:

```java
@Test
public void gettingLettersUsedInNames() {
   List<String> names = Arrays.asList("Alex", "Paul", "Viktor");
   List<String> lettersUsed = Collections.emptyList();

   assertThat(lettersUsed)
      .hasSize(12)
.containsExactly("a","l","e","x","p","u","v","i","k","t","o","r");
}
```

One possible solution could be:

```
List<String> lettersUsed = names.stream()
    .map(String::toLowerCase)
    .flatMap(name -> Stream.of(name.split("")))
    .distinct()
    .collect(Collectors.toList());
```

This time we have used `Stream.of()`, a convenient method for creating Streams. Another really nice feature is the method `distinct()`, which returns a collection of unique elements, comparing them using the method `equals()`.

reduce

In the previous example, the function returns the list of letters used in all the names passed as input. But if we are only interested in the number of different letters, there's an easier way to proceed. reduce basically applies a function to all elements and combines them into one single result. Let's see an example:

```
@Test
public void countingLettersUsedInNames() {
    List<String> names = Arrays.asList("Alex", "Paul", "Viktor");
    long count = 0;

    assertThat(count).isEqualTo(12);
}
```

This solution is very similar to the one we used for the previous exercise:

```
long count = names.stream()
    .map(String::toLowerCase)
    .flatMap(name -> Stream.of(name.split("")))
    .distinct()
    .mapToLong(l -> 1L)
    .reduce(0L, (v1, v2) -> v1 + v2);
```

Even though the preceding code snippet solves the problem, there is a much nicer way to do it:

```
long count = names.stream()
    .map(String::toLowerCase)
    .flatMap(name -> Stream.of(name.split("")))
    .distinct()
    .count();
```

The function `count()` is another built-in tool that Streams includes. It's a particular shortcut for a `reduction` function that counts the number of elements the stream contains.

Summary

Functional programming is an old concept that is gaining popularity, because it's easier to use when trying to increase performance by executing tasks in parallel. In this chapter some concepts from the functional world were presented along with some of the test tools that AssertJ provides.

Testing functions without side effects is very easy because the test scope is reduced. Instead of testing changes that the function might cause on different objects, the only thing that needs to be verified is the outcome of the invocation. No side-effects means that the outcome of the function is the same as long as the parameters are the same. Therefore, the execution is repeatable as many times as needed and leads to the same result on every execution. Additionally, tests are easier to read and comprehend.

To conclude, Java includes a good API for functional programming if you need to use this paradigm within your projects. But there are some languages, some of them purely functional, that offer more powerful features with better syntax and less boilerplate. You should evaluate whether using one of those other languages might make sense if your project or approach can be purely functional.

All of the examples presented in this chapter can be found at `https://bitbucket.org/alexgarcia/tdd-java-funcprog.git`.

Now it is time to take a look at legacy code and how to adapt it and make it more TDD friendly.

8
BDD – Working Together with the Whole Team

"I'm not a great programmer; I'm just a good programmer with great habits."

– Kent Beck

Everything we have done until now is related to techniques that can be applied only by developers, for developers. Customers, business representatives, and other parties that are not capable of reading and understanding code were not involved in the process.

TDD can be much more than what we have done up to now. We can define requirements, discuss them with the client, and get agreement as to what should be developed. We can use those same requirements and make them executable so that they drive and validate our development. We can use ubiquitous language to write acceptance criteria. All this, and more, is accomplished with a flavor of TDD called **behavior-driven development** (**BDD**).

We'll develop a book store application using a BDD approach. We'll define acceptance criteria in English, make the implementation of each feature separately, confirm that it is working correctly by running BDD scenarios and, if required, refactor the code to accomplish the desired level of quality. The process still follows the Red-Green-Refactor that is the essence of TDD. The major difference is the definition level. While, until this moment, we have been mostly working at the units level, this time we'll move a bit higher and apply TDD through functional and integration tests.

Our frameworks of choice will be JBehave and Selenide.

The following topics will be covered in this chapter:

- The different types of specifications
- Behavior-driven development (BDD)
- The book store BDD story
- JBehave

Different specifications

We have already mentioned that one of the benefits of TDD is executable documentation that is always up to date. However, documentation obtained through unit tests is often not enough. When working at such a low-level, we get insights into details; however, it is all too easy to miss the big picture. If, for example, you were to inspect specifications that we created for the Tic-Tac-Toe game, you might easily miss the point of the application. You would understand what each unit does and how it interoperates with other units, but would have a hard time grasping the idea behind it. To be precise, you would understand that unit X does Y and communicates with Z; however, the functional documentation and the idea behind it would be, at best, hard to find.

The same can be said for development. Before we start working on specifications in the form of unit tests, we need to get a bigger picture. Throughout this book, you were presented with requirements that we used for writing specifications that resulted in their implementation. Those requirements were later on discarded; they are nowhere to be seen. We did not put them in to the repository, nor did we use them to validate the result of our work.

Documentation

In many of the organizations that we worked with, the documentation was created for the wrong reasons. The management tends to think that documentation is somehow related to project success—that without a lot of (often short-lived) documentation, the project will fail. Thus, we are asked to spend a lot of time planning, answering questions, and filling in questionnaires that are often designed not to help the project but to provide an illusion that everything is under control. Someone's existence is often justified with documentation (the result of my work is this document). It also serves as a reassurance that everything is going as planned (there is an Excel sheet that states that we are on schedule). However, by far the most common reason for the creation of documentation is a process that simply states that certain documents need to be created. We might question the value of those documents, however, since the process is sacred, they need to be produced.

Not only might that documentation be created for the wrong reasons and not provide enough value, but, as is often the case, it might also do a lot of damage. If we created the documentation, it is natural that we trust it. However, what happens if that documentation is not up to date? The requirements are changing, bugs are getting fixed, new functionalities are being developed, and some are being removed. If given enough time, all traditional documentation becomes obsolete. The sheer task of updating documentation with every change we make to the code is so big and complex that, sooner or later, we must face the fact that static documents do not reflect the reality. If we are putting our trust into something that is not accurate, our development is based on wrong assumptions.

The only accurate documentation is our code. The code is what we develop, what we deploy, and is the only source that truthfully represents our application. However, code is not readable by everyone involved with the project. Besides coders, we might work with managers, testers, business people, end users, and so on.

In search of a better way to define what would constitute better documentation, let us explore a bit further into who the potential documentation consumers are. For the sake of simplicity, we'll divide them into coders (those capable of reading and understanding code) and non-coders (everyone else).

Documentation for coders

Developers work with code and, since we have established that code is the most accurate documentation, there is no reason to not utilize it. If you want to understand what some method does, take a look at the code of that method. In doubt about what some class does? Take a look at that class. Having trouble understanding a piece of code? We have a problem! However, the problem is not that the documentation is missing, but that the code itself is not written well.

Looking at the code to understand the code is still often not enough. Even though you might understand what the code does, the purpose of that code might not be so obvious. Why was it written in the first place?

That's where specifications come in. Not only are we using them to continuously validate the code, but they also act as executable documentation. They are always up to date because if they aren't, their execution will fail. At the same time, while code itself should be written in a way that is easy to read and understand, specifications provide a much easier and faster way to understand the reasons, logic, and motivations that lead us to write some piece of implementation code.

Using code as documentation does not exclude other types. Quite the contrary, the key is not to avoid using static documentation, but to avoid duplication. When code provides the necessary details, use it before anything else. In most cases, this leaves us with higher-level documentation, such as an overview, the general purpose of the system, the technologies used, the environment set-up, the installation, building, and packaging, and other types of data that tend to serve more like guidelines and quick-start information than detailed information. For those cases, a simple `README` in markdown format (`http://whatismarkdown.com/`) tends to be the best.

For all code-based documentation, TDD is the best enabler. Until now, we worked only with units (methods). We are yet to see how to apply TDD on a higher-level, such as, for example, functional specifications. However, before we get there, let's speak about other roles in the team.

Documentation for non-coders

Traditional testers tend to form groups completely separated from developers. This separation leads to an increased number of testers who are not familiar with code and assume that their job is to be quality checkers. They are validators at the end of the process and act as a kind of border police who decide what can be deployed and what should be returned back. There is, on the other hand, an increasing number of organizations that are employing testers as integral members of the team, with the job of ensuring that quality is built in. This latter group requires testers to be proficient with code. For them, using code as documentation is quite natural. However, what should we do with the first group? What should we do with testers who do not understand the code? Also, it is not only (some) testers that fall into this group. Managers, end-users, business representatives, and so on are also included. The world is full of people that cannot read and understand code.

We should look for a way to retain the advantages that the executable documentation provides, but write it in a way that can be understood by everyone. Moreover, in TDD fashion, we should allow everyone to participate in the creation of executable documentation from the very start. We should allow them to define requirements that we'll use to develop applications and, at the same time, to validate the result of that development. We need something that will define what we'll do on a higher-level, since low-level is already covered with unit tests. To summarize, we need documentation that can serve as requirements, that can be executed, that can validate our work, and that can be written and understood by everyone.

Say hello to BDD.

Behavior-driven development

Behavior-driven development (BDD) is an agile process designed to keep the focus on stakeholder value throughout the whole project; it is a form of TDD. Specifications are defined in advance, the implementation is done according to those specifications, and they are run periodically to validate the outcome. Besides those similarities, there are a few differences as well. Unlike TDD, which is based on unit tests, BDD encourages us to write multiple specifications (called scenarios) before starting the implementation (coding). Even though there is no specific rule, BDD tends to levitate towards higher-level functional requirements. While it can be employed at a unit level as well, the real benefits are obtained when taking a higher approach that can be written and understood by everyone. The audience is another difference—BDD tries to empower everyone (coders, testers, managers, end users, business representatives, and so on).

While TDD, which is based on unit level, can be described as inside-out (we begin with units and build up towards functionalities), BDD is often understood as outside-in (we start with features and go inside towards units). BDD acts as an **acceptance criteria** that acts as an indicator of readiness. It tells us when something is finished and ready for production.

We start by defining functionalities (or behaviors), work on them by employing TDD with unit tests, and, once a complete behavior has finished, validate with BDD. One BDD scenario can take hours or even days to finish. During all that time, we can employ TDD and unit testing. Once we're done, we run BDD scenarios to do the final validation. TDD is for coders and has a very fast cycle, while BDD is for everyone and has a much slower turnout time. For each BDD scenario, we have many TDD unit tests.

At this point, you might have gotten confused about what BDD really is, so let us go back a bit. We'll start with the explanation of its format.

Narrative

A BDD story consists of one narrative followed by at least one scenario. A narrative is only informative, and its main purpose is to provide just enough information that can serve as a beginning of communication between everyone involved (testers, business representatives, developers, analysts, and so on). It is a short and simple description of a feature, told from the perspective of a person who requires it.

The goal of a narrative is to answer three basic questions:

1. **In order to**: What is the benefit or value of the feature that should be built?
2. **As a**: Who needs the feature that was requested?
3. **I want to**: What is the feature or goal that should be developed?

Once we have those questions answered, we can start defining what we think would be the best solution. This thinking process results in scenarios that provide a lower-level of detail.

Until now, we were working at a very low-level using unit tests as a driving force. We were specifying what should be built from the coder's perspective. We assumed that high-level requirements were defined earlier and that our job was to do the code specific to one of them. Now, let us take a few steps back and start from the beginning.

Let us act, let's say, as a customer or a business representative. Someone got this great idea and we are discussing it with the rest of the team. In short, we want to build an online book store. It is only an idea and we're not even certain of how it will develop, so we want to work on a **Minimum Viable Product** (**MVP**). One of the roles that we want to explore is the one of a store administrator. This person should be able to add new books and update or remove the existing ones. All those actions should be doable, because we want this person to be able to manage our book store collection in an efficient way. The narrative that we came up with for this role is the following:

```
In order to manage the book store collection efficiently
As a store administrator
I want to be able to add, update, and remove books
```

Now that we know what the benefit is (managing books), who needs it (administrator), and finally what the feature that should be developed is (insert, update, and delete operations). Keep in mind that this was not a detailed description of what should be done. The narrative's purpose is to initiate a discussion that will result in one or more scenarios.

Unlike TDD unit tests, narratives, and indeed the rest of the BDD story, can be written by anyone. They do not require coding skills, nor do they have to go into too many details. Depending on the organization, all narratives can be written by the same person (a business representative, product owner, customer, and so on) or it might be a collaborative effort by the whole team.

Now that we have a clearer idea regarding narratives, let us take a look at scenarios.

Scenarios

A narrative acts as a communication enabler, and scenarios are the result of that communication. They should describe interactions that the role (specified in the *Narrative* section) has with the system. Unlike unit tests, which were written as code by developers for developers, BDD scenarios should be defined in plain language and with minimum technical details so that all those involved with the project (developers, testers, designers, managers, customers, and so on) can have a common understanding about behaviors (or features) that will be added to the system.

Scenarios act as the acceptance criteria of the narrative. Once all scenarios related to the narrative are run successfully, the job can be considered done. Each scenario is very similar to a unit test, with the main difference being the scope (one method against a whole feature) and the time it takes to implement it (a few seconds or minutes against a few hours or even days). Similarly to unit tests, scenarios drive the development; they are defined first.

Each scenario consists of a description and one or more steps that start with the words `Given`, `When`, or `Then`. The description is short and only informative. It helps us to understand, at a glance, what the scenario does. Steps, on the other hand, are a sequence of the preconditions, events, and expected outcomes of the scenario. They help us define the behavior unambiguously and it's easy to translate them to automated tests.

Throughout this chapter, we'll focus more on the technical aspects of BDD and the ways they fit into the developer's mindset. For broader usage of BDD and much deeper discussion, consult the book, *Specification by Example: How Successful Teams Deliver the Right Software* by Gojko Adzic.

The `Given` step defines a context or preconditions that need to be fulfilled for the rest of the scenario to be successful. Going back to the book's administration narrative, one such precondition might be the following:

```
Given user is on the books screen
```

This is a very simple but pretty necessary precondition. Our website might have many pages, and we need to make sure that the user is on the correct screen before we perform any action.

The `When` step defines an action or some kind of an event. In our narrative, we defined that the `administrator` should be able to `add`, `update`, and `remove` books. Let's see what should be an action related to, for example, the `delete` operation:

```
When user selects a book
When user clicks the deleteBook button
```

In this example, we multiplied actions defined with the When steps. First, we should select a book and then we should click on the `deleteBook` button. In this case, we used an ID (`deleteBook`) instead of text (Delete the book) to define the button that should be clicked. In most cases, IDs are preferable because they provide multiple benefits. They are unique (only one ID can exist on a given screen), they provide clear instructions for developers (create an element with an ID `deleteBook`), and they are not affected by other changes on the same screen. The text of an element can easily change; if this happens, all scenarios that used it would fail as well. In the case of websites, an alternative could be XPath. However, avoid this whenever possible. It tends to fail with the smallest change to the HTML structure.

Similarly to unit tests, scenarios should be reliable and fail when a feature is not yet developed or when there is a real problem. Otherwise, it is a natural reaction to start ignoring specifications when they produce false negatives.

Finally, we should always end the scenario with some kind of verification. We should specify the desired outcome of actions that were performed. Following the same scenario, our Then step could be the following:

```
Then book is removed
```

This outcome strikes a balance between providing just enough data and not going into design details. We could have, for example, mentioned the database or, even more specifically, MongoDB. However, in many cases, that information is not important from the behavioral point of view. We should simply confirm that the book is removed from the catalog, no matter where it is stored.

Now that we are familiar with the BDD story format, let us write the book store BDD story.

The book store BDD story

Before we start, clone the code that is available at https://bitbucket.org/vfarcic/tdd-java-ch08-books-store. It is an empty project that we'll use throughout this chapter. As with previous chapters, it contains branches for each section, in case you miss something.

We'll write one BDD story that will be in a pure text format, in plain English and without any code. That way, all stakeholders can participate and get involved independently of their coding proficiency. Later on, we'll see how to automate the story we're writing.

Let us start by creating a new file called `administration.story` inside the `stories` directory:

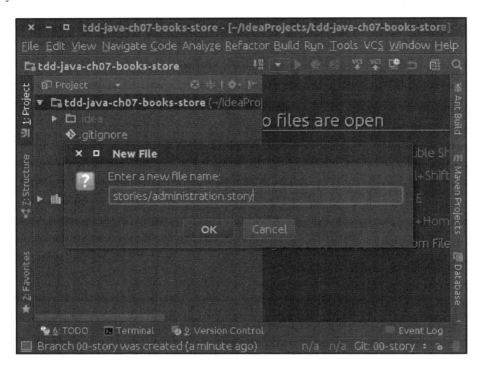

We already have the narrative that we wrote earlier, so we'll build on top of that:

```
Narrative:
In order to manage the book store collection efficiently
As a store administrator
I want to be able to add, update, and remove books
```

We'll be using JBehave format for writing stories. More details regarding JBehave are coming soon. Until then, visit `http://jbehave.org/` for more info.

A narrative always starts with the `Narrative` line and is followed with the `In order to`, `As a`, and `I want to` lines. We already discussed the meaning of each of them.

Now that we know the answers to why, who, and what, it is time to sit with the rest of the team and discuss possible scenarios. We're still not talking about steps (`Given`, `When`, and `Then`), but simply what would be the outlines or short descriptions of the potential scenarios. The list could be the following:

```
Scenario: Book details form should have all fields
Scenario: User should be able to create a new book
Scenario: User should be able to display book details
Scenario: User should be able to update book details
Scenario: User should be able to delete a book
```

We're following the JBehave syntax by using `Scenario` followed by a short description. There is no reason to go into detail at this stage; the purpose of this stage is to serve as a quick brainstorming session. In this case, we came up with those five scenarios. The first one should define fields of the form that we'll use to administer books. The rest of the scenarios are trying to define different administrative tasks. There's nothing truly creative about them. We're supposed to develop an MVP of a very simple application. If it proves to be successful, we can expand and truly employ our creativity. With the current objective, the application will be simple and straightforward.

Now that we know what our scenarios are, in general terms, it is time to properly define each of them. Let us start working on the first one:

```
Scenario: Book details form should have all fields

Given user is on the books screen
Then field bookId exists
Then field bookTitle exists
Then field bookAuthor exists
Then field bookDescription exists
```

This scenario does not contain any actions; there are no `When` steps. It can be considered a sanity check. It tells developers what fields should be present in the book form. Through those fields, we can decide what data schema we'll use. IDs are descriptive enough that we know what each field is about (one ID and three text fields). Keep in mind that this scenario (and those that will follow) are pure texts without any code. The main advantage is that anyone can write them, and we'll try to keep it that way.

Let's see what the second scenario should look like:

```
Scenario: User should be able to create a new book

Given user is on the books screen
When user clicks the button newBook
When user sets values to the book form
When user clicks the button saveBook
Then book is stored
```

This scenario is a bit better formed than the previous one. There is a clear prerequisite (`user` should be on a certain screen); there are several actions (click on the `newBook` button, fill in the form, and click on the `saveBook` button); finally, there is the verification of the outcome (book is stored).

The rest of the scenarios are as follows (since they all work in a similar way, we feel that there is no reason to explain each of them separately):

```
Scenario: User should be able to display book details

Given user is on the books screen
When user selects a book
Then book form contains all data

Scenario: User should be able to update book details

Given user is on the books screen
When user selects a book
When user sets values to the book form
Then book is stored

Scenario: User should be able to delete a book

Given user is on the books screen
When user selects a book
When user clicks the deleteBook button
Then book is removed
```

The only thing that might be worth noticing is that we are using the same steps when appropriate (for example, `When user selects a book`). Since we'll soon try to automate all those scenarios, having the same text for the same step will save us some time by duplicating the code. It is important to strike a balance between the freedom to express scenarios in the best possible way and the ease of automation. There are a few more things that we can modify in our existing scenarios, however, before we refactor them, let us introduce you to JBehave.

The source code can be found in the `00-story` branch of the `tdd-java-ch08-books-store` Git repository,
at https://bitbucket.org/vfarcic/tdd-java-ch08-books-store/branch/00-story.

JBehave

There are two major components required for JBehave to run BDD stories—runners and steps. A runner is a class that will parse the story, run all scenarios, and generate a report. Steps are code methods that match steps written in scenarios. The project already contains all Gradle dependencies, so we can dive right into creating the JBehave runner.

JBehave runner

JBehave is no exception to the rule that every type of test needs a runner. In the previous chapters, we used JUnit and TestNG runners. While neither of those needed any special configuration, JBehave is a bit more demanding and forces us to create a class that will hold all the configuration required for running stories.

The following is the `Runner` code that we'll use throughout this chapter:

```java
public class Runner extends JUnitStories {

  @Override
  public Configuration configuration() {
    return new MostUsefulConfiguration()
            .useStoryReporterBuilder(getReporter())
            .useStoryLoader(new LoadFromURL());
  }

  @Override
  protected List<String> storyPaths() {
    String path = "stories/**/*.story";
    return new StoryFinder().findPaths(
            CodeLocations.codeLocationFromPath("").getFile(),
            Collections.singletonList(path),
            new ArrayList<String>(),
            "file:");
  }

  @Override
  public InjectableStepsFactory stepsFactory() {
    return new InstanceStepsFactory(configuration(), new Steps());
```

```
            }

    private StoryReporterBuilder getReporter() {
        return new StoryReporterBuilder()
            .withPathResolver(new
FilePrintStreamFactory.ResolveToSimpleName())
            .withDefaultFormats()
            .withFormats(Format.CONSOLE, Format.HTML);
    }
}
```

It is very uneventful code, so we'll comment only on a few important parts. The overridden method `storyPaths` has the location to our story files set to the `stories/**/*.story` path. This is a standard Apache Ant (http://ant.apache.org/) syntax that, when translated to plain language, means that any file ending with `.story` inside the `stories` directory or any subdirectory (`**`) will be included. Another important overridden method is `stepsFactory`, which is used to set classes containing the steps definition (we'll work with them very soon). In this case, we set it to the instance of a single class called `Steps` (the repository already contains an empty class that we'll use later on).

The source code can be found in the `01-runner` branch of the `tdd-java-ch08-books-store` Git repository, at https://bitbucket.org/vfarcic/tdd-java-ch08-books-store/branch/01-runner.

Now that we have our runner done, it is time to fire it up and see what the result is.

Pending steps

We can run our scenarios with the following Gradle command:

```
$ gradle clean test
```

Gradle only runs tasks that changed from the last execution. Since our source code will not always change (we often modify only stories in text format), the `clean` task is required to be run before the `test` so that the cache is removed.

JBehave creates a nice report for us and puts it into the `target/jbehave/view` directory. Open the `reports.html` file in your favorite browser.

The initial page of the report displays a list of our stories (in our case, only **Administration**) and two predefined ones called **BeforeStories** and **AfterStories**. Their purpose is similar to the @BeforeClass and @AfterClass JUnit annotated methods. They are run before and after stories, and can be useful for setting up and tearing down data, servers, and so on.

This initial reports page shows that we have five scenarios and all of them are in the **Pending** status. This is JBehave's way of telling us that they were neither successful nor failed, but that there is code missing behind the steps we used:

Story Reports

Stories		Scenarios				
Name	Excluded	Total	Successful	Pending	Failed	Excluded
Administration	0	5	5	5	0	0
AfterStories	0	0	0	0	0	0
BeforeStories	0	0	0	0	0	0
3	0	5	5	5	0	0

The last column in each row contains a link that allows us to see details of each story:

Narrative:

In order to manage the book store collection
As a store administrator
I want to be able to perform insert, update and delete operations

Scenario: Book details form should have all fields

Given user is on the books screen   (PENDING)
Then field bookId exists   (PENDING)
Then field bookTitle exists   (PENDING)
Then field bookAuthor exists   (PENDING)
Then field bookDescription exists   (PENDING)

```
@Given("user is on the books screen")
@Pending
public void givenUserIsOnTheBooksScreen() {
  // PENDING
}
```

In our case, all the steps are marked as pending. JBehave even puts a suggestion of a method that we need to create for each pending step.

To recapitulate, at this point, we wrote one story with five scenarios. Each of those scenarios is equivalent to a specification that will be used both as a definition that should be developed and to verify that the development was done correctly. Each of those scenarios consists of several steps that define preconditions (`Given`), actions (`When`), and the expected outcome (`Then`).

Now it is time, to write the code behind our steps. However, before we start coding, let us get introduced to Selenium and Selenide.

Selenium and Selenide

Selenium is a set of drivers that can be used to automate browsers. We can use them to manipulate browsers and page elements by, for example, clicking on a button or a link, filling up a form field, opening a specific URL, and so on. There are drivers for almost any browser—Android, Chrome, FireFox, Internet Explorer, Safari, and many more. Our favorite is PhantomJS, which is a headless browser that works without any UI. Running stories with it is faster than with traditional browsers, and we often use it to get fast feedback on the readiness of web applications. If it works as expected, we can proceed and try it out in all the different browsers and versions that our application is supposed to support.

More information about Selenium can be found at http://www.seleniumhq.org/, with the list of supported drivers at http://www.seleniumhq.org/projects/webdriver/.

While Selenium is great for automating browsers, it has its downsides, one of them being that it is operating at a very low-level. Clicking on a button, for example, is easy and can be accomplished with a single line of code:

```
selenium.click("myLink")
```

If the element with the ID `myLink` does not exist, Selenium will throw an exception and the test will fail. While we want our tests to fail when the expected element does not exist, in many cases it is not so simple. For example, our page might load dynamically with that element appearing only after an asynchronous request to the server got a response. For this reason, we might not only want to click on that element, but also wait until it is available, and fail only if a timeout is reached. While this can be done with Selenium, it is tedious and error prone. Besides, why would we do the work that is already done by others? Say hello to Selenide.

Selenide (http://selenide.org/) is a wrapper around Selenium `WebDrivers` with a more concise API, support for Ajax, selectors that use JQuery style, and so on. We'll use Selenide for all our Web steps, and you'll get more familiar with it soon.

Now, let us write some code.

JBehave steps

Before we start writing steps, install the PhantomJS browser. The instructions for your operating system can be found at http://phantomjs.org/download.html.

With PhantomJS installed, it is time to specify a few Gradle dependencies:

```
dependencies {
    testCompile 'junit:junit:4.+'
    testCompile 'org.jbehave:jbehave-core:3.+'
    testCompile 'com.codeborne:selenide:2.+'
    testCompile 'com.codeborne:phantomjsdriver:1.+'
}
```

You are already familiar with JUnit and JBehave Core, which was set up earlier. Two new additions are Selenide and PhantomJS. Refresh Gradle dependencies so that they are included in your IDEA project.

Now, it is time to add the PhantomJS `WebDriver` to our `Steps` class:

```
public class Steps {

  private WebDriver webDriver;

  @BeforeStory
  public void beforeStory() {
    if (webDriver == null) {
      webDriver = new PhantomJSDriver();
      webDriverRunner.setWebDriver(webDriver);
      webDriver.manage().window().setSize(new Dimension(1024, 768));
    }
  }
}
```

We're utilizing the `@BeforeStory` annotation to define the method that we're using to do some basic setup. If a driver is not already specified, we're setting it up to be `PhantomJSDriver`. Since this application will look different on smaller devices (phones, tablets, and so on), it is important that we specify clearly what the size of the screen is. In this case, we're setting it to be a reasonable desktop/laptop monitor screen resolution of 1024 x 768.

With setup out of the way, let us code our first pending step. We can simply copy and paste the first method JBehave suggested for us in the report:

```
@Given("user is on the books screen")
public void givenUserIsOnTheBooksScreen() {
// PENDING
}
```

Imagine that our application will have a link that will open the book's screen.
To do that, we'll need to perform two steps:

1. Open the website home page.
2. Click on the books link in the menu.

We'll specify that this link will have the ID `books`. IDs are very important as they allow us to easily locate an element on the page.

The steps we described earlier can be translated to the following code:

```
private String url = "http://localhost:9001";

@Given("user is on the books screen")
public void givenUserIsOnTheBooksScreen() {
  open(url);
  $("#books").click();
}
```

We're assuming that our application will run on the `9001` port on the `localhost`. Therefore, we are first opening the home page URL and then clicking on the element with the ID `books`. Selenide/JQuery syntax for specifying an ID is `#`.

If we run our runner again, we'd see that the first step failed and the rest is still in the `Pending` state. Now, we are in the red state of the Red-Green-Refactor cycle.

Let us continue working on the rest of the steps used in the first scenario. The second one can be the following:

```
@Then("field bookId exists")
public void thenFieldBookIdExists() {
  $("#books").shouldBe(visible);
}
```

The third one is almost the same, so we can refactor the previous method and convert an element ID into a variable:

```
@Then("field $elementId exists")
public void thenFieldExists(String elementId) {
  $("#" + elementId).shouldBe(visible);
}
```

With this change, all the steps in the first scenario are done. If we run our tests again, the result is the following:

```
Scenario: Book details form should have all fields

Given user is on the books screen   (FAILED)
Element not found {#books} Expected: visible Screenshot:
file:/home/vfarcic/IdeaProjects/tdd-java-ch07-books-
store/build/reports/tests/1430688921325.15.png Timeout: 4 s. Caused by:
NoSuchElementException: Error Message => 'Unable to find element with css selector
'#books'
Then field bookId exists   (NOT PERFORMED)
Then field bookTitle exists   (NOT PERFORMED)
Then field bookAuthor exists   (NOT PERFORMED)
Then field bookDescription exists   (NOT PERFORMED)
```

The first step failed since we did not even start working on the implementation of our book store application. Selenide has a nice feature that creates a screenshot of the browser every time there is a failure. We can see the path in the report. The rest of the steps are in the not performed state since the execution of the scenario stopped on failure.

What should be done next depends on the structure of the team. If the same person is working both on functional tests and the implementation, he could start working on the implementation and write just enough code to make this scenario pass. In many other situations, separate people are working on the functional specification and the implementation code. In that case, one could continue working on the missing steps for the rest of the scenarios, while the other would start working on the implementation. Since all scenarios are already written in text form, a coder already knows what should be done and the two can work in parallel. We'll take the former route and write the code for the rest of the pending steps.

Let's go through the next scenario:

```
Scenario: User should be able to create a new book

Given user is on the books screen   (FAILED)
Element not found {#books} Expected: visible Screenshot:
file:/home/vfarcic/IdeaProjects/tdd-java-ch07-books-
store/build/reports/tests/1430690653894.32.png Timeout: 4 s. Caused by:
NoSuchElementException: Error Message => 'Unable to find element with css selector
'#books''
When user clicks the button newBook   (NOT PERFORMED)
When user sets values to the book form   (PENDING)
When user clicks the button saveBook   (NOT PERFORMED)
Then book is stored   (PENDING)
```

We already have half of the steps done from the previous scenario, so there are only two pending. After we click on the `newBook` button, we should set some values to the form, click on the `saveBook` button, and verify that the book was stored correctly. We can do the last part by checking whether it appeared in the list of available books.

The missing steps can be the following:

```
@When("user sets values to the book form")
public void whenUserSetsValuesToTheBookForm() {
  $("#bookId").setValue("123");
  $("#bookTitle").setValue("BDD Assistant");
  $("#bookAuthor").setValue("Viktor Farcic");
  $("#bookDescription")
      .setValue("Open source BDD stories editor and runner");
}

@Then("book is stored")
public void thenBookIsStored() {
  $("#book123").shouldBe(present);
}
```

The second step assumes that each of the available books will have an ID in the format `book[ID]`.

Let us take a look at the next scenario:

> **Scenario: User should be able to display book details**
>
> Given user is on the books screen   (FAILED)
> Element not found {#books} Expected: visible Screenshot:
> file:/home/vfarcic/IdeaProjects/tdd-java-ch07-books-
> store/build/reports/tests/1430691141869.46.png Timeout: 4 s. Caused by:
> NoSuchElementException: Error Message => 'Unable to find element with css selector
> '#books''
> When user selects a book   (PENDING)
> Then book form contains all data   (PENDING)

Like in the previous scenario, there are two steps pending development. We need to have a way to select a book and to verify that data in the form is correctly populated:

```
@When("user selects a book")
public void whenUserSelectsABook() {
  $("#book1").click();
}

@Then("book form contains all data")
public void thenBookFormContainsAllData() {
  $("#bookId").shouldHave(value("1"));
  $("#bookTitle").shouldHave(value("TDD for Java Developers"));
  $("#bookAuthor").shouldHave(value("Viktor Farcic"));
  $("#bookDescription").shouldHave(value("Cool book!"));
}
```

These two methods are interesting because they not only specify the expected behavior (when a specific book link is clicked, then a form with its data is displayed), but also expect certain data to be available for testing. When this scenario is run, a book with the ID 1, title `TDD for Java Developers`, author `Viktor Farcic`, and description `Cool book!` should already exist. We can choose to add that data to the database or use a mock server that will serve the predefined values. No matter what the choice of how to set test data is, we can finish with this scenario and jump into the next one:

> **Scenario: User should be able to update book details**
>
> Given user is on the books screen   (FAILED)
> Element not found {#books} Expected: visible Screenshot:
> file:/home/vfarcic/IdeaProjects/tdd-java-ch07-books-
> store/build/reports/tests/1430692088078.61.png Timeout: 4 s. Caused by:
> NoSuchElementException: Error Message => 'Unable to find element with css selector
> '#books''
> When user selects a book   (NOT PERFORMED)
> When user sets new values to the book form   (PENDING)
> Then book is updated   (PENDING)

The implementation of the pending steps could be the following:

```
@When("user sets new values to the book form")
public void whenUserSetsNewValuesToTheBookForm() {
  $("#bookTitle").setValue("TDD for Java Developers revised");
  $("#bookAuthor").setValue("Viktor Farcic and Alex Garcia");
  $("#bookDescription").setValue("Even better book!");
  $("#saveBook").click();
}

@Then("book is updated")
public void thenBookIsUpdated() {
  $("#book1").shouldHave(text("TDD for Java Developers revised"));
  $("#book1").click();
  $("#bookTitle").shouldHave(value("TDD for Java Developers revised"));
  $("#bookAuthor").shouldHave(value("Viktor Farcic and Alex Garcia"));
  $("#bookDescription").shouldHave(value("Even better book!"));
}
```

Finally, there is only one scenario left:

> **Scenario: User should be able to delete a book**
>
> Given user is on the books screen   (FAILED)
> Element not found {#books} Expected: visible Screenshot: file:/home/vfarcic/IdeaProjects/tdd-java-ch07-books-store/build/reports/tests/1430692818420.77.png Timeout: 4 s. Caused by: NoSuchElementException: Error Message => 'Unable to find element with css selector '#books''
> When user selects a book   (NOT PERFORMED)
> When user clicks the button deleteBook   (NOT PERFORMED)
> Then book is removed   (PENDING)

We can verify that a book is removed by verifying that it is not in the list of available books:

```
@Then("book is removed")
public void thenBookIsRemoved() {
  $("#book1").shouldNotBe(visible);
}
```

We're finished with the steps code. Now, the person who is developing the application not only has requirements but also has a way to validate each behavior (scenario). He can move through the Red-Green-Refactor cycle one scenario at a time.

The source code can be found in the `02-steps` branch of the `tdd-java-ch08-books-store` Git repository: https://bitbucket.org/vfarcic/tdd-java-ch08-books-store/branch/02-steps.

Final validation

Let us imagine that a different person worked on the code that should fulfill the requirements set by our scenarios. This person picked one scenario at the time, developed the code, ran that scenario, and confirmed that his implementation was correct. Once the implementation of all scenarios has been done, it is time to run the whole story and do the final validation.

For that matter, the application has been packed as a `Docker` file and we have prepared a virtual machine with Vagrant for executing the application.

Check out the branch at https://bitbucket.org/vfarcic/tdd-java-ch08-books-store/branch/03-validation and run Vagrant:

```
$ vagrant up
```

The output should be similar to the following:

```
==> default: Importing base box 'ubuntu/trusty64'...
==> default: Matching MAC address for NAT networking...
==> default: Checking if box 'ubuntu/trusty64' is up to date...
...
==> default: Running provisioner: docker...
    default: Installing Docker (latest) onto machine...
    default: Configuring Docker to autostart containers...
==> default: Starting Docker containers...
==> default: -- Container: books-fe
```

Once Vagrant is finished, we can see the application by opening http://localhost:9001 in our browser of choice:

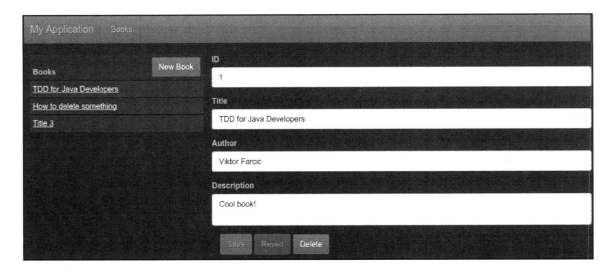

Now, let us run our scenarios again:

```
$ gradle clean test
```

This time there were no failures and all scenarios ran successfully:

> **Narrative:**
>
> **In order to** manage the book store collection
> **As a** store administrator
> **I want to** be able to perform insert, update and delete operations
>
> **Scenario: Book details form should have all fields**
>
> Given user is on the books screen
> Then field **bookId** exists
> Then field **bookTitle** exists
> Then field **bookAuthor** exists
> Then field **bookDescription** exists
>
> **Scenario: User should be able to create a new book**
>
> Given user is on the books screen
> When user clicks the button **newBook**
> When user sets values to the book form
> When user clicks the button **saveBook**
> Then book is stored

Once all scenarios are passing, we meet the acceptance criteria and the application can be delivered to production.

Summary

BDD, in its essence, is a flavor of TDD. It follows the same basic principle of writing tests (scenarios) before the implementation code. It drives the development and helps to us better understand what should be done.

One of the major differences is the life cycle duration. While with TDD, which is based on unit tests, we're moving from red to green very fast (in minutes if not seconds) BDD often takes a higher-level approach that might require hours or days until we get from the red to the green state. Another important difference is the audience. While unit tests-based TDD is done by developers for developers, BDD intends to involve everyone through its ubiquitous language.

While a whole book can be written on this subject, our intention was to give you just enough information so that you can investigate BDD further.

Now it is time to take a look at legacy code and how to adapt it and make it more TDD friendly.

9
Refactoring Legacy Code – Making It Young Again

TDD may not adjust to legacy code straight away. You may have to fiddle a bit with the steps to make it work. Understand that your TDD may change in this case, because somehow, you are no longer performing the TDD you were used to. This chapter will introduce you to the world of legacy code, taking as much as we can from TDD.

We'll start afresh, with a legacy application that is currently in production. We'll alter it in small ways without introducing defects or regressions, and we'll even have time to have an early lunch!

The following topics are covered in this chapter:

- Legacy code
- Dealing with legacy code
- REST communication
- Dependency injection
- Tests at different levels: end-to-end, integration, and unit

Legacy code

Let's start with the definition of legacy code. While there are many authors with different definitions, such as lack of trust in your application or your tests, code that is no longer supported, and so on. We like the one created by Michael Feathers the most:

> "Legacy code is code without tests. The reason for this definition is that it is objective: either there are or there aren't tests."
>
> – Michael Feathers

How do we detect legacy code? Although legacy code usually equates to bad code, Michael Feathers exposes some smells in his book, *Working Effectively with Legacy Code*, by Dorling Kindersley (India) Pvt. Ltd. (1993).

Code smell.
Smells are certain structures in the code that indicate violation of fundamental design principles and negatively impact design quality.

Code smells are usually not bugs—they are not technically incorrect and do not currently prevent the program from functioning. Instead, they indicate weaknesses in design that may be slowing down development or increasing the risk of bugs or failures in the future.

Source: http://en.wikipedia.org/wiki/Code_smell.

One of the common smells for legacy code is *I can't test this code*. It is accessing outside resources, introducing other side effects, using a new operator, and so on. In general, good design is easy to test. Let's see some legacy code.

Legacy code example

Software concepts are often easiest to explain through code, and this one is no exception. We have seen and worked with the Tic-Tac-Toe application (see `Chapter 3`, *Red-Green-Refactor – From Failure Through Success until Perfection*). The following code performs position validation:

```
public class TicTacToe {

  public void validatePosition(int x, int y) {
    if (x < 1 || x > 3) {
      throw new RuntimeException("X is outside board");
    }
    if (y < 1 || y > 3) {
      throw new RuntimeException("Y is outside board");
    }
  }
}
```

The specification that corresponds with this code is as follows:

```
public class TicTacToeSpec {
  @Rule
  public ExpectedException exception =
      ExpectedException.none();
  private TicTacToe ticTacToe;

  @Before
  public final void before() {
    ticTacToe = new TicTacToe();
  }

  @Test
  public void whenXOutsideBoardThenRuntimeException() {
    exception.expect(RuntimeException.class);
    ticTacToe.validatePosition(5, 2);
  }

  @Test
  public void whenYOutsideBoardThenRuntimeException() {
    exception.expect(RuntimeException.class);
    ticTacToe.validatePosition(2, 5);
  }
}
```

The JaCoCo report indicates that everything is covered (except the last line, the method's closing bracket):

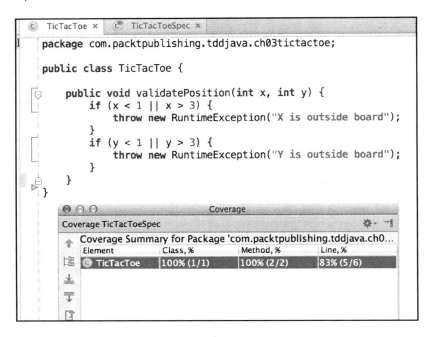

As we believe we have good coverage, we can perform an automatic and safe refactor (fragment):

```
public class TicTacToe {

  public void validatePosition(int x, int y) {
    if (isOutsideTheBoard(x)) {
      throw new RuntimeException("X is outside board");
    }
    if (isOutsideTheBoard(y)) {
      throw new RuntimeException("Y is outside board");
    }
  }

  private boolean isOutsideTheBoard(final int position) {
    return position < 1 || position > 3;
  }
}
```

This code should be ready, as the tests are successful and it has very good test coverage.

Maybe you have already realized as much, but there is a catch. The message in the RuntimeException block is not checked for correctness; even the code coverage shows it as covering all the branches in that line.

What is coverage all about?
Coverage is a measure used to describe the degree to which the source code of a program is tested by a particular test suite. Source: http://en.wikipedia.org/wiki/Code_coverage.

Let's imagine a single end-to-end test that covers an easy part of the code. This test will get you a high coverage percentage, but not much security, as there are many other parts that are still not covered.

We have already introduced legacy code in our codebase—the exception messages. There might be nothing wrong with this as long as this is not an expected behavior—no one should depend on exception messages, not programmers to debug their programs, or logs, or even users. Those parts of the program that are not covered by tests are likely to suffer regressions in the near future. This might be fine if you accept the risk. Maybe the exception type and the line number are enough.

We have decided to remove the exception message, as it is not tested:

```
public class TicTacToe {

  public void validatePosition(int x, int y) {
    if (isOutsideTheBoard(x)) {
      throw new RuntimeException("");
    }
    if (isOutsideTheBoard(y)) {
      throw new RuntimeException("");
    }
  }

  private boolean isOutsideTheBoard(final int position) {
    return position < 1 || position > 3;
  }
}
```

Other ways to recognize legacy code

You may be familiar with some of the following common signs of legacy applications:

- A patch on top of a patch, just like a living Frankenstein application
- Known bugs
- Changes are expensive
- Fragile
- Difficult to understand
- Old, outdated, static or, often, non-existent documentation
- Shotgun surgery
- Broken windows

Regarding the team that maintains it, these are some of the effects it produces on the members of the team:

- Resignation: The people in charge of the software see a huge task in front of them
- No one cares anymore: If you already have broken windows in your system, it is easier to introduce new ones

As legacy code is usually more difficult than other kinds of software, you would want your best people to work on it. However, we are often in a hurry imposed by deadlines, with the idea of programming the required functionalities as fast as possible and ignoring the quality of the solution.

Therefore, to avoid wasting our talented developers in such a bad way, we expect a non-legacy application to fulfill just the opposite. It should be:

- Easy to change
- Generalizable, configurable, and expansible
- Easy to deploy
- Robust
- No known defects or limitations
- Easy to teach to others/learn from others
- Extensive suite of tests
- Self-validating
- Able to use keyhole surgery

As we have outlined some of the properties of legacy and non-legacy code, it should be easy to replace some qualities with others. Right? Stop shotgun surgery and use keyhole surgery, a few more details and you are done. Isn't that right?

It is not as easy as it sounds. Luckily, there are some tricks and rules that, when applied, improve our code and the application comes closer to a non-legacy one.

A lack of dependency injection

This is one of the smells often detected in a legacy codebase. As there is no need to test the classes in isolation, the collaborators are instantiated where they are needed, putting the responsibility for creating collaborators and using them in the same class.

Here's an example, using the `new` operator:

```java
public class BirthdayGreetingService {

  private final MessageSender messageSender;

  public BirthdayGreetingService() {
    messageSender = new EmailMessageSender();
  }

  public void greet(final Employee employee) {
    messageSender.send(employee.getAddress(),
      "Greetings on your birthday");
  }
}
```

In the current state, the `BirthdayGreeting` service is not unit-testable. It has the dependency to `EmailMessageSender` hardcoded in the constructor. It is not possible to replace this dependency without modifying the codebase (except for injecting objects using reflection or replacing objects on the `new` operator).

Modifying the codebase is always a source of possible regressions, so it should be done with caution. Refactoring requires tests, except when it is not possible.

The Legacy Code Dilemma.

When we change code, we should have tests in place. To put tests in place, we often have to change code.

The legacy code change algorithm

When you have to make a change in a legacy codebase, here is an algorithm you can use:

- Identify change points
- Find test points
- Break dependencies
- Write tests
- Make changes and refactor

Applying the legacy code change algorithm

To apply this algorithm, we usually start with a suite of tests and always keep it green while refactoring. This is different from the normal cycle of TDD because refactoring should not introduce any new features (that is, it should not write any new specifications).

To better explain the algorithm, imagine that we received the following change request: To greet my employees in a more informal way, I want to send them a tweet instead of an email.

Identifying change points

The system is only able to send emails right now, so a change is necessary. Where? A quick investigation shows that the strategy for sending the greeting is decided in the constructor for the `BirthdayGreetingService` class following the strategy pattern (https://en.wikipedia.org/?title=Strategy_pattern):

```
public class BirthdayGreetingService {

  public BirthdayGreetingService() {
    messageSender = new EmailMessageSender();
  }
  [...]
}
```

Finding test points

As the `BirthdayGreetingService` class does not have a collaborator injected that could be used to attach additional responsibilities to the object, the only option is to go outside this service class to test it. An option would be to change the `EmailMessageSender` class for a mock or fake implementation, but this would risk the implementation in that class.

Another option is to create an end-to-end test for this functionality:

```java
public class EndToEndTest {

  @Test
  public void email_an_employee() {
    final StringBuilder systemOutput =
      injectSystemOutput();
    final Employee john = new Employee(
      new Email("john@example.com"));

    new BirthdayGreetingService().greet(john);

    assertThat(systemOutput.toString(),
      equalTo("Sent email to "
        + "'john@example.com' with "
        + "the body 'Greetings on your "
        + "birthday'\n"));
  }

  // This code has been used with permission from
  //GMaur's LegacyUtils:
  // https://github.com/GMaur/legacyutils
  private StringBuilder injectSystemOutput() {
    final StringBuilder stringBuilder =
      new StringBuilder();
    final PrintStream outputPrintStream =
      new PrintStream(
        new OutputStream() {
        @Override
        public void write(final int b)
          throws IOException {
          stringBuilder.append((char) b);
        }
      });
    System.setOut(outputPrintStream);
    return stringBuilder;
  }
}
```

This code has been used with permission from https://github.com/GMaur/legacyutils. This library helps you perform the technique of capturing the system out (System.out).

The name of the file does not end in Specification (or Spec), such as TicTacToeSpec, because this is not a specification. It is a test, to ensure the functionality remains constant. The file has been named EndToEndTest because we try to cover as much functionality as possible.

Breaking dependencies

After having created a test that guarantees the expected behavior does not change, we will break the hardcoded dependency between BirthdayGreetingService and EmailMessageSender. For this, we will use a technique called **extract and override call**, which is first explained in Michael Feathers' book:

```
public class BirthdayGreetingService {

  public BirthdayGreetingService() {
    messageSender = getMessageSender();
  }

  private MessageSender getMessageSender() {
    return new EmailMessageSender();
  }

[...]
```

Execute the tests again and verify that the lonely test we previously created still is green. Additionally, we need to make this method protected or more open to be able to override it:

```
public class BirthdayGreetingService {

  protected MessageSender getMessageSender() {
    return new EmailMessageSender();
  }

[...]
```

Now that the method can be overridden, we create a fake service to replace the original instance of the service. Introducing fakes in code is a pattern that consists of creating an object that could replace an existing one, with the particularity that we can control its behavior. This way, we can inject some customized fakes to achieve what we need. More information is available at http://xunitpatterns.com/.

In this particular case, we should create a fake service that extends the original service. The next step is to override complicated methods in order to bypass irrelevant parts of code for testing purposes:

```java
public class FakeBirthdayGreetingService
  extends BirthdayGreetingService {

  @Override
  protected MessageSender getMessageSender() {
    return new EmailMessageSender();
  }
}
```

Now we can use the fake, instead of the `BirthdayGreetingService` class:

```java
public class EndToEndTest {

  @Test
  public void email_an_employee() {
    final StringBuilder systemOutput =
      injectSystemOutput();
    final Employee john = new Employee(
      new Email("john@example.com"));

    new FakeBirthdayGreetingService().greet(john);

    assertThat(systemOutput.toString(),
      equalTo("Sent email to "
        + "'john@example.com' with "
        + "the body 'Greetings on "
        + "your birthday'\n"));
  }
```

The test is still green.

We can now apply another dependency-breaking technique, parameterize constructor, explained in Feathers paper at https://archive.org/details/WorkingEffectivelyWithLegacyCode. The production code may look like this:

```java
public class BirthdayGreetingService {

  public BirthdayGreetingService(final MessageSender
    messageSender) {
    this.messageSender = messageSender;
  }
  [...]
}
```

Test code that corresponds to this implementation may be as follows:

```
public class EndToEndTest {

  @Test
  public void email_an_employee() {
    final StringBuilder systemOutput =
      injectSystemOutput();
    final Employee john = new Employee(
      new Email("john@example.com"));

    new BirthdayGreetingService(new
        EmailMessageSender()).greet(john);

    assertThat(systemOutput.toString(),
      equalTo("Sent email to "
        + "'john@example.com' with "
        + "the body 'Greetings on "
        + "your birthday'\n"));
  }
  [...]
```

We can also remove `FakeBirthday`, as it is no longer used.

Writing tests

While keeping the old end-to-end test, create an interaction to verify the integration of `BirthdayGreetingService` and `MessageSender`:

```
    @Test
    public void the_service_should_ask_the_messageSender() {
      final Email address =
        new Email("john@example.com");
      final Employee john = new Employee(address);
      final MessageSender messageSender =
        mock(MessageSender.class);

      new BirthdayGreetingService(messageSender)
        .greet(john);

      verify(messageSender).send(address,
          "Greetings on your birthday");
    }
```

At this point, a new `TweetMessageSender` can be written, completing the last step of the algorithm.

The kata exercise

The only way a programmer will be able to improve is through practice. Creating programs of different types and using different technologies usually provide a programmer with new insights into software construction. Based on this idea, a kata is an exercise that defines some requirements or fixed features to be implemented in order to achieve some goals.

The programmer is asked to implement a possible solution and then compare it with others trying to find the best. The key value of this exercise is not getting the fastest implementation but discussing decisions taken while designing the solution. In most cases, all programs created in kata are dropped at the end.

The kata exercise in this chapter is about a legacy system. This is a sufficiently simple program to be processed in this chapter but also complex enough to pose some difficulties.

Legacy kata

You have been given a task to adopt a system that is already in production, a working piece of software for a book library: the Alexandria project.

The project currently lacks documentation, and the old maintainer is no longer available for discussion. So, should you accept this mission, it is going to be entirely your responsibility, as there is no one else to rely on.

Description

We have been able to recover these specification snippets from the time the original project was written:

- The Alexandria software should be able to store books and lend them to users, who have the power to return them. The user can also query the system for books, by author, book title, status, and ID.
- There is no time frame for returning the books.
- The books can also be censored as this is considered important for business reasons.
- The software should not accept new users.
- The user should be told, at any moment, the server's time.

Technical comments

The Alexandria is a backend project written in Java, which communicates information to the frontend using a REST API. For the purpose of this kata exercise, persistence has been implemented as an in-memory object, using the fake test double explained at `http://xunitpatterns.com/Fake%20Object.html`.

The code is available at `https://bitbucket.org/vfarcic/tdd-java-alexandria`.

Adding a new feature

Until the point of adding a new feature, the legacy code might not be a disturbance to the programmer's productivity. The codebase is in a state that is worse than desired, but the production systems work without any inconvenience.

Now is the time when the problems start to appear. The **product owner** (**PO**) wants to add a new feature.

For example, as a library manager, I want to know all the history for a given book so that I can measure which books are more in demand than others.

Black-box or spike testing

As the old maintainer of the Alexandria project is no longer available for questions and there is no documentation, black-box testing is more difficult. Thus, we decide to get to know the software better through investigation and then doing some spikes that will leak internal knowledge to us about the system.

We will later use this knowledge to implement the new feature.

Black-box testing is a method of software testing that examines the functionality of an application without peering into its internal structures or workings. This type of test can be applied to virtually every level of software testing: unit, integration, system, and acceptance. It typically most if not all higher-level testing, but can dominate unit testing as well.

Source: `http://en.wikipedia.org/wiki/Black-box_testing`.

Preliminary investigation

When we know the required feature, we will start looking at the Alexandria project:

- 15 files
- Gradle-based (`build.gradle`)
- 0 tests

Firstly, we want to confirm that this project has never been tested, and the lack of a test folder reveals so:

```
$ find src/test
find: src/test: No such file or directory
```

These are the folder contents for the Java part:

```
$ cd src/main/java/com/packtpublishing/tddjava/ch09/alexandria/
$ find .
.
./Book.java
./Books.java
./BooksEndpoint.java
./BooksRepository.java
./CustomExceptionMapper.java
./MyApplication.java
./States.java
./User.java
./UserRepository.java
./Users.java
```

Here is the rest:

```
$ cd src/main
$ find resources webapp
resources
resources/applicationContext.xml
webapp
webapp/WEB-INF
webapp/WEB-INF/web.xml
```

This seems to be a web project (indicated by the `web.xml` file) using Spring (indicated by the `applicationContext.xml`). The dependencies in the `build.gradle` show the following (fragment):

```
compile 'org.springframework:spring-web:4.1.4.RELEASE'
```

Having Spring is already a good sign, as it can help with the dependency injection, but a quick look showed that the context is not really being used. Maybe something that was used in the past?

In the web.xml file, we can find this fragment:

```xml
<?xml version="1.0" encoding="UTF-8"?>
<web-app version="3.0" xmlns="http://java.sun.com/xml/ns/javaee"
        xmlns:xsi="http://www.w3.org/2001/XMLSchema-instance"
        xsi:schemaLocation="http://java.sun.com/xml/ns/javaee
          http://java.sun.com/xml/ns/javaee/web-app_3_0.xsd">

    <module-name>alexandria</module-name>

    <context-param>
        <param-name>contextConfigLocation</param-name>
        <param-value>classpath:applicationContext.xml</param-value>
    </context-param>

    <servlet>
        <servlet-name>SpringApplication</servlet-name>
        <servlet-class>
 org.glassfish.jersey.servlet.ServletContainer</servlet-class>
        <init-param>
            <param-name>javax.ws.rs.Application</param-name>
            <param-value>com.packtpublishing.tddjava.alexandria.MyApplication</param-value>
        </init-param>
        <load-on-startup>1</load-on-startup>
    </servlet>
```

In this file, we discover the following:

- The context in applicationContext.xml will be loaded
- There is an application file (com.packtpublishing.tddjava.alexandria.MyApplication) that will be executed inside a servlet

The `MyApplication` file is as follows:

```
public class MyApplication extends ResourceConfig {
  public MyApplication() {
    register(RequestContextFilter.class);
    register(BooksEndpoint.class);
    register(JacksonJaxbJsonProvider.class);
    register(CustomExceptionMapper.class);
  }
}
```

This configures the necessary classes for executing the `BooksEndpoint` endpoint (fragment):

```
@Path("books")
@Component
public class BooksEndpoint {
  private BooksRepository books = new BooksRepository();

  private UserRepository users = new UserRepository();
```

In this last snippet, we can find one of the first indicators that this is a legacy codebase—both dependencies (`books` and `users`) are created inside the endpoint and not injected. This makes unit testing more difficult.

We can start by writing down the element that will be used during refactoring; we write the code for the **dependency injection** in `BooksEndpoint`.

How to find candidates for refactoring

There are different paradigms of programming (for example, functional, imperative, and object-oriented) and styles (for example, compact, verbose, minimalistic, and too clever). Therefore, the candidates for refactoring are different from one person to the other.

There is another way, as opposed to subjectively, of finding candidates for refactoring—objectively. There are many papers investigating how to find candidates for refactoring objectively. This is just an introduction and it is left to the reader to learn more about these techniques.

Introducing the new feature

After getting to know the code more, it seems that the most important functional change is to replace the current status (fragment):

```
@XmlRootElement
public class Book {

    private final String title;
    private final String author;
    private int status; //<- this attribute
    private int id;
```

And replace it with a collection of them (fragment):

```
@XmlRootElement
public class Book {
    private int[] statuses;
    // ...
```

This might seem to work (after changing all access to the field to the array, for example), but this also prompts a functional requirement.

The Alexandria software should be able to store books and lend them to users who have the power to return them. The user can also query the system for books, by author, book title, status, and ID.

The PO confirms that searching books via status has now changed now, it also allows searching for any previous status.

This change is getting bigger and bigger. Whenever we feel that the time for removing this legacy code has come, we start applying the legacy code algorithm.

We have also detected a primitive obsession and feature envy smell: storing the status as an integer (primitive obsession) and then actuating on another object's state (feature envy). We will add this to the following to-do list:

- Dependency injection in BooksEndpoint for books
- Change status for statuses
- Remove the primitive obsession with status (optional)

Applying the legacy code algorithm

In this case, the whole middle-end works as a standalone, using in-memory persistence. The same algorithm could be used if the persistence was saved into a database, but we would require some extra code to clean and populate the database between test runs.

We'll use DbUnit. More information can be found at `http://dbunit.sourceforge.net/`.

Writing end-to-end test cases

The first step we've decided to take to ensure that behavior is maintained during refactoring is to write end-to-end tests. In other applications that include frontends, this could be using a higher-level tool, such as Selenium/Selenide.

In our case, as the frontend is not subject to refactoring, the tool can be lower-level. We have chosen to write HTTP requests for the purpose of end-to-end tests.

These requests should be automatic and testable, and should follow all existing rules for automatic tests or specifications. As we were discovering the real application behavior while writing these tests, we have decided to write a spike in a tool called Postman. The product website is here: `https://www.getpostman.com/`. This is also possible with a tool called curl (`http://curl.haxx.se/`).

What is curl?
curl is a command-line tool and library for transferring data with URL syntax, supporting [...] HTTP, HTTPS, [...], HTTP POST, HTTP PUT, and [...].

What's curl used for?
curl is used in command lines or scripts to transfer data.

Source: `http://curl.haxx.se/`.

To do this, we decide to execute the legacy software locally with the following line:

```
./gradlew clean jettyRun
```

This fires up a local jetty server that processes requests. The big benefit is that deployment is done automatically and there is no need to package everything and manually deploy to an application server (for example, JBoss AS, GlassFish, Geronimo, and TomEE). This can greatly speed up the process of making changes and seeing the effects, therefore decreasing the feedback lead time. Later on, we will start the server programmatically from Java code.

We start looking for functionalities. As we discovered earlier that the `BooksEndpoint` class contains the webservice endpoint definitions, this is a good place to start looking for functionalities. They are listed as follows:

1. Add a new book
2. List all the books
3. Search for books by ID, by author, by title, and by status
4. Prepare this book to be rented
5. Rent this book
6. Censor this book
7. Uncensor the book

We launch the server manually and start writing requests:

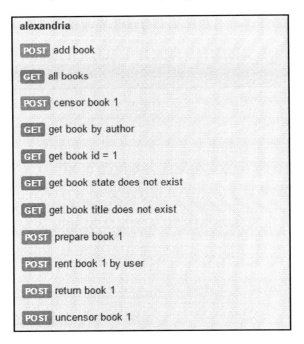

These tests seem good enough for a spike. One thing that we have realized is that each response contains a timestamp, so this makes our automation more difficult:

For the tests to have more value, they should be automated and exhaustive. For the moment, they are not, so we consider them spikes. They will be automated in the future.

Each and every single test that we perform is not automated. In this case, the tests from the Postman interface are much faster to write than the automated ones. Also, the experience is far more representative of what production use would be like. The test client (thankfully, in this case) could introduce some problems with the production one, and therefore not return trusted results.

In this particular case, we have found that the Postman tests are a better investment because, even after writing them, we will throw them away. They give very rapid feedback on the API and results. We also use this tool for prototyping the REST APIs, as its tools are both effective and useful.

The general idea here is this: depending on whether you want to save those tests for the future or not, use one tool or another. This also depends on how often you want to execute them, and in which environment.

After writing down all the requests, these are the states that we have found in the application, represented by a state diagram:

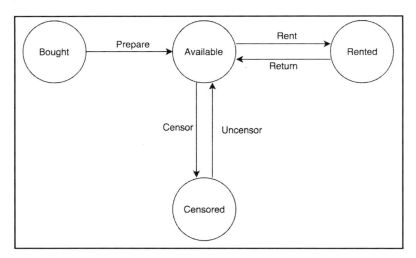

After these tests are ready and we start to understand the application, it is time to automate the tests. After all, if they are not automated, we don't really feel confident enough for refactoring.

Automating the test cases

We start the server programmatically. For this, we have decided to use a Grizzly (https://javaee.github.io/grizzly/), which allows us to start the server using the configuration from Jersey's `ResourceConfig` (FQCN: `org.glassfish.jersey.server.ResourceConfig`), as shown in the test `BooksEndpointTest` (fragment).

The code can be found at https://bitbucket.org/vfarcic/tdd-java-alexandria:

```
public class BooksEndpointTest {
    public static final URI FULL_PATH =
        URI.create("http://localhost:8080/alexandria");
    private HttpServer server;

    @Before
    public void setUp() throws IOException {
        ResourceConfig resourceConfig =
            new MyApplication();
        server = GrizzlyHttpServerFactory
            .createHttpServer(FULL_PATH, resourceConfig);
        server.start();
    }

    @After
    public void tearDown(){
        server.shutdownNow();
    }
```

This prepares a local server at the address http://localhost:8080/alexandria. It will only be available for a short period of time (while the tests run), so, if you need to manually access the server, whenever you want to pause the execution, insert a call to the following method:

```
public void pauseTheServer() throws Exception {
    System.in.read();
}
```

When you want to stop the server, stop the execution or hit *Enter* in the allocated console.

Now we can start the server programmatically, pause it (with the preceding method), and execute the spike again. The results are the same, so the refactor is successful.

We add the first automated test to the system.

The code can be found at https://bitbucket.org/vfarcic/tdd-java-alexandria:

```java
public class BooksEndpointTest {

  public static final String AUTHOR_BOOK_1 =
    "Viktor Farcic and Alex Garcia";
  public static final String TITLE_BOOK_1 =
    "TDD in Java";
  private final Map<String, String> TDD_IN_JAVA;

  public BooksEndpointTest() {
    TDD_IN_JAVA = getBookProperties(TITLE_BOOK_1,
      AUTHOR_BOOK_1);
  }

  private Map<String, String> getBookProperties
    (String title, String author) {
      Map<String, String> bookProperties =
        new HashMap<>();
      bookProperties.put("title", title);
      bookProperties.put("author", author);
      return bookProperties;
  }

  @Test
  public void add_one_book() throws IOException {
      final Response books1 = addBook(TDD_IN_JAVA);
      assertBooksSize(books1, is("1"));
  }

   private void assertBooksSize(Response response,
      Matcher<String> matcher) {
      response.then().body(matcher);
  }

  private Response addBook
    (Map<String, ?> bookProperties) {
      return RestAssured
         .given().log().path()
         .contentType(ContentType.URLENC)
         .parameters(bookProperties)
         .post("books");
  }
```

For testing purposes, we're using a library called RestAssured (https://github.com/rest-assured/rest-assured) that allows for easier testing of REST and JSON.

To complete the automated test suite, we create these tests:

- add_one_book()
- add_a_second_book()
- get_book_details_by_id()
- get_several_books_in_a_row()
- censor_a_book()
- cannot_retrieve_a_censored_book()

The code can be found at https://bitbucket.org/vfarcic/tdd-java-alexandria/.

Now that we have a suite that ensures that no regression is introduced, we take a look at the following to-do list:

1. Dependency injection in BooksEndpoint for books
2. Change status for statuses
3. Remove the primitive obsession with status (optional)

We will tackle dependency injection first.

Injecting the BookRepository dependency

The code for the BookRepository dependency is in BooksEndpoint (fragment):

```
@Path("books")
@Component
public class BooksEndpoint {

    private BooksRepository books =
        new BooksRepository();
[...]
```

Extract and override call

We will apply the already introduced refactoring technique extract and override call. For this, we create a failing specification, as shown here:

```
@Test
public void add_one_book() throws IOException {
    addBook(TDD_IN_JAVA);
```

```
        Book tddInJava = new Book(TITLE_BOOK_1,
          AUTHOR_BOOK_1,
            States.fromValue(1));

        verify(booksRepository).add(tddInJava);
}
```

To pass this red specification, also known as a failing specificiation, we will first extract the dependency creation to a `protected` method in the `BookRepository` class:

```
@Path("books")
@Component
public class BooksEndpoint {

    private BooksRepository books =
      getBooksRepository();

    [...]

     protected BooksRepository
       getBooksRepository() {
         return new BooksRepository();
    }

    [...]
```

We copy the `MyApplication` launcher to this:

```
public class TestApplication
    extends ResourceConfig {

    public TestApplication
      (BooksEndpoint booksEndpoint) {
        register(booksEndpoint);
        register(RequestContextFilter.class);
        register(JacksonJaxbJsonProvider.class);
        register(CustomExceptionMapper.class);
    }

    public TestApplication() {
        this(new BooksEndpoint(
          new BooksRepository()));
    }
}
```

This allows us to inject any `BooksEndpoint`. In this case, in the test `BooksEndpointInteractionTest`, we will override the dependency getter with a mock. In this way, we can check that the necessary calls are being made (fragment from `BooksEndpointInteractionTest`):

```java
@Test
public void add_one_book() throws IOException {
    addBook(TDD_IN_JAVA);
    verify(booksRepository)
      .add(new Book(TITLE_BOOK_1,
          AUTHOR_BOOK_1, 1));
}
```

Run the tests; everything is green. Even though the specifications are successful, we have introduced a piece of design only for test purposes, and the production code is not executing this new launcher, `TestApplication`, but is still executing the old `MyApplication`. To solve this, we have to unify both launchers into one. This can be solved with the refactor parametrize constructor, also explained in Roy Osherove's book, *The Art of Unit Testing* (http://artofunittesting.com).

Parameterizing a constructor

We can unify the launchers by accepting a `BooksEndpoint` dependency. If we don't specify it, it will register the dependency with the real instance of `BooksRepository`. Otherwise, it will register the received one:

```java
public class MyApplication
    extends ResourceConfig {

  public MyApplication() {
     this(new BooksEndpoint(
       new BooksRepository()));
  }

  public MyApplication
    (BooksEndpoint booksEndpoint) {
      register(booksEndpoint);
      register(RequestContextFilter.class);
      register(JacksonJaxbJsonProvider.class);
      register(CustomExceptionMapper.class);
  }
}
```

In this case, we have opted for **constructor chaining** to avoid repetition in the constructors.

After doing this refactor, the `BooksEndpointInteractionTest` class is as follows in its final state:

```java
public class BooksEndpointInteractionTest {

    public static final URI FULL_PATH = URI.
        create("http://localhost:8080/alexandria");
    private HttpServer server;
    private BooksRepository booksRepository;

    @Before
    public void setUp() throws IOException {
        booksRepository = mock(BooksRepository.class);
        BooksEndpoint booksEndpoint =
          new BooksEndpoint(booksRepository);
        ResourceConfig resourceConfig =
          new MyApplication(booksEndpoint);
        server = GrizzlyHttpServerFactory
           .createHttpServer(FULL_PATH, resourceConfig);
        server.start();
    }
}
```

The first test passed, so we can mark the dependency injection task as done.

Tasks performed:

- Dependency injection in `BooksEndpoint` for books

The to-do list:

- Change `status` for `statuses`
- Remove the primitive obsession with `status` (optional)

Adding a new feature

Once we have the necessary test environment in place, we can add the new feature.

As a library manager, I want to know all the history for a given book so that I can measure which books are more in demand than others.

We will start with a red specification:

```java
public class BooksSpec {

    @Test
```

```
public void should_search_for_any_past_state() {
    Book book1 = new Book("title", "author",
        States.AVAILABLE);
    book1.censor();

    Books books = new Books();
    books.add(book1);

    String available =
       String.valueOf(States.AVAILABLE);
    assertThat(
      books.filterByState(available).isEmpty(),
      is(false));
}
}
```

Run all the tests and see the last one fail.

Implement the search on all states (fragment):

```
public class Book {

    private ArrayList<Integer> status;

    public Book(String title, String author, int status) {
        this.title = title;
        this.author = author;
        this.status = new ArrayList<>();
        this.status.add(status);
    }

    public int getStatus() {
        return status.get(status.size()-1);
    }

    public void rent() {
        status.add(States.RENTED);
    }
    [...]

    public List<Integer> anyState() {
        return status;
    }
    [...]
```

In this fragment, we have omitted the irrelevant parts—things that were not modified, or more modifier methods, such as `rent`, that have changed the implementation in the same fashion:

```
public class Books {
    public Books filterByState(String state) {
        Integer expectedState = Integer.valueOf(state);
        return new Books(
            new ConcurrentLinkedQueue<>(
                books.stream()
                  .filter(x
                  -> x.anyState()
                  .contains(expectedState))
                  .collect(toList())));
    }
    [...]
```

The outside methods, especially the serialization to JSON, are not affected, as the `getStatus` method still returns an `int` value.

We run all the tests and everything is green.

Tasks performed:

- Dependency injection in `BooksEndpoint` for books
- Change `status` for `statuses`

The to-do list:

- Remove the primitive obsession with `status` (optional)

Removing the primitive obsession with status as int

We have decided to also tackle the optional item in our to-do list.

The to-do list:

- Dependency injection in `BooksEndpoint` for books
- Change `status` for `statuses`
- Remove the primitive obsession with `status` (optional)

The smell: **Primitive obsession** involves using primitive data types to represent domain ideas. For example, we use a string to represent a message, an integer to represent an amount of money, or a struct/dictionary/hash to represent a specific object.

The source is http://c2.com/cgi/wiki?PrimitiveObsession.

As this is a refactor step (that is, we are not introducing any new behavior into the system), we don't need any new specification. We will proceed and try to always stay green, or leave it for as little time as possible.

We have converted `States` from a Java class with constants:

```
public class States {
    public static final int BOUGHT = 1;
    public static final int RENTED = 2;
    public static final int AVAILABLE = 3;
    public static final int CENSORED = 4;
}
```

And turned it into an `enum`:

```
enum States {
    BOUGHT (1),
    RENTED (2),
    AVAILABLE (3),
    CENSORED (4);

    private final int value;

    private States(int value) {
        this.value = value;
    }

    public int getValue() {
        return value;
    }

    public static States fromValue(int value) {
        for (States states : values()) {
            if(states.getValue() == value) {
                return states;
            }
        }
        throw new IllegalArgumentException(
          "Value '" + value
```

```
                + "' could not be found in States");
        }
    }
```

Adapt the tests as follows:

```
        public class BooksEndpointInteractionTest {
            @Test
            public void add_one_book() throws IOException {
                addBook(TDD_IN_JAVA);
                verify(booksRepository).add(
                    new Book(TITLE_BOOK_1, AUTHOR_BOOK_1,
                        States.BOUGHT));
            }
            [...]
        public class BooksTest {

            @Test
            public void should_search_for_any_past_state() {
                Book book1 = new Book("title", "author",
                    States.AVAILABLE);
                book1.censor();

                Books books = new Books();
                books.add(book1);

                assertThat(books.filterByState(
                    String.valueOf(
                        States.AVAILABLE.getValue()))
                    .isEmpty(), is(false));
            }
            [...]
```

Adapt the production code. The code snippet is as follows:

```
        @XmlRootElement
        public class Books {
            public Books filterByState(String state) {
                State expected =
                    States.fromValue(Integer.valueOf(state));
                return new Books(
                    new ConcurrentLinkedQueue<>(
                        books.stream()
                            .filter(x -> x.anyState()
                                .contains(expected))
                            .collect(toList())));
            }
            [...]
```

Also the following:

```
@XmlRootElement
public class Book {

    private final String title;
    private final String author;
    @XmlTransient
    private ArrayList<States> status;
    private int id;

    public Book
       (String title, String author, States status) {
         this.title = title;
         this.author = author;
         this.status = new ArrayList<>();
         this.status.add(status);
    }

    public States getStatus() {
        return status.get(status.size() - 1);
    }

    @XmlElement(name = "status")
    public int getStatusAsInteger(){
        return getStatus().getValue();
    }

    public List<States> anyState() {
        return status;
    }
    [...]
```

In this case, the serialization has been done using the annotation:

```
@XmlElement(name = "status")
```

This converts the result of the method into the field named `status`.

Also, the `status` field, now `ArrayList<States>`, is marked with `@XmlTransient` so it is not serialized to JSON.

We execute all the tests and they are green, so we can now cross off the optional element in our to-do list.

Tasks performed:

- Dependency injection in `BooksEndpoint` for books
- Change `status` for `statuses`
- Remove the primitive obsession with `status` (optional)

Summary

As you already know, inheriting a legacy codebase may be a daunting task.

We stated that legacy code is code without tests, so the first step in dealing with it is to create tests to help you preserve the same functionality during the process. Unfortunately, creating tests is not always as easy as it sounds. Many times, legacy code is tightly coupled and presents other symptoms that show a poor design or at least a lack of interest in the code's quality in the past. Worry not: you can perform some of the tedious tasks step by step, as shown in `http://martinfowler.com/bliki/ParallelChange.html`. Moreover, it is also well known that software development is a learning process. Working code is a side effect. Therefore, the most important part is to learn more about the codebase, to be able to modify it with security. Please visit `http://www.slideshare.net/ziobrando/model-storming` for more information.

Finally, we encourage you to read Michael Feathers book called *Working Effectively with Legacy Code*. It has plenty of techniques for this kind of codebase, and as a result is very useful for understanding the whole process.

10
Feature Toggles – Deploying Partially Done Features to Production

"Do not let circumstances control you. You change your circumstances."

– Jackie Chan

We have seen so far how TDD makes the development process easier and decreases the amount of time spent on writing quality code. But there's another particular benefit to this. As code is being tested and its correctness is proven, we can go a step further and assume that our code is production-ready once all tests have passed.

There are some software life cycle approaches based on this idea. Some **extreme programming (XP)** practices such as **continuous integration (CI)**, continuous delivery, and **continuous deployment (CD)** will be introduced. The code examples can be found at https://bitbucket.org/alexgarcia/packt-tdd-java/src/, in the folder `10-feature-toggles`.

The following topics will be covered in this chapter:

- Continuous integration, delivery, and deployment
- Testing the application in production
- Feature Toggles

Continuous integration, delivery, and deployment

TDD goes hand in hand with CI, continuous delivery, or CD. Differences aside, all three techniques have similar goals. They are all trying to foster the continuous verification of production readiness of our code. In that respect, they are very similar to TDD. They each promote very short development cycles, continuous verification of the code we're producing, and the intention to continuously keep our application in a production-ready state.

The scope of this book does not permit us to go into the details of those techniques. Indeed, a whole book could be written on this subject. We'll just briefly explain the differences between the three. Practicing CI means that our code is at (almost) all times integrated with the rest of the system, and if there is a problem it will surface quickly. If such a thing happens, the priority is to fix the cause of that problem, meaning that any new development must take lower priority. You might have noticed a similarity between this definition and the way TDD works. The major difference is that with TDD, our primary focus is not the integration with the rest of the system. The rest is the same. Both TDD and CI try to detect problems fast and treat fixing them as the highest priority, putting everything else on hold. CI does not have the whole pipeline automated, and additional manual verifications are needed before the code is deployed to production.

Continuous delivery is very similar to CI, except that the former goes a bit further and has the whole pipeline automated, except the actual deployment to production. Every push to the repository that passed all verifications is considered valid for deployment to production. However, the decision to deploy is made manually. Someone needs to choose one of the builds and promote it to the production environment. The choice is political or functional. It depends on what and when we want our users to receive, even though each is production-ready.

> "*Continuous Delivery is a software development discipline where you build software in such a way that the software can be released to production at any time.*"
>
> *– Martin Fowler*

Finally, CD is accomplished when the decision about what to deploy is automated as well. In this scenario, every commit that passed all verifications is deployed to production—no exceptions.

In order to continuously integrate or deliver our code to production, branches cannot exist, or the time between creating them and integrating them with the mainline must be very short (less than a day, preferably a few hours). If that is not the case, we are not continuously verifying our code.

The true connection with TDD comes from the necessity to create validations before the code is committed. If those verifications are not created in advance, code pushed to the repository is not accompanied with tests and the process fails. Without tests, there is no confidence in what we did. Without TDD, there are no tests to accompany our implementation code. Alternatively, a delay in pushing commits to repository until tests are created but in that case, there is no continuous part of the process. Code is sitting on someone's computer until someone else is finished with tests. Code that sits somewhere is not continuously verified against the whole system.

To summarize, continuous integration, delivery, and deployment rely on tests to accompany the integration code (thus, relying on TDD) and on the practice of not using branches or having them very short-lived (very often merged to the mainline). The problem lies with the fact that some features cannot be developed that fast. No matter how small our features are, in some cases it might take days to develop them. During all that time, we cannot push to the repository because the process would deliver them to production. Users do not want to see partial features. There is no point having, for example, part of the login process delivered. If one were to see a login page with a username, password, and login button, but the process behind that button does not actually store that info and provides, let's say, an authentication cookie, then at best we would have confused the users. In some other cases, one feature cannot work without the other. Following the same example, even if a login feature is fully developed, without registration it is pointless. One cannot be used without the other.

Imagine playing a puzzle. We need to have a rough idea of the final picture, but we are focused on one piece at the time. We pick a piece that we think is the easiest to place and combine it with its neighbors. Only when all of them are in place is the picture complete and we are finished.

The same applies to TDD. We develop our code by being focused on small units. As we progress, they start taking a shape and working with each other until they are all integrated. While we're waiting for that to happen, even though all our tests are passing and we are in a green state, the code is not ready for the end users.

The easiest way to solve those problems and not compromise on TDD and CI/CD is to use Feature Toggles.

Feature Toggles

You might have also heard about this as **Feature Flipping** or **Feature Flags**. No matter which expression we use, they are all based on a mechanism that permits you to turn on and off the features of your application. This is very useful when all code is merged into one branch and you must deal with partially finished (or integrated) code. With this technique, unfinished features can be hidden so that users cannot access them.

Due to its nature, there are other possible uses for this functionality. As a circuit breaker when something is wrong with a particular feature, providing graceful degradation of the application, shutting down secondary features to preserve hardware resources for business core operations, and so on. Feature Toggles, in some cases, can go even further. We might use them to enable features only to certain users, based on, for example, geographic location or their role. Another use is that we can enable new features for our testers only. That way, end users would continue to be oblivious of the existence of some new features, while testers would be able to validate them on a production server.

Moreover, there are some aspects to remember when using Feature Toggles:

- Use toggles only until they are fully deployed and proven to work. Otherwise, you might end up with spaghetti code full of if/else statements containing old toggles that are not in use any more.
- Do not spend too much time testing toggles. It is, in most cases, enough to confirm that the entry point into some new feature is not visible. That can be, for example, a link to the new feature.
- Do not overuse toggles. Do not use them when there is no need for them. For example, you might be developing a new screen that is accessible through a link in the home page. If that link is added at the end, there might be no need to have a toggle that hides it.

There are many good frameworks and libraries for application feature handling. Two of them are the following:

- **Togglz** (http://www.togglz.org/)
- **FF4J** (http://ff4j.org/)

These libraries offer a sophisticated way to manage features, even adding role-based or rules-based feature access. In many cases, you aren't going to need it, but these capabilities bring us the possibility of testing a new feature in production without opening it to all users. However, implementing a custom basic solution for feature toggling is quite simple, and we are going to go through an example to illustrate this.

A Feature Toggle example

Here we go with our demo application. This time, we're going to build a simple and small **REpresentational State Transfer (REST)** service to compute, on demand, a concrete N^{th} position of Fibonacci's sequence. We will keep track of enabled/disabled features using a file. For simplicity, we will use Spring Boot as our framework of choice and Thymeleaf as a template engine. This is also included in the Spring Boot dependency. Find more information about Spring Boot and related projects at http://projects.spring.io/spring-boot/. Also, you can visit http://www.thymeleaf.org/ to read more about the template engine.

This is how the `build.gradle` file looks:

```
apply plugin: 'java'
apply plugin: 'application'

sourceCompatibility = 1.8
version = '1.0'
mainClassName = "com.packtpublishing.tddjava.ch09.Application"

repositories {
    mavenLocal()
    mavenCentral()
}

dependencies {
    compile group: 'org.springframework.boot',
            name: 'spring-boot-starter-thymeleaf',
            version: '1.2.4.RELEASE'

    testCompile group: 'junit',
    name: 'junit',
    version: '4.12'
}
```

Note that application plugin is present because we want to run the application using the Gradle command `run`. Here is the application's `main` class:

```
@SpringBootApplication
public class Application {
    public static void main(String[] args) {
        SpringApplication.run(Application.class, args);
    }
}
```

We will create the properties file. This time, we are going to use **YAML Ain't Markup Language (YAML)** format, as it is very comprehensive and concise. Add a file called `application.yml` in the `src/main/resources` folder, with the following content:

```
features:
    fibonacci:
        restEnabled: false
```

Spring offers a way to load this kind of property file automatically. Currently, there are only two restrictions: the name must be `application.yml` and/or the file should be included in the application's class path.

This is our implementation of the feature's `config` file:

```
@Configuration
@EnableConfigurationProperties
@ConfigurationProperties(prefix = "features.fibonacci")
public class FibonacciFeatureConfig {
    private boolean restEnabled;

    public boolean isRestEnabled() {
        return restEnabled;
    }

    public void setRestEnabled(boolean restEnabled) {
        this.restEnabled = restEnabled;
    }
}
```

This is the `fibonacci` service class. This time, the computation operation will always return -1, just to simulate a partially done feature:

```
@Service("fibonacci")
public class FibonacciService {

    public int getNthNumber(int n) {
        return -1;
    }
}
```

We also need a wrapper to hold the computed values:

```
public class FibonacciNumber {
    private final int number, value;

    public FibonacciNumber(int number, int value) {
        this.number = number;
```

```
            this.value = value;
        }

        public int getNumber() {
            return number;
        }

        public int getValue() {
            return value;
        }
    }
```

This is the `FibonacciRESTController` class, responsible for handling the `fibonacci` service queries:

```
@RestController
public class FibonacciRestController {
    @Autowired
    FibonacciFeatureConfig fibonacciFeatureConfig;

    @Autowired
    @Qualifier("fibonacci")
    private FibonacciService fibonacciProvider;

    @RequestMapping(value = "/fibonacci", method = GET)
    public FibonacciNumber fibonacci(
            @RequestParam(
                    value = "number",
                    defaultValue = "0") int number) {
        if (fibonacciFeatureConfig.isRestEnabled()) {
            int fibonacciValue = fibonacciProvider
                    .getNthNumber(number);
            return new FibonacciNumber(number, fibonacciValue);
        } else throw new UnsupportedOperationException();
    }

    @ExceptionHandler(UnsupportedOperationException.class)
    public void unsupportedException(HttpServletResponse response)
            throws IOException {
        response.sendError(
                HttpStatus.SERVICE_UNAVAILABLE.value(),
                "This feature is currently unavailable"
        );
    }

    @ExceptionHandler(Exception.class)
    public void handleGenericException(
```

```
                HttpServletResponse response,
                Exception e) throws IOException {
        String msg = "There was an error processing " +
                "your request: " + e.getMessage();
        response.sendError(
                HttpStatus.BAD_REQUEST.value(),
                msg
        );
    }
}
```

Note that the `fibonacci` method is checking whether the `fibonacci` service should be enabled or disabled, throwing an `UnsupportedOperationException` for convenience in the last case. There are also two error-handling functions; the first one is for processing `UnsupportedOperationException` and the second is for generic exceptions handling.

Now that all the components have been set, all we need to do is execute Gradle's `run` command:

```
$> gradle run
```

The command will launch a process that will eventually set a server up on the following address: `http://localhost:8080`. This can be observed in the console output:

```
...
    2015-06-19 03:44:54.157  INFO 3886 --- [           main]
o.s.w.s.handler.SimpleUrlHandlerMapping  : Mapped URL path [/webjars/**]
onto handler of type [class
org.springframework.web.servlet.resource.ResourceHttpRequestHandler]
    2015-06-19 03:44:54.160  INFO 3886 --- [           main]
o.s.w.s.handler.SimpleUrlHandlerMapping  : Mapped URL path [/**] onto
handler of type [class
org.springframework.web.servlet.resource.ResourceHttpRequestHandler]
    2015-06-19 03:44:54.319  INFO 3886 --- [           main]
o.s.w.s.handler.SimpleUrlHandlerMapping  : Mapped URL path
[/**/favicon.ico] onto handler of type [class
org.springframework.web.servlet.resource.ResourceHttpRequestHandler]
    2015-06-19 03:44:54.495  INFO 3886 --- [           main]
o.s.j.e.a.AnnotationMBeanExporter        : Registering beans for JMX
exposure on startup
    2015-06-19 03:44:54.649  INFO 3886 --- [           main]
s.b.c.e.t.TomcatEmbeddedServletContainer : Tomcat started on port(s): 8080
(http)
    2015-06-19 03:44:54.654  INFO 3886 --- [           main]
c.p.tddjava.ch09.Application             : Started Application in 6.916
seconds (JVM running for 8.558)
> Building 75% > :run
```

Once the application has started, we can perform a query using a regular browser. The URL of the query is `http://localhost:8080/fibonacci?number=7`.

This gives us the following output:

As you can see, the error received corresponds to the error sent by the REST API when the feature is disabled. Otherwise, the return should be -1.

Implementing the Fibonacci service

Most of you might be familiar with Fibonacci's numbers. Here's a brief explanation anyway for those who don't know what they are.

Fibonacci's sequence is an integer sequence resulting from the recurrence $f(n) = f(n-1) - f(n - 2)$. The sequence starts with being $f(0) = 0$ and $f(1) = 1$. All other numbers are generated applying the recurrence as many times as needed until a value substitution can be performed using either 0 or 1 known values.

That is: 0, 1, 1, 2, 3, 5, 8, 13, 21, 34, 55, 89, 144,...

More info about Fibonacci's sequence can be found here: `http://www.wolframalpha.com/input/?i=fibonacci+sequence`

As an extra functionality, we want to limit how long the value computation takes, so we impose a constraint on the input; our service will only compute Fibonacci's numbers from 0 to 30 (both numbers included).

This is a possible implementation of a class computing Fibonacci's numbers:

```
@Service("fibonacci")
public class FibonacciService {
    public static final int LIMIT = 30;

    public int getNthNumber(int n) {
        if (isOutOfLimits(n) {
        throw new IllegalArgumentException(
        "Requested number must be a positive " +
           number no bigger than " + LIMIT);
        if (n == 0) return 0;
        if (n == 1 || n == 2) return 1;
        int first, second = 1, result = 1;
        do {
            first = second;
            second = result;
            result = first + second;
            --n;
        } while (n > 2);
        return result;
    }

    private boolean isOutOfLimits(int number) {
        return number > LIMIT || number < 0;
    }
}
```

For the sake of brevity, the TDD Red-Green-Refactor process is not explicitly explained in the demonstration, but has been present through development. Only the final implementation with the final tests is presented:

```
public class FibonacciServiceTest {
    private FibonacciService tested;
    private final String expectedExceptionMessage =
        "Requested number " +
            "must be a positive number no bigger than " +
            FibonacciService.LIMIT;

    @Rule
    public ExpectedException exception = ExpectedException.none();

    @Before
    public void beforeTest() {
        tested = new FibonacciService();
    }
```

```
@Test
public void test0() {
    int actual = tested.getNthNumber(0);
    assertEquals(0, actual);
}

@Test
public void test1() {
    int actual = tested.getNthNumber(1);
    assertEquals(1, actual);
}

@Test
public void test7() {
    int actual = tested.getNthNumber(7);
    assertEquals(13, actual);
}

@Test
public void testNegative() {
    exception.expect(IllegalArgumentException.class);
    exception.expectMessage(is(expectedExceptionMessage));
    tested.getNthNumber(-1);
}

@Test
public void testOutOfBounce() {
    exception.expect(IllegalArgumentException.class);
    exception.expectMessage(is(expectedExceptionMessage));
    tested.getNthNumber(31);
}
}
```

Also, we can now turn on the `fibonacci` feature in the `application.yml` file, perform some queries with the browser, and check how is it going:

```
features:
    fibonacci:
        restEnabled: true
```

Execute Gradle's `run` command:

```
$>gradle run
```

Now we can fully test our REST API using the browser, with a number between 0 and 30:

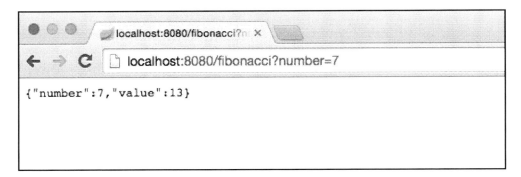

Then, we test it with a number bigger than 30, and lastly by introducing characters instead of numbers:

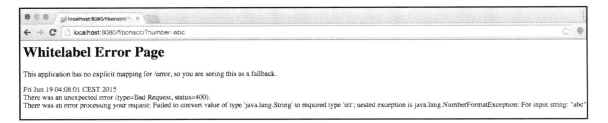

Working with the template engine

We are enabling and disabling the `fibonacci` feature, but there are many other cases where the Feature Toggle can be very useful. One of them is hiding a web link that links to an unfinished feature. This is an interesting use because we can test what we released to production using its URL, but it will be hidden for the rest of the users for as long as we want.

To illustrate this behavior, we are going to create a simple web page using the already mentioned Thymeleaf framework.

First of all, we add a new `control` flag:

```
features:
    fibonacci:
        restEnabled: true
        webEnabled: true
```

Next, map this new flag in a configuration class:

```
private boolean webEnabled;
public boolean isWebEnabled() {
    return webEnabled;
}

public void setWebEnabled(boolean webEnabled) {
    this.webEnabled = webEnabled;
}
```

We are going to create two templates. The first one is the home page. It contains some links to different Fibonacci number computations. These links should be visible only when the feature is enabled, so there's an optional block to simulate this behavior:

```
<!DOCTYPE html>
<html xmlns:th="http://www.thymeleaf.org">
<head lang="en">
    <meta http-equiv="Content-Type"
          content="text/html; charset=UTF-8" />
    <title>HOME - Fibonacci</title>
</head>
<body>
<div th:if="${isWebEnabled}">
    <p>List of links:</p>
    <ul th:each="number : ${arrayOfInts}">
        <li><a
            th:href="@{/web/fibonacci(number=${number})}"
            th:text="'Compute ' + ${number} + 'th fibonacci'">
        </a></li>
    </ul>
</div>
</body>
</html>
```

The second one just shows the value of the computed Fibonacci number and also a link to go back to the home page:

```
<!DOCTYPE html>
<html xmlns:th="http://www.thymeleaf.org">
<head lang="en">
    <meta http-equiv="Content-Type"
          content="text/html; charset=UTF-8" />
    <title>Fibonacci Example</title>
</head>
<body>
<p th:text="${number} + 'th number: ' + ${value}"></p>
```

```html
<a th:href="@{/}">back</a>
</body>
</html>
```

In order to get both templates to work, they should be in a specific location. They are `src/main/resources/templates/home.html` and `src/main/resources/templates/fibonacci.html` respectively.

Finally, the masterpiece, which is the controller that connects all this and makes it work:

```java
@Controller
public class FibonacciWebController {
    @Autowired
    FibonacciFeatureConfig fibonacciFeatureConfig;

    @Autowired
    @Qualifier("fibonacci")
    private FibonacciService fibonacciProvider;

    @RequestMapping(value = "/", method = GET)
    public String home(Model model) {
        model.addAttribute(
            "isWebEnabled",
            fibonacciFeatureConfig.isWebEnabled()
        );
        if (fibonacciFeatureConfig.isWebEnabled()) {
            model.addAttribute(
                "arrayOfInts",
                Arrays.asList(5, 7, 8, 16)
            );
        }
        return "home";
    }

    @RequestMapping(value ="/web/fibonacci", method = GET)
    public String fibonacci(
            @RequestParam(value = "number") Integer number,
            Model model) {
        if (number != null) {
            model.addAttribute("number", number);
            model.addAttribute(
                "value",
                fibonacciProvider.getNthNumber(number));
        }
        return "fibonacci";
    }
}
```

Note that this controller and the previous one seen in the REST API example share some similarities. This is because both are constructed with the same framework and use the same resources. However, there are slight differences between them; one is annotated as `@Controller` instead of both being `@RestController`. This is because the web controller is serving template pages with custom information, while the REST API generates a JSON object response.

Let's see this working, again using this Gradle command:

```
$> gradle clean run
```

This is the generated home page:

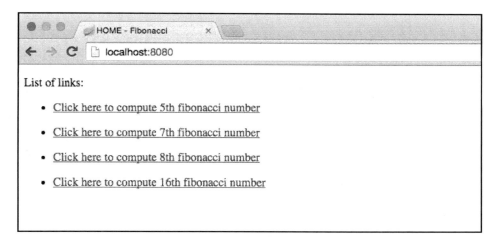

This is shown when visiting the Fibonacci number link:

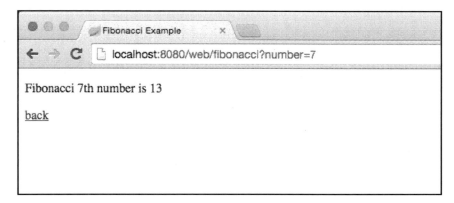

But we turn off the feature using the following code:

```
features:
    fibonacci:
        restEnabled: true
        webEnabled: false
```

Relaunching the application, we browse to the home page and see that those links are not shown anymore, but we can still access the page if we already know the URL. If we manually write `http://localhost:8080/web/fibonacci?number=15`, we can still access the page:

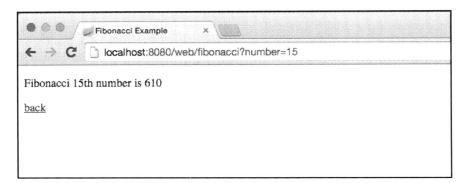

This practice is very useful, but it usually adds unnecessary complexity to your code. Don't forget to refactor the code, deleting old toggles that you won't use anymore. It will keep your code clean and readable. Also, a good point is getting this working without restarting the application. There are many storage options that do not require a restart, databases being the most popular.

Summary

Feature Toggles are a nice way to hide and/or handle partially finished functionalities in production environments. This may sound weird for those deploying code to production on demand, but it is quite common to find this situation when practicing continuous integration, delivery, or deployment.

We have introduced the technique and discussed the pros and cons. We have also enumerated some of the typical cases where toggling features can be helpful. Finally, we have implemented two different use cases: a Feature Toggle with a very simple REST API, and a Feature Toggle in a web application.

Although the code presented in this chapter is fully functional, it isn't very common to use a file-based property system for this matter. There are many libraries more suitable for production environments that can help us to implement this technique, providing a lot of capabilities, such as using a web interface to handle features, storing preferences in a database, or allowing access to concrete user profiles.

In the next chapter we are going to put the TDD concepts described in the book all together. We are going to name some good practices and recommendations that are very useful when programming in the TDD way.

11
Putting It All Together

"If you always do what you always did, then you will always get what you always got."

– Albert Einstein

We have gone through a lot of theory followed by even more practice. The entire journey was like a speeding train and we have hardly had an opportunity to repeat what we learned. There was no time for rest.

The good news is that the time for the reflection is now. We'll summarize everything we learned and go through TDD best practices. Some of those have already been mentioned, while others will be new.

Topics covered in this chapter include:

- TDD in a nutshell
- Common conventions and good practices, such as in naming tests
- Tools
- Next steps

TDD in a nutshell

Red-Green-Refactor is the pillar of TDD that wraps it into a short and repeatable cycle. By short, we mean very short. The time dedicated to each phase is often counted in minutes, if not seconds. Write a test, see it fail, write just enough implementation code to make the last test pass, run all tests, and pass into the green phase. Once the minimum code is written so that we have safety in the form of passing tests, it is time to refactor the code until it is as good as we're hoping it to be. While in this phase, tests should always pass. Neither new functionalities nor new tests can be introduced while refactoring is in progress. Doing all this in such a short period of time is often scary, or might sound impossible. We hope that, through the exercises we did together, your skills have improved, as well as your confidence and speed.

While there is the word **test** in **TDD**, it is not the main benefit nor objective. TDD is, first and foremost, a concept of a better way to design our code. On top of that, we end up with tests that should be used to continuously check that the application continues working as expected.

The importance of speed was mentioned often previously. While part of this is accomplished by us being ever more proficient in TDD, another contributor is **test doubles** (mocking, stubbing, spying, and so on). With these, we can remove the need for external dependencies such as databases, file systems, third-party services, and so on.

What are the other benefits of TDD? Documentation is one of them. Since code itself is the only accurate and always up-to-date representation of the applications we're working on, specifications written using TDD (being code as well) is the first place we should turn to when we need to better understand what a piece of code does.

How about design? You noticed how TDD produces code that is designed better. Rather than defining design in advance, with TDD it tends to emerge as we progress from one specification to another. At the same time, code that is easy to test is well-designed code. Tests force us to apply some coding best practices.

We also learned that TDD does not need to be practiced only on small units (methods). It can also be used at a much higher-level, where the focus is on a feature or a behavior that can span multiple methods, classes, or even applications and systems. One of the forms of TDD practiced at such a high-level is **behavior-driven development** (**BDD**). Unlike TDD, which is based on the unit tests that are done by developers for developers, BDD can be used by almost everyone in your organization. Since it tackles behaviors and it's written in natural (ubiquitous) language, testers, managers, business representatives, and others can participate in its creation and use it as a reference later on.

We defined legacy code as code without tests. We faced some of the challenges legacy code puts in front of us and learned some of the techniques that can be used to make it testable.

With all this in mind, let's go through TDD best practices.

Best practices

Coding best practices are a set of informal rules that the software development community has developed over time, which can help to improve the quality of software. While each application needs a level of creativity and originality (after all, we're trying to build something new or better), coding practices help us avoid some of the problems others faced before us. If you're just starting with TDD, it is a good idea to apply some (if not all) of the best practices generated by others.

For easier classification of TDD best practices, we divided them into four categories:

- Naming conventions
- Processes
- Development practices
- Tools

As you'll see, not all of them are exclusive to TDD. Since a big part of TDD consists of writing tests, many of the best practices presented in the following sections apply to testing in general, while others are related to general coding best practices. No matter the origin, all of them are useful when practicing TDD.

Take the advice with a certain dose of skepticism. Being a great programmer is not only about knowing how to code, but also about being able to decide which practice, framework, or style best suits the project and the team. Being agile is not about following someone else's rules, but about knowing how to adapt to circumstances and choose the best tools and practices that suit the team and the project.

Naming conventions

Naming conventions help to organize tests better, so that it is easier for developers to find what they're looking for. Another benefit is that many tools expect that those conventions are followed. There are many naming conventions in use, and those presented here are just a drop in the ocean. The logic is that any naming convention is better than none. Most important is that everyone on the team knows what conventions are being used and are comfortable with them. Choosing more popular conventions has the advantage that newcomers to the team can get up to speed fast, since they can leverage existing knowledge to find their way around.

Separate the implementation from the test code.
Benefits: It avoids accidentally packaging tests together with production binaries; many build tools expect tests to be in a certain source directory.

Common practice is to have at least two source directories. Implementation code should be located in `src/main/java` and test code in `src/test/java`. In bigger projects, the number of source directories can increase, but the separation between implementation and tests should remain as is.

Build tools such as Gradle and Maven expect source directory separation as well as naming conventions.

You might have noticed that the `build.gradle` files that we used throughout this book did not explicitly specify what to test, nor what classes to use to create a `.jar` file. Gradle assumes that tests are in `src/test/java` and that the implementation code that should be packaged into a JAR file is in `src/main/java`.

Place test classes in the same package as implementation.
Benefits: Knowing that tests are in the same package as the code helps you to find code faster.

As stated in the previous practice, even though packages are the same, classes are in separate source directories.

All exercises throughout this book followed this convention.

Name test classes in a similar fashion to the classes they test.
Benefits: Knowing that tests have a similar name to the classes they are testing helps you find the classes faster.

One commonly used practice is to name tests the same as the implementation classes, with the suffix Test. If, for example, the implementation class is TickTackToe, the test class should be TickTackToeTest.

However, in all cases, with the exception of those we used throughout the refactoring exercises, we prefer the suffix Spec. It helps to make a clear distinction that test methods are primarily created as a way to specify what will be developed. Testing is a great sub-product of those specifications.

Use descriptive names for test methods.
Benefits: It helps in understanding the objective of tests.

Using method names that describe tests is beneficial when trying to figure out why some tests failed or when the coverage should be increased with more tests. It should be clear what conditions are set before the test, what actions are performed, and what the expected outcome is.

There are many different ways to name test methods, and our preferred method is to name them using the Given/When/Then syntax used in the BDD scenarios. Given describes (pre)conditions, When describes actions, and Then describes the expected outcome. If a test does not have preconditions (usually set using @Before and @BeforeClass annotations), Given can be skipped.

Let's take a look at one of the specifications we created for our Tic-Tac-Toe application:

```
@Test
public void whenPlayAndWholeHorizontalLineThenWinner() {
    ticTacToe.play(1, 1); // X
    ticTacToe.play(1, 2); // O
    ticTacToe.play(2, 1); // X
    ticTacToe.play(2, 2); // O
    String actual = ticTacToe.play(3, 1); // X
    assertEquals("X is the winner", actual);
}
```

Just by reading the name of the method, we can understand what it is about. When we play and the whole horizontal or vertical and diagonal line is populated, then we have a winner.

Do not rely only on comments to provide information about the test objective. Comments do not appear when tests are executed from your favorite IDE, nor do they appear in reports generated by CI or build tools.

Processes

TDD processes are the core set of practices. Successful implementation of TDD depends on practices described in this section.

Write a test before writing the implementation code.
Benefits: It ensures that testable code is written; it ensures that every line of code gets tests written for it.

By writing or modifying the test first, the developer is focused on requirements before starting to work on the implementation code. This is the main difference compared to writing tests after the implementation is done. The additional benefit is that with the tests written first, we are avoiding the danger that the tests work as **quality checking** (**QC**) instead of **quality assurance** (**QA**). We're trying to ensure that quality is built in, as opposed to checking later whether we met quality objectives.

Only write new code when the test is failing.
Benefits: It confirms that the test does not work without the implementation.

If tests are passing without the need to write or modify the implementation code, then either the functionality is already implemented or the test is defective. If new functionality is indeed missing, then the test always passes and is therefore useless. Tests should fail for the expected reason. Even though there are no guarantees that the test is verifying the right thing, with fail first and for the expected reason, confidence that verification is correct should be high.

Rerun all tests every time the implementation code changes.
Benefits: It ensures that there are no unexpected side effects caused by code changes.

Every time any part of the implementation code changes, all tests should be run. Ideally, tests are fast to execute and can be run by the developer locally. Once code is submitted to version control, all tests should be run again to ensure that there was no problem due to code merges. This is especially important when more than one developer is working on the code. **Continuous integration** (CI) tools should be used to pull the code from the repository, compile it, and run tests, such as:

- Jenkins (https://jenkins.io/)
- Hudson (http://hudson-ci.org/)
- Travis (https://travis-ci.org/)
- Bamboo (https://www.atlassian.com/software/bamboo)

All tests should pass before a new test is written.
Benefits: The focus is maintained on a small unit of work; implementation code is (almost) always in working condition.

It is sometimes tempting to write multiple tests before the actual implementation. In other cases, developers ignore problems detected by existing tests and move towards new features. This should be avoided whenever possible. In most cases, breaking this rule will only introduce technical debt that will need to be paid with interest. One of the goals of TDD is that the implementation code is (almost) always working as expected. Some projects, due to pressures to reach the delivery date or maintain the budget, break this rule and dedicate time to new features, leaving the task of fixing the code associated with failed tests for later. These projects usually end up postponing the inevitable.

Refactor only after all tests are passing.
Benefits: This type of refactoring is safe.

If all implementation code that can be affected has tests and they are all passing, it is relatively safe to refactor. In most cases, there is no need for new tests. Small modifications to existing tests should be enough. The expected outcome of refactoring is to have all tests passing both before and after the code is modified.

Development practices

Practices listed in this section are focused on the best way to write tests. Write the simplest code to pass the test as it ensures cleaner and clearer design and avoids unnecessary features.

The idea is that the simpler the implementation, the better and easier it is to maintain the product. The idea adheres to the **keep it simple, stupid** (**KISS**) principle. This states that most systems work best if they are kept simple rather than made complex; therefore, simplicity should be a key goal in design, and unnecessary complexity should be avoided. Write assertions first, act later as it clarifies the purpose of the requirements and tests early.

Once the assertion is written, the purpose of the test is clear and the developer can concentrate on the code that will accomplish that assertion and, later on, on the actual implementation. Minimize assertions in each test as it avoids assertion roulette; it allows the execution of more asserts.

If multiple assertions are used within one test method, it might be hard to tell which of them caused a test failure. This is especially common when tests are executed as part of the CI process. If the problem cannot be reproduced on a developer's machine (as may be the case if the problem is caused by environmental issues), fixing the problem may be difficult and time consuming.

When one assert fails, execution of that test method stops. If there are other asserts in that method, they will not be run and information that can be used in debugging is lost.

Last but not least, having multiple asserts creates confusion about the objective of the test.

This practice does not mean that there should always be only one `assert` per test method. If there are other asserts that test the same logical condition or unit of functionality, they can be used within the same method.

Let's go through a few examples:

```
@Test
public final void
whenOneNumberIsUsedThenReturnValueIsThatSameNumber() {
    Assert.assertEquals(3, StringCalculator.add("3"));
}

@Test
public final void whenTwoNumbersAreUsedThenReturnValueIsTheirSum()
{
    Assert.assertEquals(3+6, StringCalculator.add("3,6"));
}
```

The preceding code contains two specifications that clearly define what the objective of the tests is. By reading the method names and looking at the `assert`, there should be clarity on what is being tested. Consider the following example:

```
@Test
public final void
whenNegativeNumbersAreUsedThenRuntimeExceptionIsThrown() {
    RuntimeException exception = null;
    try {
        StringCalculator.add("3,-6,15,-18,46,33");
    } catch (RuntimeException e) {
        exception = e;
    }
    Assert.assertNotNull("Exception was not thrown", exception);
    Assert.assertEquals("Negatives not allowed: [-6, -18]",
            exception.getMessage());
}
```

This specification has more than one `assert`, but they are testing the same logical unit of functionality. The first `assert` is confirming that the exception exists, and the second that its message is correct. When multiple asserts are used in one test method, they should all contain messages that explain the failure. This way, debugging the failed `assert` is easier. In the case of one `assert` per test method, messages are welcome but not necessary, since it should be clear from the method name what the objective of the test is:

```
@Test
public final void whenAddIsUsedThenItWorks() {
    Assert.assertEquals(0, StringCalculator.add(""));
    Assert.assertEquals(3, StringCalculator.add("3"));
    Assert.assertEquals(3+6, StringCalculator.add("3,6"));
    Assert.assertEquals(3+6+15+18+46+33,
```

Putting It All Together

```
                StringCalculator.add("3,6,15,18,46,33"));
        Assert.assertEquals(3+6+15,  StringCalculator.add("3,6n15"));
        Assert.assertEquals(3+6+15,
                StringCalculator.add("//;n3;6;15"));
    Assert.assertEquals(3+1000+6,
                StringCalculator.add("3,1000,1001,6,1234"));
    }
```

This test has many asserts. It is unclear what the functionality is, and if one of them fails, it is not known whether the rest would work or not. It might be hard to understand the failure when this test is executed through some CI tools.

Do not introduce dependencies between tests.
Benefits: The tests work in any order independently, whether all or only a subset is run.

Each test should be independent of the others. Developers should be able to execute any individual test, a set of tests, or all of them. Often, due to the test runner's design, there is no guarantee that tests will be executed in any particular order. If there are dependencies between tests, they might easily be broken with the introduction of new ones.

Tests should run fast.
Benefits: These tests are used often.

If it takes a lot of time to run tests, developers will stop using them or run only a small subset related to the changes they are making. The benefit of fast tests, besides fostering their usage, is quick feedback. The sooner the problem is detected, the easier it is to fix it. Knowledge about the code that produced the problem is still fresh. If the developer already started working on the next feature while waiting for the completion of the execution of the tests, they might decide to postpone fixing the problem until that new feature is developed. On the other hand, if they drops their current work to fix the bug, time is lost in context switching.

Tests should be so quick that developers can run all of them after each change without getting bored or frustrated.

Use test doubles.
Benefits: This reduces code dependency and test execution will be faster.

[276]

Mocks are prerequisites for the fast execution of tests and the ability to concentrate on a single unit of functionality. By mocking dependencies external to the method that is being tested, the developer is able to focus on the task at hand without spending time in setting them up. In the case of bigger teams, those dependencies might not even be developed. Also, the execution of tests without mocks tends to be slow. Good candidates for mocks are databases, other products, services, and so on.

Use setup and teardown methods.
Benefits: This allows setup and teardown code to be executed before and after the class or each method.

In many cases, some code needs to be executed before the test class or before each method in a class. For this purpose, JUnit has `@BeforeClass` and `@Before` annotations that should be used as the setup phase. `@BeforeClass` executes the associated method before the class is loaded (before the first test method is run).
`@Before` executes the associated method before each test is run. Both should be used when there are certain preconditions required by tests. The most common example is setting up test data in the (hopefully in-memory) database.

At the opposite end are `@After` and `@AfterClass` annotations, which should be used as the teardown phase. Their main purpose is to destroy data or a state created during the setup phase or by the tests themselves. As stated in one of the previous practices, each test should be independent from the others. Moreover, no test should be affected by the others. The teardown phase helps to maintain the system as if no test was previously executed.

Do not use base classes in tests.
Benefits: It provides test clarity.

Developers often approach test code in the same way as implementation. One of the common mistakes is to create base classes that are extended by tests. This practice avoids code duplication at the expense of test clarity. When possible, base classes used for testing should be avoided or limited. Having to navigate from the test class to its parent, to the parent of the parent, and so on in order to understand the logic behind
tests often introduces unnecessary confusion. Clarity in tests should be more important than avoiding code duplication.

Tools

TDD, coding, and testing in general, are heavily dependent on other tools and processes. Some of the most important ones are as follows. Each of them is too big a topic to be explored in this book, so they will be described only briefly.

Code coverage and CI.
Benefits: It gives assurance that everything is tested.

Code coverage practices and tools are very valuable in determining that all code, branches, and complexity is tested. Some of these tools are as follows:

- JaCoCo (http://www.eclemma.org/jacoco/)
- Clover (https://www.atlassian.com/software/clover)
- Cobertura (http://cobertura.github.io/cobertura/)

CI tools are a must for all except the most trivial projects. Some of the most used tools are:

- Jenkins (https://jenkins.io/)
- Hudson (http://hudson-ci.org/)
- Travis (https://travis-ci.org/)
- Bamboo (https://www.atlassian.com/software/bamboo).

Use TDD together with BDD.
Benefits: Both developer unit tests and functional customer facing tests are covered.

While TDD with unit tests is a great practice, in many cases it does not provide all the testing that projects need. TDD is fast to develop, helps the design process, and gives confidence through fast feedback. On the other hand, BDD is more suitable for integration and functional testing, provides a better process for requirement gathering through narratives, and is a better way of communicating with clients through scenarios. Both should be used, and together they provide a full process that involves all stakeholders and team members. TDD (based on unit tests) and BDD should be driving the development process. Our recommendation is to use TDD for high code coverage and fast feedback, and BDD as automated acceptance tests. While TDD is mostly oriented towards white-box, BDD often aims at black-box testing. Both TDD and BDD are trying to focus on QA instead of QC.

Summary

In this chapter, we first went through a brief overview of TDD. We learned about the four best practices that can help to improve the quality of software.

Moving on to the final chapter, we will be introduced to the concepts of CI and continuous delivery, and the importance of TDD all through the pipeline process will be highlighted with an example.

12
Leverage TDD by Implementing Continuous Delivery

"Nothing speaks like results. If you want to build the kind of credibility that connects with people, then deliver results before you deliver a message. Get out and do what you advise others to do. Communicate from experience."

– John C. Maxwell

Throughout this book, concepts and good practices have been presented with isolated examples. The goal of this chapter is to put into practice some of these concepts by applying them to a more realistic scenario.

To accomplish that, we are introducing a fictitious company called Awesome Gambling Corp. This company is struggling with a few problems in its software development life cycle that could be easily solved by applying some of the things we have learned in this book. As a disclaimer, any similarity with a real company is pure coincidence. Furthermore, for the sake of brevity, the codebase is not very extensive and some of the problems have been exaggerated in order to better represent the issue that needs to be addressed.

The topics covered not necessarily in order, are:

- Continuous integration
- Continuous delivery
- Benefits of test-driven development
- Identifying quick wins

Case study – Awesome Gambling Corp

You are Alice, a software developer, and you just joined the software development team of Awesome Gambling Corp. Your teammates are trying to bring you up to speed in the shortest time possible. It's your first day and your teammate, John, who has been designated as your mentor, is going to be guiding you during the first few hours in the company.

After a pleasant cup of coffee, he rapidly sets the topic of your conversation to all the tasks and procedures that will comprise your day-to-day work. Your team is developing and maintaining a very simple `thimblerig-service`. As soon as you hear the word *thimblerig*, you ashamedly admit this is the first time you have heard that word. John laughs and says he didn't know it either when he joined the company two years ago.

The Thimblerig game, also known as **three shells and a pea**, is an ancient gambling game. The rules are pretty simple, there are three shells, and the pea is covered by one of the three. The three shells are shuffled at really high speed and, when finished, the player has to guess which shell hides the pea.

After the explanation, he kindly offers to help you downloading the code project from the repository and briefly explains to you the overall concepts.

Once he is done with the explanation, he asks you to read the code on your own. He also tells you he is the person for you to go to in case you have any questions or concerns. You express your gratitude for his time and start browsing the project.

Exploring the codebase

As you start browsing the project, you realise that the application is not very complex. In fact, the project contains roughly a dozen Java classes and, as you start opening and looking at the files, you notice that none of them is longer than one hundred lines. That is pretty good, the codebase is small so you will be able to develop new features in no time.

Provided that this is a Gradle project, you quickly open the `build.gradle` file to acknowledge the frameworks and libraries being used within the project:

```
apply plugin: 'java'
apply plugin: 'org.springframework.boot'

sourceCompatibility = 1.8
targetCompatibility = 1.8
```

```
bootRepackage.executable = true

repositories {
  mavenLocal()
  mavenCentral()
}

dependencies {
  compile 'org.springframework.boot:spring-boot-starter-actuator'
  compile 'org.springframework.boot:spring-boot-starter-web'
  testCompile 'junit:junit:4.12'
  testCompile 'org.hamcrest:hamcrest-all:1.3'
  testCompile 'org.mockito:mockito-core:1.10.19'
}
```

The Gradle build field looks good. The project you are going to work on is a Spring-based web service. It uses `spring-boot-starter-web`, so it's very likely you will be able to run it locally without hassle. Moreover, there are some test dependencies which means there should be some tests in the test folder as well.

A couple of minutes later you already have a mental map of the application. There is a class called `ThimblerigService` which handles the logic of the game. It has a dependency on a `RandomNumberGenerator` and it only has one public method, which is `placeBet`. Methods and classes have an understandable name, so it isn't hard to figure out what they do:

```
@Service
public class ThimblerigService {
  private RandomNumberGenerator randomNumberGenerator;

  @Autowired
  ThimblerigService(RandomNumberGenerator randomNumberGenerator) {
    this.randomNumberGenerator = randomNumberGenerator;
  }

  public BetResult placeBet(int position, BigDecimal betAmount) {
    ...
  }
}
```

Besides that class, there is only one controller class that implements an API: it is
`ThimblerigAPI`. It exposes only one method, which is `placeBet`. Other company services
invoke that `POST` method in order to play one game in this service. The service resolves the
bet and includes in the response details such as whether there's a prize won, the amount,
and so forth:

```
@RestController
@RequestMapping("/v1/thimblerig")
public class ThimblerigAPI {
  private ThimblerigService thimblerigService;

  @Autowired
  public ThimblerigAPI(ThimblerigService thimblerigService) {
    this.thimblerigService = thimblerigService;
  }

  @ResponseBody
  @PostMapping(value = "/placeBet",
      consumes = MediaType.APPLICATION_JSON_VALUE)
  public BetReport placeBet(@RequestBody NewBet bet) {
    BetResult betResult =
        thimblerigService.placeBet(bet.getPick(), bet.getAmount());
    return new BetReport(betResult);
  }
}
```

This is a fairly easy setup and everything is crystal-clear, so you decide to move on and start
looking at the tests.

As you open the `test` folder and start looking for tests, you are very surprised when you
discover there is only one test class: `ThimblerigServiceTest`. One single good test is
worth more than hundred bad ones but still, you think this application is poorly unit-tested:

```
public class ThimblerigServiceTest {
  @Test
  public void placingBetDoesNotAcceptPositionsLessThanOne() {
    ...
  }

  @Test
  public void placingBetDoesNotAcceptPositionsGreaterThan3() {
    ...
  }

  @Test
  public void placingBetOnlyAcceptsAmountsGreaterThanZero() {
```

```
        ...
    }

    @Test
    public void onFailedBetThePrizeIsZero() {
        ...
    }

    @Test
    public void
    whenThePositionIsGuessedCorrectlyThePrizeIsDoubleTheBet() {
        ...
    }
}
```

After opening the class and going over all the tests it contains, your impression changes slightly for the good. The tests cover the core service completely and they seem meaningful and exhaustive. But despite that, you can't avoid turning your head to John and asking him why there's only one test. He tells you they didn't have much time to create tests because they were in a hurry, so only the critical parts have tests. Whether a piece of code is critical or not is very subjective, but you understand the situation; in fact, you have been in that situations many times.

Only one second later, before you have time to go back to your task, John adds another interesting point to his answer: the **quality assurance** (**QA**) department. The aim of this department is to test all release candidates before they reach a production environment. Their mission is to find errors and bugs that might affect the application and report them. In some cases, if any of the errors found are very critical, the release is stopped and it will never be deployed to production. This procedure usually takes from three to five days. You think that could be a bottleneck in some scenarios, so you ask him to give you further details of the release process.

Release procedure

Provided that the project is a simple **REpresentational State Transfer** (**REST**) service, the creation of a release is not complex at all. According to the current procedure, a developer compiles the code and sends the artifact to the team that manages all deployments. That team coordinates the testing and deployment to production with the customer and QA departments.

You decide to ask John if he is happy with the process. Before you even get the answer, you know John is not happy at all with it. You can see on his face that he is making an effort to hide his feelings about it. John gulps back his emotions and starts describing the current situation of the team.

It turns out that not everything is joy and candy in the development team. All developers, when they start coding, create their own branch from the master branch in the repository. This is not bad at all, but it has happened that some branches have been merged back to the master many weeks later. The issue is that the master branch has changed a lot since then and the code base diverges a lot, meaning the merge is very difficult, unpleasant, and error prone.

Besides the occasional merging problems, it has happened that one developer compiled his local branch by mistake and it was deployed to production, generating chaos, carnage, and uncertainty for a short period.

On top of that, the customer is not very happy with the time new features take to be implemented. They are complaining about this from time to time, saying that every single tiny change takes at least a week to be applied.

You are puzzled how this can happen to a very tiny REST service, but of course John was referring to other bigger projects in the company. You know this kind of problem can be solved, or at least mitigated, by implementing **continuous integration** (**CI**) and continuous delivery. In fact, automating processes as much as possible enables you to focus on other problems by getting rid of those that are trivial.

After this small reflection, you now know you need more information about the deployment procedure and you also know that John is willing to give you the details.

Deployments to production

With the release process covered, John starts explaining to you how the service is deployed to production. It is very manual work: one member of the **infrastructure team** (**IT**) department copies the artifact to the server and executes a few commands to get it running.

John also takes the opportunity to add some stories of errors that they suffered in the past, like the time when, instead of deploying the latest version, the infrastructure operator mistakenly redeployed an old version. A bunch of old bugs reappeared and stayed in production until somebody found out what had happened.

While listening to those stories, you can't help but start thinking about what you have learned from previous projects and companies. You know that putting code into a production environment could be a very easy and straightforward task, a never-ending nightmare, or something in the middle. It depends on many factors and sometimes it is not up to us to change it. In some scenarios, deploying an application to production needs to be acknowledged by people who have the power to decide when and what is deployed. In others, there is strict regulation that turns what should be an easy procedure into a tedious and verbose task.

Furthermore, automating deployments is a way to reduce the risk factor that human interaction can add. Creating a repeatable process can be as easy as writing all the necessary steps in a script and scheduling its execution. It is well known that any single script can't replace a human completely, but, needless to say, the goal is not to replace humans with scripts. The main purpose of this is to provide a tool that can be executed autonomously and humans can supervise it, with manual intervention just in case it is necessary. For this, implementing continuous delivery is very suitable.

After John's brief but intense introduction, you feel that you are ready to start working on your own. You have many possible improvements in your head and you are definitely eager to implement them.

Conclusions

Even though the situation in this company has been exaggerated for didactic purposes, there are still companies struggling with these problems. Indeed, Alice knew that the way software developers at Awesome Gambling Corp work is not ideal. There are many techniques, some of them covered in this book, that could help the company stop focusing on unconscious mistakes and start focusing on other things that can add more value to their final product.

In the next section, we are going to address some of the problems described by proposing one possible solution. This is not a unique solution; actually, the solution proposed includes some tools, and there are many options for each of the tools used. Moreover, every company has its own culture and restrictions, and because of that, the proposed solution might not be fully suitable.

Possible improvements

In this section and the following subsections, we are going to tackle some of the problems described in Alice's story. Because the code we inherited from the example is already implemented, we can't apply TDD here. Instead, we are going to set the basis and prepare the ground for future developments where applying TDD will become very useful.

Although there are always many things that can be improved, the pain points being addressed are code merging issues, lots of manual testing, manual releases, and the length of time taken to develop changes or new features.

For the first two, we are going to increase the test coverage of the application and implement CI. A Jenkins server is going to be configured to address the third issue, manual releases. And finally, the last issue, which is the long **time to market** (TTM), is going to be mitigated by implementing the rest of the solutions.

Increasing test coverage

Among the metrics for measuring code quality, there is one that is especially difficult to understand, and that is test coverage. Test coverage is a dangerous metric because a really high coverage does not imply the code is well tested. As the name says, it only contemplates whether a piece of code has been triggered and hence executed by a test. For that reason, the goal of testing is basically a combination of good tests and good coverage. To summarize, it is the quality of tests that matters, the code coverage is secondary.

There are some scenarios though where code coverage is indeed a good indicator. These are when the code coverage is really low. In those, the number means a greater part of the codebase is not being tested and therefore tests are not ensuring we are not introducing errors.

Additionally, creating good automated tests can reduce the amount of time spent by the QA team on performing regression tests. This very likely reduces the time they spend testing the same code over and over again, increasing the team's delivery velocity.

Implementing continuous integration

In large companies with multiple teams working in parallel, it is very common to end up having tons of integration conflicts. This occurs more frequently when the codebase is under heavy development.

In order to mitigate this, it is highly recommended to use CI. The main idea is that development branches should not diverge much from the master branch. One way to do it is splitting the changes or new features into really small chunks so they can be finished and merged back pretty fast. Another way is to merge regularly; this is more suitable when features are difficult to break down into small ones.

When facing indivisible features, such as architectural changes, Feature Toggles are very helpful. With Feature Toggles, unfinished features can be merged and will not be accessible until the flag is turned on.

Towards continuous delivery

One of the problems developers were facing in the story is the manual creation of releases. There are many tools that help automate such tasks, such as Jenkins, Travis, or Bamboo, just to name a few. As part of the proposed solution, we are going to configure an instance of Jenkins to run all of these tasks automatically. On every execution of the Jenkins job, a new release of the `thimblerig-service` will be created.

Moreover, since we already moved to CI, the status of the master branch should be always ready for production. And, in case some unfinished features have been merged, they are hidden thanks to Feature Toggles.

At this point, to solve the problem of the releases, we could have implemented either continuous delivery or **continuous deployment (CD)**, but for the sake of simplicity we are going to implement continuous delivery. Let's get into it.

Jenkins installation

Jenkins is a very powerful tool and easy to learn. In this section, we are going to prepare the environment, which consists of a virtual machine running a Docker image of Jenkins. This setup is for demonstration purposes; for real scenarios, it will be better to install it in a dedicated server with more resources, or get it as a service from a company like CloudBees. In this particular case, all the configuration is located in the Vagrantfile:

```
Vagrant.configure("2") do |config|

  config.vm.box = "ubuntu/trusty64"
  config.vm.box_check_update = false

  config.vm.network "forwarded_port", guest: 8080, host: 9090

  config.vm.provider "virtualbox" do |vb|
    vb.gui = false
    vb.memory = 2048
  end

  config.vm.provision "docker" do |d|
    d.run "jenkins/jenkins",
      args: "-p 8080:8080 -p 50000:50000 -v jenkins_home:/var/jenkins_home"
  end
end
```

So, to get it up and running, we just need to execute the following command:

```
$> vagrant up
```

> If, after a restart or whatever the reason might be, Jenkins appears offline or you can't reach it, try running the same command with provision flag:
> ```
> $> vagrant up --provision
> ```

Once finished, we can open `http://localhost:9090` in our favorite browser to continue the setup:

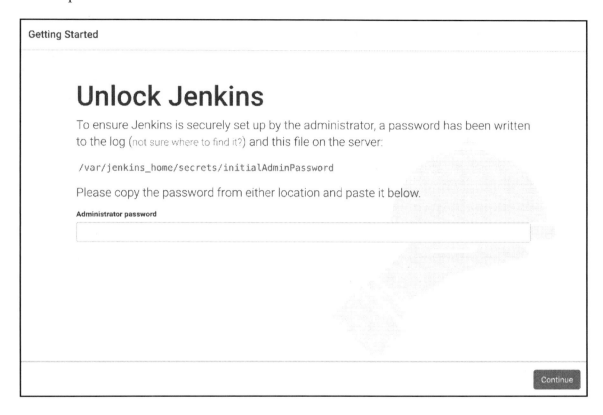

Since we are not installing it in the server but running it in a Docker image, this password is a bit tricky to get. Probably the easiest way is to access the Docker machine and get the password from the file, and that could be done like this:

```
$> vagrant ssh
$> docker exec jenkins-jenkins cat /var/jenkins_home/secrets/initialAdminPassword
```

Copy the password, paste in the password field, and we move to the next step, which is configuring plugins. For now, we are going to install the recommended ones only. Other plugins can be installed later on in the administration panel:

Getting Started				
✔ Folders	○ OWASP Markup Formatter	○ Build Timeout	○ Credentials Binding	** Script Security ** Command Agent Launcher **Folders** ** bouncycastle API
○ Timestamper	○ Workspace Cleanup	○ Ant	○ Gradle	
○ Pipeline	○ GitHub Branch Source	○ Pipeline: GitHub Groovy Libraries	○ Pipeline: Stage View	
○ Git	○ Subversion	○ SSH Slaves	○ Matrix Authorization Strategy	
○ PAM Authentication	○ LDAP	○ Email Extension	○ Mailer	
				** - required dependency

Jenkins 2.108

Then, when the setup has finished installing plugins, another screen is shown. This is the last step of the configuration, creating an admin user. It's recommended to create a user with a password that is easy to remember:

This step can be skipped, but then the admin password will remain the same as the initial password, which is really difficult to remember. Now we are ready to use our brand new Jenkins installation.

Automating builds

Once we have Jenkins up and running, it is time to start using it. We are going to create a task on Jenkins that will download the `thimblerig-service` master branch, execute the tests, build it, and archive the resultant artifact.

Leverage TDD by Implementing Continuous Delivery

Let's start by creating a **Freestyle project**:

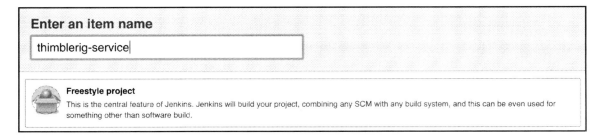

We have to tell Jenkins where the repository is located. In this example, we don't need authentication, but is very likely we would need it in a real-world scenario:

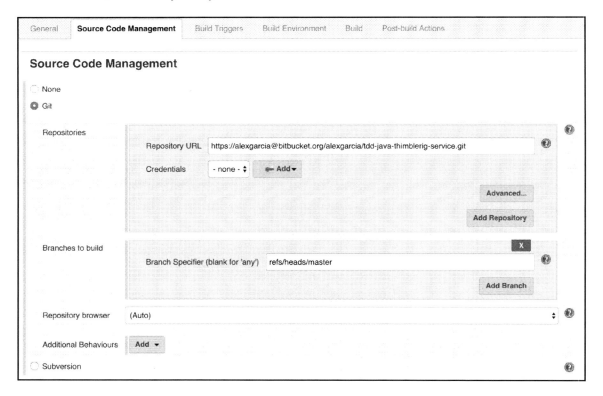

The `thimblerig-service` project is a Gradle project. We are going to use the Jenkins Gradle plugin for compiling, testing, and building our service:

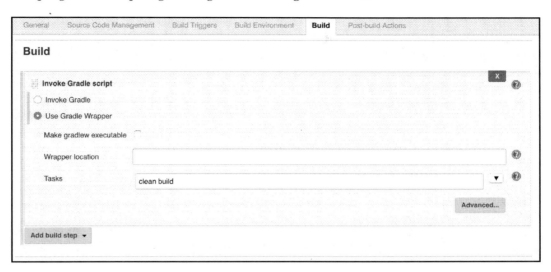

Finally, we have to specify the location of the test reports and the artifact built:

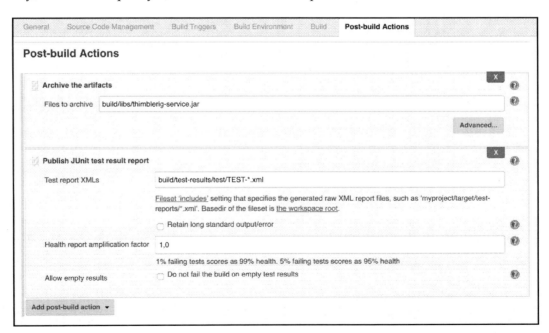

And we are done. This is not very different when compared to what we usually do in our local environment. It downloads the code from the master branch and uses Gradle for building the service, as developers were doing, according to John in the story.

First execution

With our project created in Jenkins, now it is time to test it. We never configured a triggered execution, so Jenkins is not monitoring the changes in the repository. For this example, launching the builds manually is more than enough, but in a real scenario we would like it to be triggered automatically on every change in the master branch:

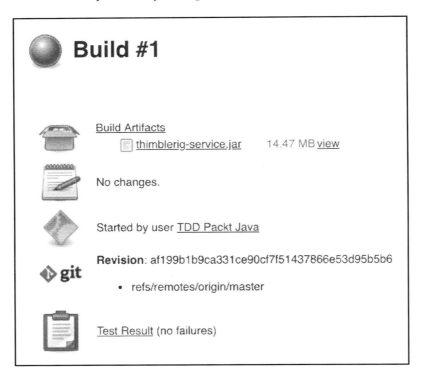

The build has finished successfully; we can see in the summary that tests were executed but none has failed. We are ready to download the artifact and try to execute it locally:

```
$> chmod u+x thimblerig-service.jar
$> ./thimblerig-service.jar
```

At some point, the logs will display a message like `Tomcat started on port(s): 8080 (http)`. This means our that service is ready and we can start using it. To make sure, we can always check the health of the service by running:

```
$> curl http://localhost:8080/health
{"status":"UP"}
```

This concludes the example of continuous delivery. Although this example is fully functional, Jenkins is not the best place to store releases of the service. For a real-world use case, there are much more powerful alternatives, such as Artifactory, or simply Dockerize the service and push new versions to a private Docker registry.

What is next?

The example here is purely academic, and parts of the solution are a bit hacky. In a real company, Jenkins would be installed in a dedicated server and would have many more tasks to build and release. To orchestrate all of this, proper management of generated artifacts is needed. As mentioned earlier, some of the solutions that companies are adopting are tools such as Artifactory or private instances of Docker Registry to store Docker images of the services. Whatever the storage of choice, the procedure will remain the same—compile, test, build, archive. It's just a matter of configuration.

For the sake of brevity, some parts that required new code have been omitted and are left for the reader to complete as an exercise. Here are some ideas of how to continue:

- Create some tests for the REST controller.
- There is an issue in the random number generator—it is not random at all. Fork the `thimblerig-service` project, create a test to reproduce the issue, fix it, and release a new version of the service by using the recently-created build project on Jenkins.
- Use Docker.

All the code snippets and the rest of the project files required can be found online in the following repository: https://bitbucket.org/alexgarcia/tdd-java-thimblerig-service

This is just the beginning

You might have expected that by the time you reached the end of this book, you'd know everything about test-driven development (TDD). If that was the case, we're sorry that we'll have to disappoint you. It takes a lot of time and practice to master any craft, and TDD is no exception. Go on, apply what you have learned to your projects. Share knowledge with your colleagues. Most importantly, practice, practice, and practice. As with karate, only through continuous practice and repetition can one fully master TDD. We have been using it for a long time, and we still often face new challenges and learn new ways to improve our craftsmanship.

This does not have to be the end

Writing this book was a long journey filled with many adventures. We hope you enjoyed reading it as much as we enjoyed writing it.

We share our experience on a wide variety of subjects at our blog, at `http://technologyconversations.com`.

Summary

Throughout Alice's fictitious story, some of the common problems which companies are facing nowadays were presented. One of them is the lack of time. In this particular case, and in the majority of cases, people lack time because they are trapped doing repetitive tasks that don't add value, thus there is this constant feeling that it's impossible to achieve more ambitious goals. One of the main excuses that developers give when asked why they are not practicing TDD is the lack of time for writing tests.

This chapter tackles a possible solution for this, which is using Jenkins. A virtual machine with an instance of Jenkins was configured to automate some of the repetitive tasks that were draining time from the team.

Once the problems have been addressed, TDD becomes really handy. Every new feature developed in the TDD way will be more than covered by tests, then future changes on that feature will be run against the test suite, and this will fail if one of the tests is not satisfied.

Other Books You May Enjoy

If you enjoyed this book, you may be interested in these other books by Packt:

Java 9 High Performance
Mayur Ramgir, Nick Samoylov

ISBN: 978-1-78712-078-5

- Work with JIT compilers
- Understand the usage of profiling tools
- Generate JSON with code examples
- Leverage the command-line tools to speed up application development
- Build microservices in Java 9
- Explore the use of APIs to improve application code
- Speed up your application with reactive programming and concurrency

Other Books You May Enjoy

Test-Driven iOS Development with Swift 4 - Third Edition
Dr. Dominik Hauser

ISBN: 978-1-78847-570-9

- Implement TDD in Swift application development
- Find bugs before you enter code using the TDD approach
- Use TDD to build models, view controllers, and views
- Test network code with asynchronous tests and stubs
- Write code that is a joy to read and maintain
- Develop functional tests to ensure the app works as planned

Leave a review - let other readers know what you think

Please share your thoughts on this book with others by leaving a review on the site that you bought it from. If you purchased the book from Amazon, please leave us an honest review on this book's Amazon page. This is vital so that other potential readers can see and use your unbiased opinion to make purchasing decisions, we can understand what our customers think about our products, and our authors can see your feedback on the title that they have worked with Packt to create. It will only take a few minutes of your time, but is valuable to other potential customers, our authors, and Packt. Thank you!

Index

A

acceptance criteria 194
acceptance test-driven development (ATDD) 14
acceptance tests 90
Alexandria project
  about 227
  black-box testing 228
  call, extracting 239, 241
  call, overriding 239, 241
  legacy code algorithm, applying 233
  new feature, adding 228
  preliminary investigation 229, 230, 231
  primitive obsession, removing with status as int 244, 247
  spike testing 228
  technical comments 228
application debugging
  avoiding 18
Awesome Gambling Corp
  about 282
  codebase, exploring 282, 285
  conclusions 287
  production, deployments 286, 287
  release procedure 285, 286

B

Bamboo
  reference link 273
behavior-driven development (BDD)
  about 13, 189, 193, 194
  book store 197, 199, 200
  narrative 194, 195
  scenarios 195, 196, 197
  specifications 190
black-box testing
  about 12
  advantages 13
  disadvantages 13
  reference link 228

C

call extraction, Alexandria project
  constructor, parameterizing 241, 242
  new feature, adding 242, 244
call override, Alexandria project
  constructor, parameterizing 241, 242
  new feature, adding 242, 244
Clover
  reference link 278
Cobertura
  reference link 278
code coverage
  reference link 219
code refactoring 89
code smell
  reference link 216
commands, remote-controlled ship development
  combined commands 109, 110
  single commands 107, 108
Connect 4 game
  about 121
  reference link 121
  requirements 121
constructor chaining 241
continuous delivery
  about 250, 251, 289
  builds, automating 293, 295
  continuous integration, implementing 289
  example 297
  executing 296, 297
  improvements 288
  Jenkins installation 290, 292, 293

test coverage, increasing 288
continuous deployment (CD) 289
continuous integration (CI) 17, 250, 251, 286
curl
  reference link 233

D

DbUnit
  reference link 233
dependency injection 141, 231
Don't Repeat Yourself (DRY) principle
  reference link 119

E

environment
  setting up, with Gradle 58
  setting up, with JUnit 58
executable documentation 16, 17, 18
extract 224
Extreme Programming (XP)
  about 9
  reference link 88

F

Feature Flags 252
Feature Flipping 252
feature toggles, example
  about 253, 257
  Fibonacci service, implementing 257, 258, 260
  template engine, working with 260, 261, 263, 264
Feature Toggles
  about 252
  FF4J 252
  Togglz 252
FF4J
  reference link 252
Fibonacci's sequence
  reference link 257
functional tests 90
functions
  about 178
  Reverse Polish Notation (RPN) 179

G

Gradle project
  setting up, in IntelliJ IDEA 58, 61
Grizzly
  reference link 237

H

helper classes 98, 99
Hudson
  reference link 273

I

infrastructure team (IT) 286
integration tests 90, 168
IntelliJ IDEA
  Gradle project, setting up 58, 61
  Java project, setting up 58, 61

J

Java Code Coverage (JaCoCo)
  reference link 278
Java Functional Programming
  environment, setting up 174
Java project
  setting up, in IntelliJ IDEA 58, 61
JBehave stories, writing
  reference link 198
JBehave
  about 201
  final validation 211, 213
  pending steps 202, 203, 204
  runner 201
  steps 205, 206, 207, 208, 209, 210, 211
Jenkins
  reference link 273
JUnit
  @AfterMethod annotation 94
  @BeforeClass annotation 94
  @BeforeMethod annotation 94
  @Test annotation 92
  @Test(expectedExceptions = SomeClass.class)
    annotation argument 94
  reference link 95

versus TestNG 94

K

kata exercise 227
keep it simple, stupid (KISS)
   about 91, 274
   reference link 119

L

legacy code algorithm, applying
   about 233
   BookRepository dependency, injecting 239
   end-to-end test cases, writing 233, 235, 236
   test cases, automating 237, 238
legacy code change algorithm 222
legacy code change algorithm, applying
   about 222
   change points, identifying 222
   dependencies, breaking 224, 225, 226
   test points, finding 223, 224
   tests, writing 226
legacy code
   about 216
   example 217, 218, 219
   lack of dependency injection 221
   recognition 220, 221
legacy kata
   about 227
   Alexandria project 227

M

markdown
   reference link 192
Mars Rover 95
method reference 186
Minimum Viable Product (MVP) 195
mocking
   about 15, 144
   features 145
   mock objects 146, 147
   terminology 145, 146
Mockito
   about 147

N

null class 174, 175

O

Occam's razor principle
   reference link 119
Optional class
   about 175, 177
   example 175
orientation, remote-controlled ship development
   direction, keeping in memory 100
   implementation 101
   position, keeping in memory 100
   refactoring 101
override call 224

P

partial mocking 154
players, Tic-Tac-Toe game
   player O 74
   player X 73, 74
   X's turn, checking 75
police syndrome 15
Postman
   reference link 233
preliminary investigation
   about 229, 230, 231
   candidates, finding for refactoring 231
   new feature, introduction 232
primitive obsession
   reference link 245
Principles of OOD
   reference link 120
product owner (PO) 228

Q

quality assurance (QA)
   about 14, 285
   versus quality checking 14

R

red-green-refactor process
   about 9, 10, 11, 61, 268

implementation code, writing 62
last test failure, confirming 62
refactoring 63
repeating 63
test, writing 62
tests, executing 62, 63
remote-controlled ship development
  about 96
  backward moves 102, 104
  commands 106
  forward moves 102, 104
  helper classes 98, 99
  obstacles detection 114
  orientation 99, 100
  project setup 96, 98
  ship, rotating 105
  spheric maps, representing 110
  starting point 99, 100
remote-controlled ship
  requirements 95
REpresentational State Transfer (REST) 285
requisites, Reverse Polish Notation (RPN)
  complex operations 183, 184
  invalid input, handling 180
  single operations 181
RestAssured
  reference link 238
Reverse Polish Notation (RPN)
  about 179
  requisites 179, 180
Rule feature, JUnit
  reference link 65

S

Selenide
  reference link 205
Selenium
  reference link 204
ship rotation, remote-controlled ship development
  specification, for turning left 105
  specification, for turning right 106
software design 118
software design principles
  about 118
  Don't Repeat Yourself (DRY) principle 119
  keep it simple, stupid (KISS) 119
  Occam's razor principle 119
  You Ain't Gonna Need It principle 118
SOLID principles
  dependency inversion principle 120
  interface segregation principle 120
  liskov substitution principle 120
  open-closed principle 120
  single responsibility principle 120
specifications, Behavior-Driven Development (BDD)
  documentation 191
  documentation, for coders 192
  documentation, for non-coders 193
spheric maps, remote-controlled ship development
  map boundaries 113
  planet information 111, 112
Spring Boot
  reference link 253
store moves, Tic-Tac-Toe v2
  clear state between games 159
  DB name, specifying 150
  drop operation feedback 160
  error handling 158, 160
  items, adding to Mongo collection 153, 154, 155
  name, defining for Mongo collection 151
  operation feedback, adding 157
store turn, Tic-Tac-Toe v2
  alternate players 166, 167
  collection, creating 162, 163
  current move, storing 163
  error handling 165
strategy pattern
  reference link 222
Streams
  about 185
  filter function 185
  flatMap function 186, 187
  map function 186
  reduce function 187
  reference link 185

T

TDD best practices
  about 269
  development practices 274, 275, 277

    naming conventions 270, 271
    processes 272, 273
    tools 278
test double 15, 90
test-driven development (TDD)
    testable code design 12
    about 7, 8, 9, 268, 269
    features 11
    red-green-refactor process 9, 10, 11
test-first implementation, of Connect 4 game
    about 130
    board 131
    discs 132
    Hamcrest, using 130
    output 135
    player shifts 134
    win condition, scenarios 137, 138, 139
test-last implementation, of Connect 4 game
    about 122
    board 122, 123
    discs 123, 124
    output 125
    player shifts 124
    win condition, scenarios 126, 128, 130
testing
    about 12
    black-box testing 12
    quality checking, versus quality assurance 14
    white-box testing 13
TestNG
    @AfterClass annotation 94
    @AfterGroups annotation 93
    @AfterSuite annotation 93
    @AfterTest annotation 93
    @BeforeGroups annotation 93
    @BeforeSuite annotation 93
    @BeforeTest annotation 93
    @Test annotation 92
    @Test(enable = false) annotation argument 94
    about 92
    reference link 95
    versus JUnit 94
tests
    separation, in Gradle 168, 169
thimblerig service 282

Thymeleaf
    reference link 253
Tic-Tac-Toe game
    board boundaries 68, 69, 70
    code coverage 84, 85
    developing 64
    integration test 169, 171
    pieces, placing 65, 67
    pieces, placing on unoccupied spaces 70, 71
    reference link 64
    requirements 64
    tie condition 82, 83
    two players support, adding 72, 73
    win conditions, adding 75, 76, 77, 78, 79, 80, 81
Tic-Tac-Toe v2 game, developing
    about 148
    moves, storing 149
    turn, storing 161
Tic-Tac-Toe v2 game
    requirements 147
time to market (TTM) 7
Togglz
    reference link 252
Travis
    reference link 273

U

unit testing
    about 88
    limitations 89
    need for 89
    with test-driven development (TDD) 91
user acceptance tests 122

W

white-box testing
    about 13
    advantages 13
    disadvantages 14

Y

YAML Ain't Markup Language (YAML) 254
You Ain't Gonna Need It principle
    reference link 118

Printed in Poland
by Amazon Fulfillment
Poland Sp. z o.o., Wrocław